MOTOR
SPIRIT

MOTOR SPIRIT

the long hunt for the zodiac

Jarett Kobek

we heard you like books • los angeles california

2022

PUBLISHED BY WE HEARD YOU LIKE BOOKS
A Division of U2603 LLC
5419 Hollywood Blvd, Ste C-231 Los Angeles CA 90027

http://weheardyoulikebooks.com/

ISBN: 978-1-7378428-1-1

February 2022

First Edition

PREFACE

WHEN YOU'RE DEAD, YOU'RE GONE—except in people's memories. But those who knew you will themselves die. It's then that you're truly done. When no one's left to remember, when the neurological echoes fall silent. The joy and anxiety and fear and love. They disappear and nothing's left. Time moves on. A person becomes one more entry in ledgers, in the census, in aging social media posts, in wedding notices and obituaries. A name carved into grave stone sitting atop a corpse reclaimed by the Earth.

Everyone gets the same thing. The good, the bad, the wretched, the rich, the poor. They get the big blank nothing. No more, no less.

In England, outside Bradford, outside Leeds, in West Yorkshire, there rests the Bingley Cemetery. It's the same as any Victorian graveyard in any market town of the post-industrial north, an enclosure of green and Christian kitsch that, generally, people don't visit unless they have a personal connection to one of the interred bodies, or if they're an odd sort who enjoys the icy silence of dirt.

The cemetery is split into sections. Half is Church of England. The rest for everyone else. In the southeast corner of the cemetery's northwest, unconsecrated, up a small slope, a grave is marked by a weather-beaten white Calvary cross decorated with a metal statue of the crucified Christ. Along the three foundational tiers, meant to symbolize Jesus' ascent to Golgotha, runs an inscription:

**TREASURED
MEMORIES**

**OF A DEAR HUSBAND
BRONISLAW ZAPOLSKI
DIED 19ᵀᴴ JUNE 1965,**

**AGED 49 YEARS.
POKÓJ JEGO DUSZY**

Pokój jego duszy is the Polish equivalent of *requiescat in pace* or *rest in peace*.

†

If anyone could rest in peace, it was Bronisław Zapolski. He lived a small life that left almost no public traces. Gone before fifty. A marriage certificate and a medal for his service as a paratrooper in the Polish Air Force, a military body formed in exile after the Nazi invasion of his homeland. Otherwise, nothing can be found of his life. No immigration records, no newspaper notices. He came, saw, and left this world without noise or fanfare.

A year or so after Zapolski died, something happened. Or, rather, something is supposed to have happened. Or, rather, something happened that we know did not happen in objective reality but was presented as a manifestation of one man's mental illness. Even in this subjective presentation, the event might not have happened. It is possible that the man in question might have been faking maladies as part of a criminal defense, hoping that, if the story worked, he'd be put in a hospital for the insane rather than sent to prison.

The man's name was Peter Sutcliffe. The Yorkshire Ripper. Between the years of 1964 and 1967, Sutcliffe worked as a gravedigger in the cemetery. For the second half the 1970s, and a bit of the 1980s, he terrorized West Yorkshire with a string of violent murders and brutal attacks on women. His weapons of choice were hammers and screwdrivers and teeth and boots.

Sutcliffe suggested that his crimes were the product of a mind laboring under diminished capacity. He was, he and his defense said, a paranoid schizophrenic told by God that he must murder prostitutes to cleanse society of its filth. Interrogated in court, Sutcliffe was asked when, and how, he first heard the divine voice.

Mr Chadwin: What was it that happened at Bingley cemetery that you particularly remember?

Mr Sutcliffe: Something that I felt was very wonderful at the time. I heard what I believed then and believe now to have been God's voice. I was in the process of digging a grave. I was digging and I just paused for a minute. It was very hard ground. I just heard something—it sounded like a voice similar to a human voice—like an echo. I looked round to see if there was anyone there, but there was no one in sight. I was in the grave with my feet about five feet below the surface. There was no one in sight when I looked round from where I was. Then I got out of the grave. The voice was not very clear. I got out and walked—the ground rose up. It was quite a steep slope. I walked to the top, but there was no one there at all. I heard again the same sound. It was like a voice saying something, but the words were all imposed on top of each other. I could not make them out, it was like echoes. The voices were coming directly in front of me from the top of a gravestone, which was Polish. I remember the name on the grave to this day. It was a man called Zipolski. Stanislaw Zipolski... I remember getting a message from the grave. I looked at several graves. I was looking round to determine where the sound came from. After looking at the grave I walked back. I was kind of transfixed because of the voice... immediately afterwards as I stepped back to the path immediately in front of the grave, I saw what I took to be a definite message about the echoing voice... I recall,

> as Jesus was speaking to me... I thought the message on
> the gravestone ["*Pokój jego duszy*"] was a direct message
> telling me it was the voice of Jesus speaking to me.

Although Sutcliffe could not remember the name on the grave, he did identify, from a photograph, Bronisław Zapolski's Calvary cross. It was this grave that talked to the Yorkshire Ripper, this grave that spoke with the Voice of God.

Thus a long dead Polish paratrooper, a man of no great importance, was thrust into posthumous infamy. Linked forever to a murderous rampage, his name embedded in True Crime entertainments, the titular figure of Nicole Ward Jouve's *Un homme nommé Zapolski.* (Ignore online reviews. The book is excellent.)

Amongst those who remember the bad old days, Zapolski's cross has a nickname. It's called "the talking grave." It spoke to Sutcliffe, once, and now it cries out to the world's murder junkies, to the curious, to the morbid, and to the morbidly curious.

When you're dead, you're gone—except in people's memories.

And, sometimes, if you're very unlucky, people who did not know you will invent stories that have no connection to who you were as a person.

These are the memories that last forever.

part one

The Year of Zodiac

chapter one

young love

IN JANUARY 1986, St. Martin's Press issues *Zodiac* by Robert Graysmith. Prior to the book's appearance, Zodiac is a dim ghost from the bad hippie days of San Francisco and the Bay Area. Graysmith takes the old stories, gives them shape, and inserts himself into the narrative. He's going to solve the mystery.

But he fails. He recycles a rogue's gallery who've floated around for years. A child molester. A film buff. A random homosexual. None of the trio are the killer.

The failure doesn't matter. The failure helps. The failure leaves the mystery unsolved. *Zodiac* is a major success and burns through multiple printings. It creates an obsession and a cottage industry. Here is a killer who tormented and terrified a small but influential part of America. Who got away with it. A regional story is expanded and transformed into a national nightmare.

The template was there from the beginning, from the moment that the killer sent in his first letters. Zodiac was always the one upon whom you could project any fantasy. If the data didn't support your conclusion, the data could be manipulated. Or excuses invented. The small details never matter. Only the big conclusions. Graysmith codifies the approach. *Zodiac* is a mixture of factual reporting and confabulated finger-pointing. The book expands the template.

Commentators will spend hours and days and weeks and months and years and decades cataloging *Zodiac*'s errors. Of which there are many. Graysmith wrote in a pre-digital era that was paleolithic in its relationship to information processing. He was neither a reporter nor trained historian. Distortions would have crept into the best intentions.

Zodiac is the foundation of an informational pyramid scheme. Subsequent layers come from other books, from digital forums, from Graysmith himself, from David Fincher's film adaption of Graysmith. Each builds upon the last. Each creates a new idea of The Zodiac that engages and critiques previous ideas of The Zodiac.

But if the original is corrupted, what does that imply about its copies?

The recycled story is the opposite of reality. Time happens backwards. Rather than one incident followed by another followed by another, *Zodiac* starts with the end and moves towards the beginning. Every detail is used to support a single conclusion: a mad occultist murderer terrorized the Bay Area, killed people, wrote letters, made cryptographic messages. And got away. It's an approach where accidents are intentional, where the killer and everything in his orbit are on a set path. It's a narrative without the fuck-ups and catastrophes that define life. It creates an idea of The Zodiac as a supergenius, a maniac who planned everything out to the last detail, a person whose murderous spree was so rigorous that even Moon phases and weather patterns are reinforcing clues.

Almost no one goes back to the original documents and analyzes the era as it happened. To see how the story played out for the people who lived through the day-to-day. The material is there. It's available.

The *Zodiac* approach is easier. Someone else has done the work.

So, now, when we come to The Zodiac, we are reading *Zodiac*. The narrative has been written. There is an implicit promise. The data has been sorted and sifted and made cohesive.

That's not what happened to the people who lived in the Bay Area in the late 1960s and early 1970s. They experienced The Zodiac with all of its dead-ends and circularities. It's a different story than the one we that think that we know.

If we're going to understand, we have to start at the beginning.

†

On 20 December 1968, David Faraday is 17-years old. He resides with his mother at 1930 Sereno Drive in the Lewis Ranch Estates. David was born in San Rafael and has lived in Vallejo, California for three-and-a-half years. He attends Vallejo High School. He's on the wrestling team. He's an Eagle Scout and a Lodge Chief of the Order of the Arrow. He's a member of the Knights Dunamis and a staff member of the Silverado Area Council Camp. His family is Presbyterian. David attends Church regularly.

On 20 December 1968, Betty Lou Jensen is 16-years old. She resides in Vallejo, California with her mother and father at 123 Ridgewood Court in the Vallejo Manor area. A native of Colorado, Betty Lou is a junior and honor student at Hogan High School. She is a Grand Royal Bride of the Prima Vere Council #132 of the Pythian Sunshine Girls. Her family is Christian Science.

They are typical White teenagers of middle class California. At least on paper. But what goes through their heads? No one can say. That's what happens when someone dies before they do anything. Nothing remains but the bare details.

†

It's not for no reason that it's called the Bay Area. Waters from the Sacramento and San Joaquin rivers flow into Suisun Bay, travel through the Carquinez Straight and meet waters from the Napa River and go into San Pablo Bay which empties out into the San Francisco Bay and then flow beneath the Golden Gate Bridge into the Pacific Ocean. This says nothing of the tributaries and the distributaries and lakes and creeks and the delta.

When Zodiac becomes known, one player will put forward what is called the Water Theory. It suggests that Zodiac chose his victims based on their proximity to bodies of water. It's mistaking causality for causation. Or putting the apple cart before the horse. If someone's in the Bay Area, they are always near water. It's a sure bet that the murders had nothing to do with glaciation.

The big city is San Francisco. On the coast, at the top of a peninsula across from Marin County. Berkeley and Oakland are east in Alameda County, directly across the San Francisco Bay. Vallejo is twenty-seven miles to the slight northeast of Berkeley. To get there from Alameda County, a person has to cross the Carquinez Straight. North of Vallejo is Napa County, where they've got the manmade Lake Berryessa. Benicia is about eight miles southeast of Vallejo on the same side of the Straight. There are two bridges that connect Benicia and Martinez.

Berkeley and Oakland are in the East Bay. Vallejo, Martinez, and Benicia are in the North Bay. Napa is the first county north of Vallejo. It's not, technically, part of the Bay Area. But it's right next door.

It all looks like this:

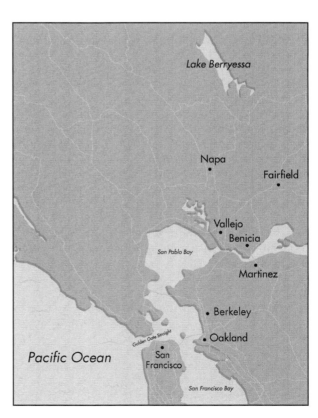

To know Zodiac, one must know the place names. Napa, Lake Berryessa, Benicia, San Francisco, Martinez, Fairfield. And Vallejo. Always Vallejo. The home of teenaged David Faraday and Betty Lou Jensen.

Vallejo is like most towns and cities in the Bay Area. It's small. The core is about five miles wide and three miles long. This is half the size of San Francisco, which is roughly seven miles by seven miles. San Francisco is dominated by hills that can stretch forty-nine square miles into what seems like infinity. Vallejo has rises and dips but Vallejo is flat. A mile in San Francisco can feel like an eternity. A mile in Vallejo feels like a mile.

And, in Vallejo, everything is a few miles from everything else. Life operates on a microscale that can't be comprehended if one is used to the dull flat endless expanses of Middle America or Los Angeles or Vienna. It's small town life and death.

The Napa River comes down the west side of Vallejo, where its mouth empties into the San Pablo Bay. On the other side of the river is Mare Island. Despite the name, it's a peninsula. It's the site of a massive US Navy installation. They build and repair ships. The naval base is the town's economy. The military-industrial complex generates beaucoup dollars. The impact can be gauged through population data. In 1950, Vallejo has 26,000 residents. In 1960, with the United States entrenched in the Cold War, the number is 60,000.

The southern border of Vallejo is the Carquinez Straight, the one that connects the Suisun and San Pablo Bays. To the east of the city, starting with Blue Rock Springs Park, there's untamed primal California nature. A few hints of human civilization but mostly hills and wetlands.

Vallejo is two cities.

There's the old California pioneer town, the one founded in 1851, the one that's left behind Victorian houses, and then there's a new Vallejo built for the exploding population. It's tract-housed, strip-malled, chained-restaurants. It puts the sub in suburban. Most of the people in this story are from the second Vallejo. They're the New Californians who rise on a prosperity bubble that follows the Second World War.

†

From about 1 December until 14 December 1968, Betty Lou was going with a boy from Hogan High named Ricky. Then, on a Saturday night, she's helping to decorate the Pythian Castle for an up-coming musical festival. David is there. Teenaged love at first sight. David digs Betty Lou, Betty Lou digs David. She tells all of her friends about this new boy and then calls Ricky and breaks the bad news. She can't go with Ricky anymore. She's met someone new. Ricky does not take it well. He starts calling Betty Lou, obsessively, and there's the possibility that he's hiding in the bushes outside her family home. He makes noise about wanting to punch David in the teeth. But he's heard the bell's toll. There's an inevitability in the sound. Even at this young age, he can tell when it's over.

David's crazy for Betty Lou. He starts cutting classes and going over to Hogan and seeing her every chance that he gets. David and Betty Lou talk on the phone. Maybe their conversations go like this: they tell each other about their families and their friends and what's going on at school. Betty Lou says they should go into San Francisco and see the crazy people who live there. David says that's a great idea but he isn't sure how much he can take. David hates drug people. They're disgusting. Betty Lou says that she isn't so sure, maybe they aren't as bad as everyone says but David shuts her up by telling her about this thing that happened over at the International House of Pancakes on Tennessee Street. A guy was dealing marijuana and David got so annoyed that he went up to the pusher and told him to clear off. Or else he'd call the cops. The guy said that David had better mind his own business and look after himself. David said, come on, come and get me if you're so rough. Right now, here, in front of everyone. Let's see what happens. The guy got scared. That's the thing with bullies, says David, they're a bunch of phoneys. They only pick on people who can't give them a licking. If someone's willing to teach them right from wrong, they back down and turn tail. I'd have thumped him into last Tuesday. Wow, says Betty Lou.

It's only about five days of Betty Lou and David knowing each other when David suggests that he and Betty Lou go on a date. Friday night. 20 December 1968. Betty Lou says that's a great idea.

Ricky keeps calling and he tells Betty Lou that if she doesn't break it off with David, Ricky's going to tell her parents that she smokes cigarettes. When he punches David's teeth, it won't be with the grace and charm of a gentleman. It'll be brass knuckles for the punk. Betty Lou doesn't know what to do. She tells her friends. She tells her sister.

†

On the afternoon of 20 December 1968, David cuts class and goes over to Hogan High. He sees Betty Lou. As they're talking, who should come along but Ricky? David and Ricky exchange words. Ricky doesn't throw a punch. An adult heads over and looks funny at David, so David hightails it back to Vallejo High.

After school, David and Betty Lou go over to a friend's house. They hang out for a while listening to records. Betty Lou's sister Melodie picks up Betty Lou at 6PM.

Betty Lou and Melodie talk about Ricky. She's scared about what he might do to David. Melodie's given Betty Lou some advice. If she wants things to go well, she'd better bring David over to the house and introduce him to their parents.

David hangs out for a while. Then he goes home. His mother and sister are there. David's parents are separated. His father lives down in Salinas. David asks to use the car like his mother promised. She says that if David wants to go out, he'll have to drive his sister Debbie to the Pythian Castle. She's got a meeting of the Rainbow Girls. Around 7:10PM, that's what David does. He drops Debbie off and comes back home. David changes into a light blue long sleeved shirt, brown corduroy jeans, black socks, and a pair of brown boots. He leaves his house around 7:30PM. He drives to where Betty Lou lives with her parents.

He rings the doorbell and Betty Lou answers. She's wearing a purple dress with a white collar and cuffs. The black hosiery is tight on her legs. Betty Lou's parents are there. The mother tries to smile. David's been a camp counselor and he's an Eagle Scout, so this is no big deal. He's prepared. He is the living vision of politeness. Yes sir, no sir, yes ma'am. He talks about how he's going to take Betty Lou to a pre-Christmas concert at Hogan High. He promises to have Betty Lou home by 11PM. He talks about the wrestling team and the Eagle Scouts. When he's passed the test, when Betty Lou's parents can't find anything wrong, David and Betty Lou leave.

They go to Sharon's house on Brentwood Avenue. Sharon is one of Betty Lou's best friends. They arrive at 8:20PM. They hang around for forty minutes before Sharon says that she has to get ready for a party. She walks them out to the car. They don't say where they're going.

In the news that follows 20 December 1968, it's reported that David and Betty Lou attended the pre-Christmas concert at Hogan High. Later, when Zodiac emerges and generational copies are written, the concert is common knowledge. It's what they did. It's where they went. This apparent fact is always present.

In the files of the Solano County Sheriff's Department, there's a report that states this concert did not take place. The report also references a ballistics analysis issued by the California Bureau of Identification and Investigation. The CII report is dated 3 January 1969.

If the Sheriff's Department references the CII document, then it must be written weeks after 20 December 1968. This is long enough to give weight to the assertion that the concert did not take place. The cops are beyond the initial fog of discovery.

The easiest assumption is that the concert was a lie told to Betty Lou's parents. A respectable pretext for her first date with David. An excuse to be alone. In the generational copies, there will be second or third hand memories of people who remember seeing the two at this concert.

Which the police state did not take place.

So. Here we are, it's 9PM on 20 December 1968.

No murder yet and we're up against it.

Scientific study has established, conclusively, that our memories are not accurate recollections of events. People forget, people invent, people obfuscate. Even those cursed with so-called photographic memories are filling in the gaps. We believe that our identities are a collection of events in our brains, that our personalities are shaped by the ineradicable truth of what we've experienced. We believe these stored memories to be truthful and accurate. But they aren't. If there's no physical evidence or footage or contemporary written record, then there's no way to know that a thing happened. It's an injustice that breeds countless injustices.

But who said that life was just?

Human memories are, at best, porous. Expose a brain to media and the media seeps in through the holes and become the memories. Recollections in the first twenty-four hours are the most accurate. Give it a week of newspaper and television reports and they're shaky. Give it a month and they're unreliable. Give it a year and they're worthless. And so much of what we think that we know about Zodiac comes from memory, from things that people somehow didn't mention in those first twenty-four hours but remembered twenty years later.

Until the development of forensic DNA testing, criminal justice was a story that society told itself. A way of fashioning order from chaos. The cornerstone of this story was a belief that what people saw, or said they saw, was accurate.

It wasn't. Our brains don't work that way.

And this says nothing of the people who lie.

†

They drive around for a little while. Just talking. Really talking. It's so good to find someone to whom you really relate. David knows a place out by the lake where some kids said they'd be getting together. Maybe they could go out there and see what's happening.

David most likely heads out on Tennessee Street and drives east until Columbus Parkway and turns onto Lake Herman Road. The road's not much more than a back route between Vallejo and Benicia. David drives until he reaches a turn-off.

It's a small area in front of a gated entrance to a dirt trail that leads to the Benicia Water Pumping Station. They're there by 10:15PM. A woman named Helen Axe drives by. She recognizes David and his car. She doesn't stop. David and Betty Lou couldn't have arrived much earlier than that. William Crow and his girlfriend were parked in the exact same spot between 9:30PM and 10PM. Crow says that he was there to examine his girlfriend's new car. But this is not true. He and his girlfriend were there for the same reason as David and Betty Lou. To examine each other's bodies. Crow's exploration was interrupted when a blue car drove past and then went up the road a little and stopped. Crow saw its tail-lights go red and realized that the blue car was moving in reverse. Crow felt like something was off, so he turned the ignition and pulled out. The blue car followed Crow before he lost it. Crow was able to observe, he thinks, that two people in the blue car.

Peggy and Homer Your drive pass the turn-off. Peggy sees David's station wagon. There's a boy in the driver's seat and a girl leans on his shoulder. Peggy and Homer drive up the road, examine a construction site that Homer is working on, turn around and come back the other way. It's around 11PM. The Rambler is still there. The girl and the boy are still there. Betty Lou has missed her curfew.

Around 11:05PM to 11:11PM, two men drive past the turn-off. They see the Rambler. At 11:14PM, James Owen drives by. He sees two vehicles in the turn-off. The Rambler and another car parked beside it.

At approximately 11:20PM, a woman named Stella Medeiros drives on Lake Herman Road. She's got two passengers. Her mother-in-law and her daughter. When she gets to the turn-out, her headlights illuminate the scene. There is only one car. The Rambler.

Beside it is the still breathing David Faraday.

In a pool of his own blood.

Some distance away is dead Betty Lou Jensen.

In a pool of her own blood.

†

It goes like this, maybe.

David and Betty Lou are in the Rambler. David's got the engine and heat on. Outside, it's around 22° Fahrenheit. They've got the front seat reclined. It can be assumed that they are engaged in what people call heavy petting. The old adolescent fumbling. As they live so close to San Francisco, ground zero for American hedonism, we should assume that this petting is freighted with a new set of hang-ups. Ten years earlier, the concern would've been about whether or not Betty Lou was going to be seen as an easy girl.

Now, thanks to relentless media coverage, it's the opposite. Everybody's doing it but are these Californian teens doing it the right way?

Enough cars have driven past that they don't pay attention to another. They hear its wheels on gravel as it pulls in beside them. It stops. Even here, maybe, they aren't paying that much attention. The turn-off is a notorious make-out spot. It's one of those liminal zones on the edge of town. A lover's lane. Cars are in and out all the time, heavy petting and sometimes even heavier. When there is nowhere else to go and screw. Maybe it's a little strange that someone pulled up this close. But David and Betty Lou aren't worried.

The front-seat of the Rambler is a split bench. They're both leaning back at something like a 45° angle. They can't see much. But they must hear it when a car door opens and closes. Footsteps in the gravel. Then there's a light shining into the Rambler. Then there's a man at David's door. There's a voice: **GET OUT OF THE CAR. GET OUT OF THE CAR NOW.** The man tries to open David's door. But it's locked. *Oh no*, whispers Betty Lou, *I don't want to get arrested.* Maybe David has enough presence of mind to look over and see that other car is not a police vehicle. Maybe he doesn't.

The man walks to the rear of the car. The voice speaks: **GET OUT OF THE CAR.** The voice fires a bullet through the Ranger's rear right window. It breaks through the glass, leaves a hole, doesn't hit anyone. **OUT. NOW.** The voice fires another bullet. This one hits the roof just above the passenger side rear door. Metal on metal screech. **OUT. NOW. THROUGH THE RIGHT DOOR. AND NO ONE GETS HURT.**

Betty Lou gets out. **THE BOY STAYS IN THE CAR.** Betty Lou is standing, petrified. Her bladder is filled with urine and she squeezes to hold it. **WAIT.** The sound of footsteps like feet across a grave. Now the voice has a body. Now the voice is beside Betty Lou. She feels the voice's breath. She hears its breathing. When she tries to look at the voice, the light shines in her face. They are surrounded by the empty dirt brown winter hills of California, the brutal land that gives no bounty but what a man pulls from it and then curses that man with madness. Weak light of waxing crescent moon. **NOW THE BOY. COME OUT.** David scrambles to the passenger side. He gets out of the car. Before he can see or say anything, there's a gun pressed to his head. Behind his left ear.

Does David speak to the voice? Does Betty Lou see the voice? Does the voice say that things will be all right if everyone keeps calm? Does the voice claim it's a robbery?

No one will ever know.

The voice fires a single bullet into David's head.

Betty Lou sees the light and hears the gas explosion from the hammer hitting the firing pin that sparks the primer that flash ignites the propellant that expels the bullet. Instinct. Now. She runs from the voice. She thinks she might really be able to make it if she just runs in a zig zag pattern like she saw on television one time when her father was watching the news and they said some thing about war and maybe if she runs she can make it if she gets to the other side of the road maybe he won't follow and oh god she has to pee and and and oh god her hosiery is so tight and there's two gunshots and the bullets didn't hit her maybe none of the bullets will hit her maybe the bullets aren't real but one just took down david just don't look back just keep going. Then there's a hot piercing hurt in her back that rips through her dress before she hears its explosion. Ten minutes earlier, David's hand was on her flesh. Now she's burning inside, her torso as porous as human memory. She keeps running. Then she feels it again. She keeps running. Then she feels it again. She keeps running. Then she feels it again. She keeps running. Then she feels it again.

Betty Lou is on the ground, five bullets through and in her body. One deformed mass of copper-plated lead has sliced through her insides and rests in her underwear. Life is bleeding away. She's not going to leave Lake Herman Road. She's never going on a second date. She's going towards the big blank nothing. Before she ever got to do anything. What's in her mind isn't the pain. You don't think about the pain. The pain reduces thought. The pain gives new consciousness. What's in her mind is broken animal fear.

Mother. I don't want to die. Father. I don't want to go.

David's not dead. David's going to linger. David's brain is damaged beyond repair. There are some bullies who won't be taught right from wrong. There are some bullies who don't offer you the chance to giving them a licking.

They were average kids. They deserved better than dying on California gravel. But that's it, they've been shot, and that's all they are, all they're given, all they ever will be. Names in this book, names on the Internet, subjects for fan fiction. Carcass meat picked to pieces and eaten by vultures.

It takes less than six minutes. Between 11:14PM and 11:20PM. The voice gets in its car and drives away. Senator Luther Gibson Highway is a three minute drive, connects to Lake Herman Road. An escape route. The vehicle unseen by anyone. The voice is gone.

No one will hear a peep for half a year.

David and Betty Lou are singled out not for whom they are but rather what and where they are. Hormonal kids in a wrong place at a bad time. Lake Herman Road generates enough traffic that the attack can be narrowed to a six minute window. One more passing car and the thing would have been witnessed.

Ballistics determines that the gun is likely a High Standard M-101 or a JC Higgins Model 80. Both are manufactured by High Standard, but the Model 80 has a different grip than the space-age number which adorns the M-101. Like all JC Higgins firearms, the Model 80 was available until 1963. It's the house brand at Sears. Both models use .22 long rifle rounds. The guns can kill a human but it's better for light hunting. The owner's manual makes this purpose explicit:

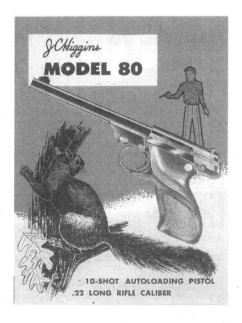

A gun for squirrels. Used to kill kids. Either the murders were unplanned and the gun was in the car. Or the voice planned the killing and wanted a challenge. Or maybe this was the only weapon available. Whatever the reason, it is the strangest of choices, the least likely way to ensure death.

At approximately 11:20PM, Stella Medeiros is passing the turn-off. Her mother-in-law and daughter are in her car. Her headlights illuminate the scene. There is only one vehicle. The Rambler. Beside it is the still breathing David Faraday. In a pool of his own blood.

Some distance away is dead Betty Lou Jensen.

In a pool of her own blood.

The women in the car scream and beg for mercy. From the universe, from Jesús Cristo, from death. But death don't. Death don't have no mercy. In this land. Medeiros drives like a demon towards Benicia. She's going to the station or a phone booth when she encounters a patrol car. She honks her horn. She flashes her lights. She gets the cops' attention.

The cops will arrive and David will be breathing. He'll be put in an ambulance and brought to a hospital where he will be pronounced dead on arrival. The cops will compile the evidence. There will be nothing to go on. Neither David nor Betty Lou have enemies. There is no rape or robbery. Other than shell casings and bullets, there's no evidence. It's an unsolvable crime.

All anyone has to tell the cops is about David arguing with a dealer at the International House of Pancakes.

And about poor stupid bigmouthed Ricky.

About his telephone calls. About his brass knuckles. About his threats.

Ricky didn't do it. Ricky has a solid alibi.

No one knows that yet.

Ricky's about to have an awful Christmas.

chapter two

generational trauma

A CATASTROPHE HAS TO START SOMEWHERE. This one begins on 2 August 1933. Three men park on Grouse Spring Road, near what is now Boggs Mountain State Forest. They're here to hunt. It's north of San Francisco in Lake County, and at this date in the history of California, they're far from anything like civilization. The men are musicians, members of an orchestra that's taken up a Summer engagement in Adams Springs. One of these men is named Leo Suennen. He's a violinist and the orchestra leader. With him are Dan Rose and Arthur Cody. Their outfit is reasonably well known, often appears in newspaper advertisements.

They walk through an orchard. Dan Rose throws a shell into his shotgun. The gun discharges. Accidentally. It blasts Leo Suennen in the right leg and the groin. Dan Rose and Arthur Cody go into shock. They attempt to will the event away. If you pretend hard enough, maybe it didn't happen. That's followed by the reality and screaming. Leo Suennen looks down at the blood seeping through his clothes. He has milliseconds to accept the stories that he's heard about bones and blood and organs and the fragility of life. When you're whole, you can pretend that they aren't real, that the skeletons are cartoon monsters. As the life leaks out, you become a believer. It's all too true. Leo Suennen is a human being. And he's dying here.

Dan Rose and Arthur Cody carry Leo Suennen the long distance back to the car. He's groaning, in and out of reality. The pain isn't so bad but he keeps seeing black spots. Dan Rose and Arthur Cody want to get Leo medical attention. Before he bleeds out.

They fail.

Leo Suennen is the first casualty of 1933's hunting season. He leaves behind a broken orchestra, two grief stricken friends, and a wife and four children.

†

One these children is Leo Suennen Jr.

He's 7-years old. There are no details of his early life but we can assume that it is not a happy one. The breadwinner is dead. The mother left alone with four mouths that demand food, clothes, and shelter. An economic depression ravages America and the world. There's never a good time to have your father killed in the woods. But it's worse when the country is broke.

As a teenager, Leo Jr. goes to work at the Mare Island Naval Shipyard. Technically, Mare Island is misnamed. It's a peninsula. To its east, it's divided from Vallejo by the mouth of the Napa River. To its west is San Pablo Bay. Suennen is taken on as an apprentice. It's 1942. America is fighting Japs and Krauts.

When he turns 18, Leo is drafted into the Navy. On his tour of duty, he meets a girl from Texas named Norma Jean Hightower. They court, they marry. He's discharged, they come back to Vallejo. Mare Island expands in proportion to the size of the war machine. With the Cold War in swing, there's plenty of work. Leo goes home with his new bride and takes up the old job. He works in Shop X38 as a machinist. He takes things apart and puts them back together again and gives use to the useless.

He and Norma Jean are prolific parents. Sources differ but they have either 8 or 10 children. The first born son is christened Leo Suennen III. The child only lives a few years. Dies as a toddler. A few months after the passing, Norma Jean gives birth to another son. They christen him Leo Suennen IV. Each child demands resources. Even with the generous square footage of California housing, there's never going to be enough room for this many kids. Shared bedrooms. Shared everything.

On 17 March 1947, Norman Jean gives birth to a daughter. They name her Darlene Elizabeth Suennen. And Darlene is why we're here.

†

The details of her early life are non-existent. Assume that the home life was complicated. She comes into focus at the end of November 1965. She's 18-years old. There is a heated family dispute. Darlene leaves home. Earlier that year, in August, she'd met a man named Jim Phillips. In the Haight-Ashbury district. When she splits home, she goes and lives with Jim. They might be in San Francisco, they might be three hours north in Redding. Jim lives a peripatetic existence, works crap jobs, is a brilliant guy with no capacity to apply the brilliance. Darlene works too. Probably as a waitress. On 1 January 1966, they marry in Reno, Nevada.

They disappear for a while. Decades later, Jim is on Internet message boards and writes about where they went. Lake Tahoe, work in a casino. Living in a trailer near the California/Nevada state line. San Francisco, where they buy a motorbike and then go on the road. They end up in Albany, New York. Jim works for *The Albany Times Union*. The newspaper gig only lasts a hot minute before Jim and Darlene go to New York City and sell the motorcycle and head to the Virgin Islands.

There is almost no evidence for any of the above. When Darlene and Jim get back to Vallejo near the end of 1966, Darlene tells her family that they've been living in the Virgin Islands for five months. Otherwise, no other location appears in contemporary police reports, which include an interview with Jim. Decades after she's dead, Darlene's address book shows up on the Internet. It lists two individuals with Albany residences. So maybe they did make it to New York state's capital city. But Jim has no credits in *The Albany Times Union*. And how do two people ride to Albany on a motorcycle in the winter?

The marriage is difficult. Jim's got his own issues, has discovered some unfortunate things about his family that have upended his sense of self. Darlene's got issues too. She likes intoxicants and running around with other men. Jim later tells the police that they lived a gypsy existence.

They come back to Vallejo around December. Jim and Darlene move in with Darlene's parents. A few weeks pass and the Suennens tell Jim that he's got a choice. Either he gets a job and stops living off Darlene's waitress earnings or they're getting bounced into the street. Jim, who claims that he owned a newspaper in the Virgin Islands, applies for a job in Fairfield, about twenty minutes northeast of Vallejo. At the *Daily Republican* newspaper. He gets the gig. He's going to help write editorials. Jim's whip-smart, can handle social situations. But Jim's uncomfortable with the strictures of social expectation. He lasts five days and never comes back. 6 January 1967 to 11 January 1967. Not long after, the paper starts getting inquiries. Jim owes people money. Gave the paper as his contact.

Darlene's parents say that around this time Darlene and Jim take off for Pennsylvania. That they're there for a few months. And then come back to Vallejo. But Darlene's divorce records tell a different story. On 22 February 1967, she moves to Reno, Nevada.

America once was ruled by Christian doctrine. One of the most sacrosanct tenants was the inviolability of marriage. Divorce was possible but the acceptable causes were burdensome in anything but extreme situations. One spouse had to be a criminal or a mental patient or the world's most brazen adulterer. None of these reasons addressed the major reason why people needed to get out. They'd woken up one day and realized that they'd involved themselves in a profound legal agreement with a stranger. Trapped inside a prison. With a person who could be abusive. Or temperamental. Or a rapist. Or worse. Or just someone whom they did not like.

America is a federalist system of government. Each of the fifty states is technically its own sovereign entity. Being part of a dynamic country, a place where people moved all the time, every state recognized legal degrees from the others. The enterprise was otherwise unworkable. Some clever individuals in Nevada realized that these preconditions could be a great source of income. By lowering the necessary standards for divorce, by making it easy to end a marriage in Nevada, a place like Reno could serve as a hub for the people who wanted out but lived in states that refused to let a marriage end.

People could come to Reno, live there for a few weeks, technically qualify as residents, and get an easy divorce. Then go home and be free.

When Darlene goes to Reno, she's there with one purpose. To break out of prison. She works as a waitress at a joint called The Huddle, where she meets Sherry, who'll soon be her roommate at 732 North Center Street. Darlene gets fired from The Huddle and starts working at a casino called The Palace Club. Somewhere around March 1967, Darlene gets knocked up. Her divorce is finalized in June.

On 3 August 1967, she marries Arthur Dean Ferrin in Carson City, Nevada. Everyone calls him Dean. He's from Vallejo. Darlene Suennen who became Darlene Phillips becomes Darlene Ferrin. It's the name that everyone uses when she's dead.

They're back in Vallejo by 24 January 1968. That's when Darlene gives birth to a daughter. Darlene and Dean stay in town, find an apartment and jobs. In April, Darlene starts working at Terry's Waffle House at the intersection of Highway 40 and Magazine Street. The restaurant is open 24 hours, has just been remodeled, losing the novelty architecture that got into record books. Terry's is not a house, it's a complex. It's divided into themed rooms. Whenever an organization wants a cheap place to host an event, they do it at the Waffle House.

The job gives Darlene opportunities to meet new people. She makes friends with other waitresses. She gets close with the male customers, a situation referred to in police files by a series of veiled euphemisms. Darlene is sleeping around. Dean knows about it and seems like he can tolerate it. But the marriage is rocky and the people coming in and out of Darlene's life cause no end of confusion and chaos. There are the men who want to use her and there are the men who want to save her and there are the men who wanted to be used by her and there are the men who are just there, the ones who don't understand what's going on and are surprised by her attentions.

Darlene sometimes goes into San Francisco, and she's running around Vallejo, and, supposedly, she pays many frequent visits to the parking lot at Blue Rock Springs Park. The park's on the eastern edge of Vallejo, across the street from a golf course of the same name. It has hiking trails that go up into undeveloped hills and mountains. Primal untamed California.

The parking lot is a lover's lane.

Maybe Darlene is reclaiming territory for herself, wringing as much from life as possible in her limited circumstances. In the contemporary moment, even with the media ethos of sexual liberation, small town people would have thought of her as a loose woman. She'll go with anyone and if they offer her grass or acid or uppers or downers, she'll take those and make it worth their while. Another interpretation belongs to True Crime vultures. The personal life is pretext for mystery. In the most denuded way, this is true. If Darlene's spending a lot of time at Blue Rock Springs, then she has a statistically higher likelihood to be killed by a murderer who haunts lover's lanes. But that's not what anyone means. What everyone means is that by sleeping around she invited the murderer into her life.

Read carefully and what one gets from Darlene's life is a person in emotional pain. She's doing the best that she can, what makes the most sense at the time. The choices are questionable. The motivation is not.

The cause is the same as every destroyed person, as every individual who acts out in ways that are not to their own benefit. The root is always family. What happens behind closed doors. Darlene's not the only Suennen with problems. Several of her siblings end up in prison.

Darlene's mother dies in 1982. Leo Suennen Jr. remarries and moves to Nevada. He lives in Fernley, a city that's about thirty miles east of Reno. Leo's obituary says that he and his new wife built their dream home.

On 4 October 1991, the *Mason Valley News* publishes an article entitled SUENNEN FOUND NOT GUILTY. Following a three-and-a-half day trial, Darlene's father was found not guilty of three counts of sexual assault on a minor child under the age of 14 and also not guilty on one count of lewdness with a minor child under the age of 14. The case was originally four counts of sexual assault but one charge was dropped at trial.

On 5 April 2002, the *Mason Valley News* publishes FERNLEY MAN PLEADS GUILTY TO LEWDNESS CHARGE. Darlene's father has pleaded guilty to a charge of open and gross lewdness and another of attempted lewdness with a minor under the age of 14. Suennen was arraigned on 4 June 2001 on one charge of open and gross lewdness and two charges of attempted lewdness with a minor under the age of 14.

And that's whom Darlene grew up with.

†

Around 4PM on 4 July 1969, after she's worked the day shift at Terry's, Darlene Ferrin calls Michael Mageau. She's 22-years old. Michael is 19. He works for his father at the Doyen Pest Control Services. Michael is paid to eliminate animal life that human beings find intolerable. He's a twin, has an identical brother named Stephen. The brother will say the most extreme things about Darlene when interviewed by the police. Which has an understandable angle. To make Michael look better. Their parents are divorced and Stephen, about three weeks ago, moved down to the Los Angeles area. To live with their mother. He and the old man don't get along. Michael stayed. He gets on okay and the job pays and he's been seeing Darlene for a while.

Darlene's interesting. You never know what she's going to say. Sometimes it's the dumbest thing and sometimes it's from another planet and then every once in a while, she'll dissect a situation with the laser precision of a genius mind. Plus, she's older, and yeah, she's married and has a kid, but Darlene says the marriage is mostly over and her husband Dean doesn't seem to mind when she steps out.

Darlene calls Michael. They make plans to go to San Francisco. To see a movie. *2001: A Space Odyssey* is playing in the Golden Gate Cinerama. *I Am Curious (Yellow)* is at the Presidio. *if....* is at the Larkin. Darlene says she'll get to Michael's house around 7:30PM.

Earlier, at 3:45PM, Darlene's husband Dean reports for work. He's an assistant cook at Caesar's Palace Italian Restaurant on Tennessee Street. He'll be working all night, won't leave until the wee morning hours. It'll give him an alibi.

Plans change after Darlene's conversation with Michael Mageau. At 7PM, her father picks up Janet Lynn and Pamela. Babysitters. Darlene's sister Christine is in the car. Leo drives the trio to Darlene's house at 1300 Virginia Avenue. Darlene's at home and she greets all the girls. They chat for a bit, nothing serious, and Darlene says that she and Christine are going into Vallejo to see the town's events. An Independence Day celebration happened that morning, presided over by this year's Miss Firecracker. Christine helped with the organization. At 9PM, there's going to be a lighted waterfront boat parade and a fireworks display at 10PM. Darlene tells the babysitters that when she gets back, she's going to San Francisco.

Darlene calls Michael and apologizes, says that she had no choice, her father dumped her sister on her. She'll call as soon as she can and see him then. Definitely tonight. It's family, you know? I don't understand, says Michael, why you do anything your father wants. It's not my father, says Darlene. It's my sister. Besides, you'll never know.

Darlene and Christine watch the boat parade and then Darlene calls the babysitters and checks in. Everything's fine, they relay a message. One of the other waitresses at Terry's called and wants Darlene to stop by the restaurant. Darlene calls Michael Mageau and says that she'll be over shortly.

Around 10:30PM, fireworks exploded and over, Darlene and Christine show up at Caesar's, where Dean works. She and Christine hang around the restaurant a little bit, chew the fat. Darlene says she's going to take Christine home. She doesn't mention that she's going to Terry's. But it's on the way to the Suennen home, where Christine lives with the family. Darlene doesn't mention Michael. She and Christine leave Caesar's and go to Terry's. Darlene talks to the other waitresses. There is no record of who asked her to come to the restaurant or what they talked about. Darlene drops off Christine and drives to 1300 Virginia Avenue. She arrives at her home around 11:30PM.

Dean and William Lee, Dean's boss, say that, about this time, they place a telephone call to 1300 Virginia Ave. They speak to Darlene and ask her to go find a fireworks stand. They want to have a party at the house after they close Caesar's. The babysitters make no mention of this call, say that when Darlene came home, she was talking about fireworks and the party. Either way, she tells the babysitters that she's going to find firecrackers and will be home around 12:30AM. She leaves and drives to 864 Beachwood Avenue. Where Michael Mageau lives with his father. It's one street over from where Betty Lou Jensen went to school.

Darlene picks Michael up. They talk about how they're hungry and right there in her Corvair they decide to go and get some food. They're heading west on Springs Road when Darlene says a fateful thing.

"I really need to talk to you about something."

When they get to Mr. Ed's restaurant on Springs Road, Michael says that they shouldn't bother with food. Why don't they go up to Blue Rock Springs and talk? Darlene turns the car around and they head east.

She drives to the Blue Rock Springs parking lot. It's a semi-circle and it's dark and on one side there's the road and then on the other, to the east, there's a great expanse of untamed California. It's summer. The hills are green but no one can see that. The hills are only outlines against faint sky illumination. Sometimes when you see a thing too much you forget how to see it. It becomes background information, easily ignored.

Darlene turns off the motor and lights but leaves on the radio. They don't talk about whatever's on Darlene's mind. It's only been a few minutes when three cars pull into the lot. The cars are full of kids, drunk or stoned. The kids laugh as they set off firecrackers. Then they leave. Michael and Darlene recollect themselves. They don't talk about whatever's on Darlene's mind. It's a stupid night to be here. Friday is always bad news for privacy because Friday's the day when the working class converts its money into leisure that blocks out the pain and hopelessness of capitalist exploitation. Friday's when you get drunk, when you fuck a stranger, when you get into a fight. It's also the 4th of July. Friday taken to the Nth degree. Tonight, the conversion of money into leisure isn't just a personal choice. It's a state-mandated obligation.

Another car pulls into the parking lot. The driver turns off the headlights and pulls up to the left side of Darlene's Corvair.

"Do you know who that is?" asks Michael.

"Oh, never mind," says Darlene.

Michael later tells the cops that he was always joshing Darlene about how many people she knew. When she says, "Oh, never mind," he has no idea if she knows the person in the car or if she's telling him to be quiet because she's tired of hearing about how many people she knows. It's one of those conversations where words have a surface meaning and then, below, there's the actual dialogue. Michael joshes Darlene because Michael doesn't want Darlene screwing every man in Vallejo. Darlene's exhausted by Michael and men in general. How many men have tried to stop her from sleeping with other men? Only her first husband was okay with it. But he was one of those San Francisco people who are okay with everything. And he was a disaster. And this one, now, here? He's a baby, just out of high school, and he's telling her how to live? Darlene's a divorcée, Darlene's been married twice, Darlene's a mother, Darlene and Dean bought their own house a couple months ago. Michael lives with his father.

Oh, never mind.

Michael sees that there's a man in the car. But it's too dark to see the man. It doesn't matter because the car drives away. Darlene and Michael collect themselves. They don't talk about what's on Darlene's mind.

Five minutes later, a vehicle pulls up behind Darlene's Corvair. In Michael's statement to the police, the implication is that this is the same car as the one that pulled up beside Darlene's Corvair. Perhaps it is. This time the vehicle's headlights remain on. In the darkness, the illumination from the car obscures the details. It could be the same vehicle, it could be different.

Michael and Darlene hear the opening of the other car's door and think that it's the cops. Whoever's in the car gets out and he's carrying a high powered flashlight, the kind with a handle. He's shining the light into Darlene's Corvair. The man from the car comes up to the passenger side and both Michael and Darlene think that he's going to check their IDs. Michael's window is down. The man is shining the light in their faces. He says nothing. Michael goes for his wallet and then no sound just pain in his back and neck. The pain robs you of human consciousness. The pain gives the animal broken fear. It's a shot in the neck and the face and it wounds his tongue and jaw but it doesn't kill him. Michael scrambles into the back seat. The man from the car fires more shots at Michael. The man from the car has had good luck. Some of his bullets pass through Michael and strike Darlene in her arms while her hands are on the steering wheel. She's incapacitated, can't drive away. Darlene's conscious mind is no no no no no. But Darlene's is her father's daughter. She knows what he taught. It was always going to come to this. The man from the car is finished with Michael. He begins shooting Darlene.

The man walks back to his car. Michael has the animal fear. Michael lets out a wail like a squealing pig. The man hears. The man from the car walks back to the Corvair. The man from the car shoots Michael. Twice. The man from the car shoots Darlene. Twice. The man walks back to his car. Unhurried, not rushed. Michael's animal fear makes him try to open the passenger door. But the handle is broken on the inside. Or Michael thinks that it is. But he left the window open. Michael is somehow back in the front seat. Michael reaches through the open window and pulls the outside handle. Michael falls on the ground. The other car backs up and takes off at a high rate of speed. Michael thinks that the car is like Darlene's. Something like a Corvair. Michael thinks the car is brown. Michael thinks the car has a California license plate. Michael can not make out the plate's numbers.

Maybe Michael or Darlene are in the front. Flashing headlights to attract attention. Michael can not tell who flashes the lights. Darlene can't speak. Darlene has nine entry wounds and seven exit wounds. Darlene is dying. What comes from Darlene is less animal than the sounds of Michael. She's not squealing like a pig. Darlene's soul is leaving her body and she sounds like the wind is rattling a door with unoiled hinges.

†

If this is who killed Betty Lou Jensen and David Faraday, then he's learning. Don't turn off the headlights, leave them blinded, approach from the rear, don't speak. Shoot them while they're trapped inside and have no chance to run. Don't use a .22LR hand pistol. Use a 9MM. Use a gun meant to kill people.

Except this gun doesn't. Darlene is a goner. But Michael survives. He's on the ground bleeding and waiting for someone to save him like in a show from Televisionland or a comic book where Superman uses heat vision to cauterize the wounds.

Salvation comes in a brown Rambler. Inside the Rambler are Jerry, Debbie and Roger. Michael later describes them as "hippy types." They were downtown watching the July 4th festivities. When the fireworks end, the trio looks for a girl Roger knows. They drive around town but this girl that Roger knows is nowhere to be seen. Someone gets the idea that maybe this girl Roger knows might be up at Blue Rock Springs. They take the freeway to Columbus Parkway and come in the back way. They get to outside of the parking lot and they see Darlene's Corvair. Its headlights are off. They decide to check to see if this girl that Roger knows is in the Corvair. The Corvair's headlights come on. They think the car's about to pull out when they hear a scream. Debbie backs up the Rambler and gets the Corvair in her headlights. There's a young man there, on the ground beside the passenger side door. He's rolling and screaming and it's not a sound like anything the three hippy types have ever heard. There's the screams of wounded men in films. This is something else, this is what it's gotta sound like when an American GI takes it in the gut from Viet Cong. Ten thousand murders seen on Televisionland were fool's gold. Televisionland is greasy kid's stuff. Televisionland doesn't prepare you for Michael's screaming or the river of blood that pours from his mouth or the smell. Debbie pulls the Rambler up beside the Corvair. Jerry jumps out and asks the young man if he's all right. It's the stupidest question. Of course he's not all right, but what else do you say? The young man says that he's been shot and the girl's been shot. He asks them to get a doctor. Jerry says all right. The young man says, "Hurry." Roger's out of the car now. He and Jerry can't take their eyes off the blood on Michael. They don't look in the car. They don't see the girl. Jerry wants to stay while Debbie and Roger get a doctor. But they make him come along. We're not leaving you here. They drive into Vallejo, go to Jerry's house at 938 Castlewood, which is next door to where Betty Lou Jensen went to school. They call the cops. They wait a while and get worried. What if the cops think the first call was a hoax? They drive to Debbie's brother-in-law's house. His name is Bob. Bob is a cop. They call the police from Bob's phone. The police dispatcher says that units are at the scene.

†

Debbie, Jerry, and Roger never tell the cops why they were looking for the girl that Roger knows. Read between the lines and it's hard to avoid the suspicion that this nameless girl was holding. She could get them grass or speed or acid. Why do they think that she's in Blue Rock Springs? Like many remote outskirts on the edge of every California town, the parking lot has become a place where people can find drugs.

Mageau's account of the attack, offered while still in the hospital, doesn't make much sense. Some of this is shock. Some of it is painkillers. But there's something else, too. Mageau is like Darlene. He's more complicated than the other victims. Of all the people attacked by the killer, Mageau is the only one with a criminal record. In a few hours, the cops will check on Mageau and discover that he was arrested on 6 September 1968. Petty theft at a grocery store located on Springs Road. At the time of his arrest, he gave the alias William James Janssen.

There's also the very strange fact that when he and Darlene are shot, Mageau is wearing three sweaters and three pairs of pants. Extant data for the nearest weather station records the highest 4 July temperature at 93.9° Fahrenheit and the lowest at 63 degrees Fahrenheit. Mageau later explains that he wore layers because he was ashamed of his puny physical stature. He wanted to look big for Darlene. But if Darlene and Michael have known each other for some time, she is more than aware of his physique. On the other hand, there's a famous example of someone who did the same thing: Nirvana frontman Kurt Cobain. Grunge fashion, of which he was the main progenitor, emerged from a deep and abiding shame about his tiny druggie body. He wore extra layers to look bigger. And did it around people who knew his body very well.

Latter day commentators have suggested some inherent criminality in Mageau's sartorial choices. That it's common criminal technique to wear multiple layers and discard the excess clothing after the crime has been committed. Or that he was wearing the layers as protection, because he and Darlene were going into a major drug deal and Michael didn't want to get slashed. Decades later, Darlene's brother will say that, on this night, he'd asked Darlene to get him pot. It's offered so far after the events that it must be considered worthless. But it does hint at a possibility. That Michael and Darlene went to Blue Rocks Springs not to engage in the typical lover's lane activity but to see if anyone was holding. The silence about the girl that Roger knows is the indicator, the small nod that the parking lot serves another function.

Why would anyone think that they can buy fireworks at 11:30PM? Why would Darlene not get fireworks and instead pick up Mageau? Why would Darlene go on a date when there's a party at her house? Why would Mageau and Darlene need food but then decide, instead, to go to a lover's lane to talk about something that Darlene never mentions? Why would Mageau be elusive about whatever he and Darlene were doing in the parking lot?

Mageau never says that Darlene is looking for fireworks. He's outside the closed loop. He doesn't know William Lee, doesn't know Dean Ferrin. If the fireworks story is concocted as excuse for the babysitters and then becomes an expediency, a convenient thing to tell the cops, a way to avoid saying that Darlene was in the commission of a harmless criminal act, there's no reason Michael would know. He is Darlene's helper in getting the real fireworks, the ones that set off chemical explosions in the human brain. Outside of the closed loop, Mageau has to offer his own elusion. He can't say why they were there. So he and Darlene were hungry. They wanted to go to the restaurant. But then decided that they needed to talk. So they went to the parking lot.

It's only a theory. There's no evidence.

But it does solve the inconsistencies.

†

Darlene arrives at Kaiser Hospital at 2600 Alameda Street around 12:38AM. She's pronounced dead on arrival. Michael is alive and, while he's being treated, gives a rudimentary account of the attack. He tells them about the man from the car.

At about the same time, a phone call comes into police dispatch. It's answered by Nancy Slover, who's working the night shift. Half an hour earlier, she took the call from Debbie and Jerry and Roger. Now she takes this one. The exact words are lost. There is an era before the United States has perfected mass surveillance, so there's no transcript or recording. This is the substance of what the caller says: "I want to report a double murder. If you will go one mile east on Columbus Parkway to the public park you will find the kids in a brown car. They were shot with a 9MM Luger. I also killed those kids last year. Goodbye."

Days later, Slover is asked to describe the voice. She writes that there was no trace of an accent, which means the voice speaks with the dull flat voice of Televisionland. Slover's impression is that the speaker was reading from a written script or had rehearsed his statement. He spoke in an even, constant voice. Soft but forceful. Slover tried getting more information from the caller but when she asked questions, he only spoke louder and never stopped until his statement was finished. The only change was when he said goodbye. His voice deepened. Got taunting. *Gooooooodbye.* Within seven minutes, the call is traced to a phone booth outside Joe Union's 76 Garage at Tuolumne Street & Springs Road. The establishment has been closed since 8:25PM.

If Slover's impression is correct and the caller is reading or reciting a prepared statement, it means that Blue Rock Springs was a pre-chosen site. If the killer also shot David Faraday and Betty Lou Jensen, then an inference is that the turn-off on Lake Herman Road was also pre-chosen.

Somewhere before 1:30AM, William Lee and Dean Ferrin leave Caesar's. Both travel in their own vehicles and drive towards 1300 Virginia Avenue. They stop at Pete's Liquor Store and pick up booze for the party. They've invited several employees from the restaurant. When they get to the Ferrin home, the babysitters say Darlene said that she'd be back at 12:30AM. Dean isn't worried. Darlene's always late.

Not long after Lee and Dean arrive at 1300 Virginia Avenue, two phone calls come into the house. When Dean picks up, no one is there. Just empty silence. No one thinks much about it. By the late 1960s, the crank call has become ubiquitous. It's the era's Internet death and/or rape threat. But. At roughly the same time, the telephone rings at the home of Arthur J. Ferrin and Mildred Ferrin. Dean's parents. When they answer, it's silence and deep breathing. They're certain that someone's there. Listening.

These calls are the only evidence of any possibility that the killer knew Darlene. Or knew her last name. They are almost certainly made by an individual looking for the surname Ferrin. The caller can't be looking for Dean. Dean answers his own phone. The caller can't be looking for Dean's parents. They answer their own phone. It can't be Dean's siblings who live in Vallejo. There's no evidence that they receive any phone calls. Which leaves Darlene. There are multiple FERRIN entries in the Vallejo phonebook. Dean, first name Arthur, and his father, same first name, are the initial listings. There is no evidence that these calls are made by the killer. But we know that the killer is using the telephone. If the calls come from one of Darlene's suitors, why contact her in-laws? If it is the killer, then it asks its own question. How does he know her last name? Maybe, if he lives in the area, he's seen her at the restaurant. Any other knowledge would be attached to her maiden name. She only spent two months in Vallejo as Darlene Phillips. She's lived in Vallejo as Darlene Ferrin for about a year and a half. The center of her life was the Waffle House. If the killer knows her from the restaurant, and is intimate enough to pick up the last name, then why call the in-laws? Maybe the killer knew that Darlene was married to Arthur. And didn't know which one. That's possible. But the least complex assumption is that the caller learned Darlene's name in a rush. Michael Mageau's memory is spotty. He doesn't mention the killer going over to Darlene's side of the car and rifling through a purse, but Michael also thought that he might have, somehow, crawled back into the front seat and turned the headlights on and off. When he never left the ground. Did the killer, having incapacitated both Darlene and Michael, examine her personal belongings? The police find her license in a quilt leather drawstring purse behind the driver's seat. Does Michael miss the examination? Or maybe the killer has the right equipment to hear police radio broadcasts. Or maybe it's not the killer at all. Maybe it's someone in the media. Or a crank who owns a police radio.

Dean brings the babysitters home. He gets them there around 2AM. He must have driven straight back to 1300 Virginia Avenue. By 2:35AM, he's gotten the bad news and he and William Lee are talking to the police.

†

The police don't know it but there's less than a month to solve the crime. There are no real leads. Darlene had her complicated personal life. The killer called the cops. Michael Mageau describes a White man who looks like half of the White men in California. Says that he could only identify the killer if he saw him again in profile. There's very meager forensic evidence. Just like David Faraday and Betty Lou Jensen. It's the perfect crime.

The cops chase down every one who knew Darlene. Dean's got an alibi and the other boyfriends don't amount to anything. Then there's George, identified and cleared. In the police files, Darlene's friends build George up as a sex pest, an annoying customer who hangs around the Waffle House. Dean sold him a car. George is the kind of man who thinks that waitresses flirt with him because they really like him. Michael's twin brother says that Darlene told Michael that George broke into Darlene's apartment and threatened to rape her. But no one else mentions it.

The reality is that no one wanted to kill Darlene. Not for being Darlene.

†

David Faraday and Betty Lou Jensen were too young to do anything, and even though the Solano County Sheriffs spend much of 1969 investigating a drug angle, there's nothing there. They are shadows. Kids who never developed. Most subsequent victims are also unremarkable. Quiet lives disrupted by violence. Notable only for their bad luck.

But Darlene?

She's got a complicated personal life. No one can keep track of it. If someone attempts to establish a personal connection between the killer and his victims, Darlene is the only real entry point. She's the one victim with loose ends. The situation is made worse in the 1980s and 1990s. Her sisters start remembering details. These are confabulations. Grief preyed upon by mass media. Put someone under the glare of lighting rigs. Smear their face with makeup. Turn on camera. They'll remember anything.

Robert Graysmith makes much out of a brief mention in files of the Vallejo Police Department. It's a name in passing. Identified by Darlene's sister Linda as "Lee." This is totality of what the files say about Lee:

> **Linda states that some of Darlenes [sic] closest friends are:**
> **Bobby a blonde who works at Terrys.**
> **Lee who used to bring Darlene presents from Tia Juana.**
> **Sue Deans [sic] cousin.**

Given that Linda's "Lee" appears between the names of two women, it's possible that "Lee" is not a man. In the files, Darlene's acquaintances and relatives tend to make a hard gender distinction between Darlene's suitors and her friends. But the most likely person, someone who appears in police reports as a helpful witness, is the employer of Darlene's second husband. William Lee. Who was working all night with Dean Ferrin.

Graysmith and others have performed acrobatic feats in their attempts to link "Lee" to a man named Arthur Leigh Allen. He's law enforcement's best suspect for the killer. Allen has everything you needed. He's a pervert with a criminal history. Perfect on paper. Decades are spent in the attempt to link Allen with the killings. Every single time that he's subjected to a new forensic test, he's excluded.

Nothing matches.

George's presence in the files and the mysterious "Lee" somehow leads to the idea that Darlene had a stalker. And if Darlene had a stalker, the stalker must have been the killer. Which means that Darlene knew the killer. Which means the killings weren't all random. Which means that Darlene is the entry point. If the details of her life can be sifted and sorted, then the case can be solved.

Her fate is more tragic than the other victims. She's the one, she's the key, she's the entry point. She's got pounds of dirty laundry. And, after her death, it's aired for the world's entertainment.

But Darlene wasn't the key. She didn't know her killer. She was like anyone else caught in the horror. In the wrong place at the wrong time. The only difference is that she's a small disaster before her killer transforms her into a giant catastrophe.

†

The police investigation is taking place in the late 1960s. There is no forensic DNA technology. Criminal justice is a story that society tells itself to fashion order from chaos. It isn't that the cops are bumbling. The cops are fine. It's criminal justice that is inadequate. Unless someone screws up, unless someone makes a threat before they commit a crime or are incapable of covering their tracks while in commission of that crime or there's a later confession, then the crime will never be solved. If it is solved, there is a reasonably decent chance that the solution will point to someone who isn't the criminal. It doesn't happen all the time. But enough. Right now, in this moment, society doesn't have a better story. Not yet. So people tell themselves that the cops always get their man. But there are so many times that they don't.

The police have until 31 July to solve this case. Until that day, the killing of Darlene Ferrin and the wounding of Michael Mageau and the earlier killings of Betty Lou Jensen and David Faraday have not drawn any attention. People around Vallejo are freaked out. But to everyone else, these are just more gruesome attacks in the Golden State, a place that is rapidly establishing itself as ground zero of American murder. There's too much violence for anyone outside of the immediate area to focus on another lover's lane killing. Not when people are being stabbed and shot and burned alive and mutilated beyond belief. Not when the Vietnam War is happening. Not when the hippies are insane in San Francisco. Not when the sexual revolution is exploding like 4 July fireworks.

Between 5 July and 31 July, the cops are insulated. They work in quiet. And while their efforts are for naught, it's different from what will happen next month. Starting on 1 August, every lunatic will have an idea about the killer. And they will share these with the cops. Who will be duly obligated to investigate each lead.

The publicly available files of the Vallejo Police Department make it clear that, from the first day, the detectives zeroed in on George. It makes sense. If this were a normal murder, everything would point to George or Dean Ferrin.

On 11 July, the VPD catches up with George in Yountville, about thirty minutes north of Vallejo. He paints an anodyne portrait of his interaction with Darlene. He called her Deedee, didn't know her very well, bought a car from her husband, and, anyway, he can account for his movements on 4 July. Presumably this alibi is verified. After this interview, George is not seen again in the police files. The best lead was a dead end. When George doesn't pan out, the cops have nowhere to go. Things stall.

In the files, there's a gap between 13 July and 21 July. This coincides with the one of the biggest things that's ever happened in Vallejo. In the early morning hours of 17 July, Vallejo's police and firefighters go on strike. It was coming, the result of broken down negotiations over salary and hours.

The strike lasts for five days. As far as anyone can tell, it's the first time in American history that police and firefighters go on strike at the same time in the same municipality. It is, definitively, the first strike of a police department anywhere in California.

A state of emergency is declared. The mayor calls in the Highway Patrol and other agencies. Only twenty of Vallejo's cops report for work. Off-duty cops from other municipalities join the picket line. In the Vallejo PD, everyone above the rank of sergeant is on basic duty. The chief and his highest ranking officers, the ones who should be investigating the murder of Darlene Ferrin, are answering the telephones and responding to routine calls and domestic disputes.

The city council caves. It takes weeks to iron out the details. The Vallejo victory sets off firefighter and police strikes around California and effectively ends investigation into the murder of Darlene Ferrin and the shooting of Michael Mageau. When the investigation picks up on 21 July, the initiative is drained out. It doesn't help that there's nothing to go on. George was the big hope. George was not the killer. There's really nothing else.

Darlene and Mageau didn't even have the better part of a month. They got nine days. From the early AM hours of 5 July until 13 July.

†

31 July is the day.
That's when the killer sends his first letters.

chapter three

a lost forgotten sad spirit

ON 31 JULY 1969, an unknown individual goes to an unknown destination somewhere in San Francisco. It might be a post office. It might be a mail box. He deposits three letters. Each is handwritten with a felt-tip blue pen and addressed to one of three newspapers. *The Vallejo Times-Herald. The San Francisco Examiner. The San Francisco Chronicle.* It's Thursday. Probably in the afternoon. If the postmarks are correct, the letters are processed in the Inner Richmond District.

The *Times-Herald* and *Examiner* letters are near identical. They're almost word for word duplicates. The *Chronicle* missive has the same thrust as the others, but different wording. All three envelopes are addressed with the note, "Please Rush To Editor." On the *Chronicle* envelope, an exclamation point is appended. *Please Rush to Editor!*

The *Chronicle* letter reads like this:

> **Dear Editor**
> This is the murderer of the 2 teenagers last Christmass at Lake Herman
> & the girl on the 4th of July near the golf course in Vallejo
> **To prove I killed them I shall state some facts which only I & the police know.**

Christmass

1 Brand name of ammo Super X

2 10 shots were fired

3 the boy was on his back with his feet to the car

4 the girl was on her right side feet to the west

4th July

1 girl was wearing paterned slacks

2 The boy was also shot in the knee.

3 Brand name of ammo was western

Over

[letter continues on back side of same page of paper:]

Here is part of a cipher the other 2 parts of this cipher are being mailed to the editors of the Vallejo Times & SF Examiner.

I want you to print this cipher on the front page of your paper. In this cipher is my idenity.

If you do not print this cipher by the afternoon of Fry. 1st of Aug 69, I will go on a kill rampage Fry. night. I will cruse around all weekend killing lone people in the night then move on to kill again, untill I end up with a dozen people over the weekend.

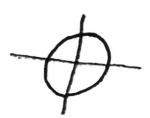

Each envelope contains one part of an encoded message. Together, the three parts look like this:

TO TIMES-HERALD

TO EXAMINER

TO CHRONICLE

When the code is broken, the order is this: *Times-Herald, Examiner, Chronicle.* While the complexity of the cryptograms necessitates that they predate the letters, their order does suggest how the letters are written. The first two read as if they've been composed off a pre-written text, or maybe the *Examiner* letter is a copy of the one sent to the *Times-Herald*. When the writer gets to the *Chronicle*, he's started to improvise. The *Times-Herald* and *Examiner* letters begin with this phrase: "I am the killer of the 2 teenagers last Christmass…" It lacks the bang of the *Chronicle* opener: "This is the murderer of the 2 teenagers last Christmass…" The former is a statement of fact, the latter is the sign-on of a television reporter.

The killer has not yet given himself the tradename. Zodiac before Zodiac. Is he the killer of the 2 teenagers or is he the murderer? The *Chronicle* letter is the only one that suggests the cipher will reveal his identity. The other two make no such promise. When it's solved, it does nothing of the sort. Neither the birth identity nor the tradename. The latter does not exist. Not yet. But it's coming.

Each of the 31 July letters end with what has come to be known as the "Zodiac symbol." A circle quadrisected by a cross. The symbol predates the invention of the tradename, the Zodiac identity. The likeliest explanation is also the simplest. The crosshairs view through a gun's scope. The symbol is shorthand for anonymous death.

In 1965, the *Chronicle* and *Examiner* enter a Joint Operating Agreement. The *Chronicle* publishes a morning edition. The *Examiner* publishes an evening edition. On Sunday, the two collaborate on an identical edition that appears under their respective mastheads. Both papers split all incoming revenues. 50/50. The *Vallejo Times-Herald* is part of a small media empire in the North Bay. Owned by former State Senator Luther E. Gibson. The micro-empire contains other papers, including the *Morning News Gazette* in Martinez, and the *Vallejo News-Chronicle*. The *Herald* is Vallejo's morning paper. The *News-Chronicle* appears in the evening.

By mailing his letters on a Thursday afternoon, the killer ensures an earliest possible delivery of Friday morning. Two of his chosen newspapers are morning editions. Their Friday editions will be typeset and printed before the letters arrive. The killer has asked for the impossible.

He asks the papers to print the ciphers but not the letters. This is the killer before he's gotten any response, before he's learned what works and what doesn't. A writer who doesn't know the strength of his own words. The killer doesn't know that the letters are as important as the codes.

†

On Friday 1 August 1969, none of the addressed newspapers run any part of his cipher. *The News-Chronicle,* sister of the *Times-Herald,* gets a cipher image and the letter's full text into its evening edition. The *Examiner* runs an article but no cipher. On 2 August, the *Chronicle* runs an article and the cipher. The *Examiner's* cipher does not run until Sunday 3 August in the joint *Examiner-Chronicle.* This is the first time that the three ciphers appear together. Only the *News-Chronicle* does what the killer asks. Only the *News-Chronicle* puts the cipher on the front page.

The killer's letters are described and excerpted, accompanied by tiny replays of the attacks at Blue Rock Springs and Lake Herman Road. The Vallejo police chief, Jack E. Stiltz, says he is not satisfied that the letters were written by the killer. He suggests that the details could have been learned through newspapers or anyone at the crime scene. Stiltz asks that the writer send in another letter and provide more details.

Another letter makes its way to the offices of the *Examiner.* The paper publishes the letter on 4 August. This new correspondence is mentioned by the papers. But the letter sparks no frenzy. This missive is the beginning of the Zodiac era. It's the tradename's debut. And no one cares.

The letter reads like this:

> **Dear Editor**
> This is the Zodiac speaking.
> In answer to your asking for more details about the good times I have had in Vallejo, I shall be very happy to supply even more material.
> By the way, are the police haveing a good time with the code? If not, tell them to cheer up; when they do crack it they will have me.
> On the 4th of July:
> I did not open the car door, The window was rolled down all ready. The boy was origionaly sitting in the front seat when I began fireing. When I fired the first shot at his head, he leaped backwards at the same time thus spoiling my aim. He ended up on the back seat then the floor in back thashing out very violently with his legs; thats how

I shot him in the knee. I did not leave the cene of the killing with squealling tires & raceing engine as described in the Vallejo paper.. I drove away quite slowly so as not to draw attention to my car.

The man who told the police that my car was brown was a negro about 40–45 rather shabbly dressed. I was at this phone booth haveing some fun with the Vallejo cops when he was walking by. When I hung the phone up the dam X@ thing began to ring & that drew his attention to me & my car.

Last Christmass

In that epasode the police were wondering as to how I could shoot & hit my victoms in the dark. They did not openly state this, but implied this by saying it was a well lit night & I could see the silowets on the horizon. Bull Shit that area is srounded by high hills &trees. What I did was tape a small pencel flash light to the barrel of my gun. If you notice, in the center of the beam of light if you aim it at a wall or celling you will see a black or darck spot in the center of the circle of light about 3 to 6 inches across. When taped to a gun barrel, the bullet will strike exactly in the center of the black dot in the light. All I had to do was spray them as if it was a water hose; there was no need to use the gun sights. I was not happy to see that I did not get front page coverage.

NO ADDRESS

When this letter is forwarded to the FBI, there is no mention of an envelope. Compound this with the letter's ending—NO ADDRESS—and it suggests that the letter was not mailed but rather hand delivered to the *Examiner*. This theory has been written about, with great plausibility, by Richard Grinell of zodiaciphers.com. What if the three pages were folded in on themselves and the Zodiac symbol/NO ADDRESS was the upward facing page?

In *Zodiac Unmasked,* Robert Graysmith's 2007 sequel to *Zodiac,* it's stated that the 4 August letter is composed on paper with a different watermark than the letters of 31 July. The FBI discovers that the 4 August correspondence was watermarked with "FIFTH AVENUE," a house brand of the Woolworth's discount chain. Graysmith writes than the earlier three letters were composed on paper with an EATON watermark.

A Woolworth's was located close to the *Examiner's* offices. Could the killer have been so enraged by Stiltz's challenge that he decided to write a response? As it's Sunday, the killer can't mail the letter. Or maybe he doesn't live in San Francisco. Maybe he's from out of town and visiting. He reads the challenge, goes to Woolworth's, buys some paper, scribbles out his response and walks over to the *Examiner.*

Scans of the 31 July letters are available on the Internet. With some manipulation, it's possible to find their watermarks. The back page of the letter sent to the *Examiner* is the easiest and clearest. Crop, flip, manipulate its contrast, invert the color palette, and the letters become identifiable:

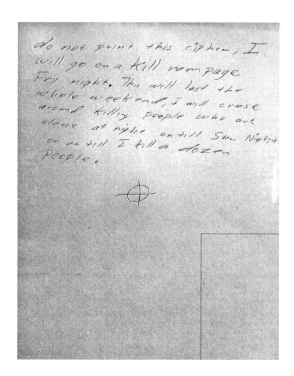

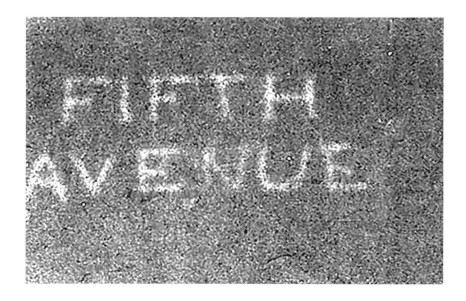

We can discard the idea of Zodiac's rage weekend. The 4 August letter was written on the same paper as his earlier three correspondences. This does not discount the possibility that the letter was hand delivered. If anything, the missing envelope only reinforces this possibility. The *Examiner* preserved the envelope of the 31 July letter. So what happened here?

The Woolworth's brand tells us about Zodiac's socioeconomic status. The gun used to kill Betty Lou Jensen and David Faraday was a JC Higgins Model 80. Available exclusively at Sears. Another brand like Woolworth's, one that caters to individuals without great wealth. If Zodiac killed the two teenagers at Lake Herman Road, then he's a man who shops at stores tailored to the working and lower middle classes. He buys on the cheap. He is not from high society.

†

The killings of Betty Lou Jensen and David Faraday and Darlene Ferrin happen around Vallejo. Zodiac doesn't happen in Vallejo. Zodiac happens in the imagination zone of the press. Here, now, as Zodiac enters his native media territory, law enforcement has zero fruitful avenues. Readers of the *Chronicle* and the *Examiner* have exactly as much information as the police. The letters are the only real lead. Zodiac has become chief of his own police investigations.

The press zone is hyperreality, a sector of information and factoids without geographical locations. Every day in California there is a litany of death and disgrace. A small article runs in the Sunday 3 August *Examiner-Chronicle*. 96 HERE THIS YEAR / FIVE MURDERS IN 12 HOURS. It's ghoul journalism, individual tragedies forced into a narrative that suggests a city and a state and a world beyond control. Every god damned week it feels as if reality has been rewritten. Lyndon Baines Johnson, that cornpone Texas racist, a Democrat of the worst kind, is no longer President. He was elected to the highest office not by ballot but bullet. Hope ended when Lee Harvey Oswald shot John F. Kennedy. The world ended. But the world is always ending. It ended in the August before Kennedy got shot, when the Civil Rights movement marched on Washington, when Martin Luther King Jr. said that America, the promise of this country, constructed for White men by White men, was an idea too powerful to be the sole domain of White men. Televisionland reduced the event. History into historicity. But the world was over. And a new world was born. Now too that new world has ended. And a new world is born. As usual, the American people do not demonstrate grace in response to these ends and rebirths.

Johnson ran for re-election in November 1964. He won. The outcome is a no-brainer. The American people aren't going to have three Presidents in less than a year. And LBJ manages the impossible. He's the most socially progressive President since Franklin Delano Roosevelt, possibly more, but he's dressed in drag. He looks, sounds, and acts like a Southern racist Democrat. But he managed a miracle. He pushed a Civil Rights Act, one with real teeth, through the Congress. If a new America is being born, and it is, then LBJ is the midwife. And yet, in August 1964, there were two incidents in the Gulf of Tonkin, in the waters outside of Vietnam, where North Vietnamese ships may or may not have attacked American naval vessels. It was the pretext for Congress authorizing Johnson to use conventional military means against the North Vietnamese, stepping up the policies of his two predecessors. Johnson not only looks and sounds like a Southern Democrat while he's passing legislation that exists in direct opposition to the goals of the Southern Democrats, he does it while operating the war machine. It's something that Abraham Lincoln knew back during the Mexican-American War. Warmongers always win American elections.

Johnson got lucky. His 1964 opponent was Barry Goldwater, a Senator from Arizona. Goldwater is a maniac. His candidacy is based on a radical set of policies. But Goldwater's like Johnson. He's in drag. He disguises the radicality by calling himself a Conservative. He wants no government, no taxes, no federal spending on social issues, and a rollback of the welfare state that's become a de facto necessity of any industrialized nation. Goldwater and his message are too early. He seems like a lunatic in an era when most people trust the government and believe that it exists to serve the people. Goldwater's argument was that government doesn't serve the people. Government is the enemy of the people. He gets crushed in the election, but not before the Republican National Convention happens in San Francisco, and not before Ronald Reagan, the Hollywood actor and vigorous anti-Communist, delivers a televised speech for Goldwater's candidacy and articulates the principles of this new radical philosophy. The speech doesn't help Goldwater but it establishes Reagan as a political force. Televisionland is coming for politics.

A wave of drug-induced violence starts around 1966 and won't end until the 1990s. The Golden State is awash in blood. The reporting is more real than the events. The country has gone mad, its people are hopeless in their insanity. All you have to do is look at what's happening in the Haight or on the campus of UC Berkeley. Just on the other side of the San Francisco Bay. The overflow of the Civil Rights movement and the natural irritation of the young have come together and caused a great deal of student unrest. Each action needs an equal and opposite reaction, so the university responded with hamfisted policies that can only inflame the moment. But that's not the Haight. There are people in that neighborhood who can only be called freaks, moving into old houses and it's not like they're getting their own apartments, it's more like ten bodies crammed into two bedrooms. Something's gone haywire. The freaks look like jumped-up Oakies escaped from the University of Southern California, if those Oakies hadn't showered in a few weeks and had abandoned any interest in a success oriented pathway. They've gotten the message. America is over. America is reborn. Must they be the same thing that was expected of them while America still lived? The old America no longer exists. They are forging the future. They hang out in bars and coffee shops and on the street corner. These new beings, these wild children of California, are defined by youth. By drugs. By sex. And, by 1969, by the time that Zodiac writes his first letter, their dream has soured. Richard Milhous Nixon is the President. He didn't get there without the world ending. In 1968, they kill Martin Luther King Jr. down in Memphis. He was the hero of American life, a man who, with a little help from his friends, transformed the country. Before they killed him he was, if not forgotten, then consigned to an earlier chapter of history. No one understood his achievements. Which was nothing more and nothing less than a total revolution without recourse to arms. There is no equivalent. Before or after. And by 1968, King was out of fashion. It was hard to see what he'd done. He kept talking about non-violence in a moment of hyperviolence, when the war ideology had infected its proponents and opponents alike. When everything was a fight. When everything was a battle. When everyone was a soldier. King preached non-violence and people thought that he was asking them to eat shit. And he was a Southern Church man when nothing was more embarrassing to the nation's cultural sophisticates than Jesus Christ. And he was middle class when all anyone wanted was the proletariat revolutionary. When they killed him, King was feeling low. He'd suffered so much and the path forward was not clear. Everyone thought that he'd been replaced by a new crop. When he was irreplaceable.

Robert Francis Kennedy, brother of JFK, gives a speech in Indianapolis after the assassination. He talks about Aeschylus and soothes the crowd. It's seen in America as a moment of genuine healing. The irony, which won't be known for years, is that RFK worked as his brother's Attorney General and was, personally, responsible for making King's life worse. He's the one who authorized the wiretaps. But no one knows this. Right now, in 1968, RFK is the great hope, a product of changing times. Something remarkable happened. The Viet Cong staged the Tet Offensive, a surprise attack of heavily coordinated forces. The Viet Cong lost, officially, but the strength and efficacy of the attack and its organization put truth to a lie. The enemy is not a bunch of rag tag guerrillas. The Viet Cong are a serious army practicing asynchronous warfare and that army has a very good chance of defeating America. Unless America commits to a full scale invasion. But that's tricky. Even though the whole country knows that America is at war in Vietnam, it's not officially a war. The Gulf of Tonkin gave LBJ the power to stage a military intervention. It gave him all the powers of a war President. But it's not officially a war. Tet tells America that if Uncle Sam is going to win, the ruse must be dropped. We can win if we restage World War Two. And that's impossible. There's no appetite. But surrender is also unpalatable. It means more American resources and lives. In service of a stalemate. The Defense Department has known this for years, but the press releases are written to deny the reality. *256 Viet Cong captured!* Now the Viet Cong have taken matters into their own hands. Now everyone knows.

Johnson realizes that he's created a total disaster and announces that he will not run for re-election. This gives RFK justification to do what he wants. Which is run for the Presidency. He's as serious of a Left candidate as America is ever going to have, he opposes the war, and he has been transformed by the same wound as everyone else. The death of his brother. He's the perfect man for the job. RFK used to be the biggest bastard in politics, a fervent anti-Communist who ruined lives and cracked nuts. Now he's learned the error of his ways. Grief has transformed him. In a mediated nation with a terminal addiction to the televised close-up, pain is the ultimate fix. RFK's been a United States Senator from New York since 1965. RFK is the promise of the Young Democrats in South Dakota co-mingled with the beautiful people in San Francisco, married to a belief in the human dignity of the poor and Blacks and Hispanics. Incredibly, he's got a real chance at winning. It won't be easy. But it can happen. At last, finally, after all these long years, controlled change has come to America.

Then Andy Warhol is shot by a maniac named Valerie Solanas. Most people, even the wild children, think that Warhol deserved it. Partly for being so faggy. Partly for the scam of his paintings. Partly for what they see as his shitty underground films. Partly because Warhol refused to take a stand on political issues. Which made him the establishment. Shooting him is a revolutionary act. For women. For us. For the antiwar movement. You can suck as much dick as you want, you can hang out with a-heads and drag queens and the Velvet Underground, but if you occupy that much cultural space and you don't take a stand, you're an enemy of the revolution. Valerie's a freedom fighter. Just like the Viet Cong. Three days later, RFK wins California's Democratic primary. It's all important. It gets him a haul of delegates for the convention. He goes to celebrate with Los Angeles's bright and beautiful in the Ambassador Hotel.

And gets shot in the head while he's in the kitchen.

Then there's the Democratic National Convention on 1968. Which should belong to RFK. And is haunted by his ghost as much as Hamlet taking orders from his father. It's in Chicago. Every resident of Televisionland turns on and tunes in. Until now, the freak kingdom of the Haight and the UC Berkeley people and their East Coast and Midwestern equivalents were a hypothetical city-state. The freak kingdom had never done the thing that legitimates any political entity. It had never gone to war. Its very existence is anti-war. Now the freak kingdom has sent out an army and invaded enemy territory. The Mayor and the police of Chicago respond with the brutality of a southern Governor trying to stop the integration of bus stations. Every citizen of Televisionland is a witness to the events, video and film rushed to satellite feed. The freak kingdom gets pummeled by police in blue uniforms. The cops are fucking crazy. It's a police riot. Here is the real face of power. Here's what happens when you fall afoul. There is no America. There is only AmeriKKKa.

All the while, the Golden State is awash in blood. The reporting is more real than the events. There is the constant presence of crime and death. People do what people always do. They react with shock and then they adapt. They become inured to the killing. They establish a manageable level of knowledge and ignore the rest.

For a killer, for someone in 1969 to break through this adaptation, to really make it, he or she must have something special. No one's going to worry over some lover's lane murders. Do you know how many people are shot in California every day?

But ciphers and letters? Now Zodiac is getting there. He's introduced a higher form of mystery, something greater than the squalid questions produced by every act of violence. It's enough to drive a few news cycles, keep him in the public eye for about ten days.

†

The debut of the tradename is done with a stylistic panache that is the envy of every beat journalist. "This is the Zodiac speaking." Despite the slight inconsistency that no one is speaking, that these are written words, the line has the force of a bold 140 point headline.

The killer calls himself Zodiac. He is speaking. And no one listens. For the next few months, when Zodiac is referred to in the press as something as other than "the letter writer" or "the Vallejo killer," he is called The Code Killer or The Cipher Killer. He debuted the tradename. And it didn't stick.

Otherwise, the letter is exactly what Stiltz wanted. The police chief asked for more details. Zodiac answered. From the 4 August letter, it's clear that Zodiac killed Darlene Ferrin and shot Michael Mageau. The open window, Mageau rolling in the back seat. It rings true. It supports evidence in the police files and adds detail that enhances rather than mirrors. The only factual error note is Zodiac's description of Darlene Ferrin's pants. He calls them patterned.

On the night of her murder, Darlene wasn't wearing pants. Her body was clad with what is cataloged in police evidence as a blue and white flowered slack dress. "Slack dress" is a less common term for a jumpsuit, for a dress with lower sleeves that cover the legs. The discrepancy reinforces Zodiac's crime scene presence. Darlene was sitting in the front seat beneath a driver's wheel. Seen from above, in the darkness, the dress is mistaken for pants.

The details about Lake Herman Road are another story. Consider what was in the 31 July letters: 1) Brand name of ammo Super X. 2) 10 shots fired. 3) Boy with his feet to the car. 4) Girl on her right side with feet to the west. Then remember what's in the 4 August letter: "What I did was tape a small pencel flash light to the barrel of my gun. If you notice, in the center of the beam of light if you aim it at a wall or celling you will see a black or darck spot in the center of the circle of light about 3 to 6 inches across. When taped to a gun barrel, the bullet will strike exactly in the center of the black dot in the light. All I had to do was spray them as if it was a water hose; there was no need to use the gun sights."

Betty Lou Jensen was found 28 feet from the Rambler. The recovery pattern of shell casings indicates that her assailant barely moved from the spot where he shot David Faraday. Betty Lou Jensen was five feet two and a half inches tall and weighed 115 pounds. Both atriums of her heart were penetrated by a bullet. Her lungs were penetrated by bullets. Her kidney and liver were penetrated by bullets.

She could not sustain this level of damage and run for thirty feet. Her killer fired as she ran. Assuming that a handheld .22LR semi-automatic pistol can be scoped with a pencil light—which is a giant assumption—the further that the target is from the gun, the bigger the black spot in the center of the illuminated beam. At twenty feet, the black spot would be huge. And how far did the beam of a crude late 1960s pencil light travel? If this technique worked so well, why didn't the killer use it when he shot Darlene Ferrin and Michael Mageau?

Here we get to something in the Zodiac letters. If a statement in the texts is not a demonstrable fact or an outright lie, then it's almost always a reference to a previously existing work. Zodiac is a reader. And Zodiac copies.

Read again, the text about the pencel light: "What I did was tape a small pencel flash light to the barrel of my gun. If you notice, in the center of the beam of light if you aim it at a wall or celling you will see a black or darck spot in the center of the circle of light about 3 to 6 inches across. When taped to a gun barrel, the bullet will strike exactly in the center of the black dot in the light. All I had to do was spray them as if it was a water hose; there was no need to use the gun sights."

In the December 1967 edition of *Popular Science,* there's an article entitled "Can New Non-Lethal Weapons Control Riots?" It's written by Erle Stanley Gardner, the man who created Perry Mason. On page 51 of the magazine, the following appears:

> **Flashlight aiming beam.** Still another development in the works is a flashlight revolver that will throw a concentrated beam of light with a small black dot in the exact center. When a button is pressed, the revolver fires a projectile at the exact point covered by the black spot.
>
> As matters now stand, an officer making an arrest at night has to hold a flashlight in one hand and, if needed, his gun in the other. If the person arrested has a firearm and tries to use it, the officer must try, simply by the feel of the weapon, to put a bullet within the circle of light thrown by his flashlight.
>
> With the new weapon, a projectile will speed unerringly to the exact point necessary to subdue the prisoner.

The 31 July letters accord with the files of the Solano County Sheriffs. But there's no unique information about Lake Herman Road. Anyone with access to the police reports would have this knowledge. Or anyone who hangs around Vallejo or Benicia and shoots the shit with cops. How did Zodiac know that Betty Lou Jensen's feet were facing west? Did he take a compass to the turn-off and make a measurement before he left? Did he later return to the scene and, working off memory of where her body fell, take another measurement and happen to get it right? Or did he get the details somewhere else?

When Captain Stiltz asks for more information, he isn't taunting Zodiac. The suspicion is genuine. These cops are many things, and the tone of their investigation will change with time, but they aren't stupid and, right now, they aren't desperate. They've been around long enough to know when something's funny.

In the response, the letter that debuts the tradename, Zodiac offers more evidence. Which is not evidence at all. It's copied out of a magazine and opens up three possibilities: (1) Zodiac did not kill Betty Lou Jensen and David Faraday but claimed them after killing Darlene Ferrin. (2) Zodiac did kill the two teenagers but did not use the pencil light technique copied from *Popular Science.* (3) Zodiac did kill the two teenagers and in the process attempted using a pencil light to emulate what he read in *Popular Science.*

The only evidence connecting Zodiac and Lake Herman Road are the killer's words. Issued almost seven months after the crime. Half of which constitute an outright lie. And this is a killer who will, in subsequent months, claim multiple murders that he did not commit.

It's probable that Zodiac killed Betty Lou Jensen and David Faraday. But it's by no means absolute.

†

On 3 August, the Sunday *Examiner-Chronicle* publishes all three parts of the cipher. Together again. For the first time. Down in Salinas, where David Faraday's father lives, a high school teacher named Donald Harden and his wife Pamela see the paper and decide to crack the code.

Pamela Harden can see a pattern in the ciphers. She and her husband have no training in cryptography but they like puzzles. They look for places where a symbol repeats. What's the one word that a murderer will use? K-I-L-L. They find what they assume are double Ls, implying the presence of K and I. They fill in letters and infer more substitutions. It takes them four days, on and off, from 6AM on 3 August until the evening hours of

6 August. Sunday through Wednesday. The killer used a homophonic substitution scheme. Each symbol stands for a specific letter and more common letters are assigned multiple symbols.

On 7 August, the Hardens mail a letter to the *Chronicle*. A staff writer gets in touch and asks for more information. When he's satisfied that the solution is legitimate, he contacts Vallejo PD with the details.

In addition to using homophonic substitution, the killer employs his trademark misspellings. He also screws up his encryption, leaving something out between the second and third pieces of the cipher. On some letters, he misuses his own key. Untouched, the message reads:

I LIKE KILLING PEOPLE BECAUSE IT IS SO MUCH FUN IT IS MORE FUN THAN KILLING WILD GAME IN THE FORREST BECAUSE MAN IS THE MOST DANGEROUE ANAMAL OF ALL TO KILL SOMETHING GIVES ME THE MOST THRILLING EXPERENCE IT IS EVEN BETTER THAN GETTING YOUR ROCKS OFF WITH A GIRL THE BEST PART OF IT IS THAE WHEN I DIE I WILL BE REBORN IN PARADICE AND THE [missing text] I HAVE KILLED WILL BECOME MY SLAVES I WILL NOT GIVE YOU MY NAME BECAUSE YOU WILL TRY TO SLOI DOWN OR ATOP MY COLLECTIOG OF SLAVES FOR MY AFTERLIFE EBEORIETEMETHHPITI

The text does not give the killer's identity. Nor does its author call himself Zodiac. The line about the most dangeroue anamal is taken as a reference to Richard Connell's short story "The Most Dangerous Game" or its 1932 RKO filmed adaptation. The plot goes like this: big-game hunter trapped on island where he's hunted by Russian Count Zoloff, a decadent aristo so bored with his social class's normal debasements that he invents new kicks. Zoloff isn't hunting animals anymore. He's hunting humans.

The story's characters don't sound much like Zodiac's letter. Their dialogue is as much about Bolsheviks and the Russian Revolution as anything else. The 1932 film tones this down. But there's not a lot of commonality between the spoken dialogue and Zodiac's cipher.

RKO filmed another adaptation. *A Game of Death*. Released in 1945. Its major scene, where the villain reveals that he's hunting people, contains the following dialogue:

KREIGER

Let me tell you, Rainsford. There is no game in the world can compare to it for a moment. At last I found something against which to pit my brain, as well as my skill. Something truly exciting. Thrillingly competitive.

Zodiac didn't hunt men. Zodiac killed kids in cars. Darlene Ferrin was the least dangerous game. The only person whom Darlene harmed was herself.

The message contains Zodiac's first flirtation with occultism. California was the breeding grounds of a New American Spirituality. Every good and bad and crazy idea about metaphysics resurfaced amongst the hippies and trickled down into the rest of the population. *TIME* magazine ran cover stories about God being dead. What comes after God? A mishmash of Eastern spirituality filtered through U$A Greed. Some people went Buddhist. Some people went Hindu. Some people went New Age. And some people went hard on the occult.

Zodiac hints at occultism and, in later letters, makes overtures towards the counterculture. But he always does it in the lamest possible way. The tradename is the key. So many commentators have wasted so much time trying to locate the origin of the name, but, in 1969, the word 'Zodiac' was everywhere. Search through the newspaper archives of the *Chronicle* and *Examiner* and there's rarely a two day period without advertisements for cheap Zodiac tat. Cups, dishes, place mats, cards, jewelry, posters, records. Zodiac was absolute American junk.

If you're someone who knows nothing about the occult and want to sound spooky, then Zodiac is where you land. It's the absolute lamest, squarest attempt to sound like a sinister freak. It's what someone's dad would come up with.

Literally:

DANTÉ PREDICTIONS
coordinated accessories with Dad's own Zodiac sign.

This goes double for the nonsense about slaves and paradise and the afterlife. Even in the craziest outcroppings, this is nothing believed by anyone in the occult scene. To exist in that culture, you need a lingo that's more complex than Zodiac's cipher. You've got to be able to talk about Aleister Crowley and *Liber Aba* and the Golden Dawn and the Enochian alphabet of Edward Kelley and John Dee. You've got to know about Kabbalah and the Babalon Working of Jack Parsons and *The Lesser Key of Solomon* and opening the Watchtowers and what to think when The Hanged Man is inverted. You've got to be able to calculate the numeric value of every word. Zodiac never, not in any of his 1969 correspondences, evidences any of this.

Instead, he offers something that a kid reads in an old comic book and, because he's got mental health issues, decides must be true. It's 12-year old girls in Wisconsin reading about Slenderman and stabbing one their friends because it'll get them into Hell. It's someone buying *Highway to Hell* and thinking that the lyrics about grotty Australian sex are a secret Satanic code.

One of the more plausible origins for the tradename is the 1939 film *Charlie Chan at Treasure Island*. Charlie Chan is a relatively benign racial stereotype who works as a detective. In *Treasure Island*, set in San Francisco, his main antagonist is a psychic named Dr. Zodiac. It's been said, by people who haven't watched the film, that Dr. Zodiac communicates with the *San Francisco Chronicle* through a series of letters. This isn't exactly true, but it's close enough. Dr. Zodiac does communicate through notes and letters. Throughout the film, he's often referred to as "Zodiac."

His final note looks like this:

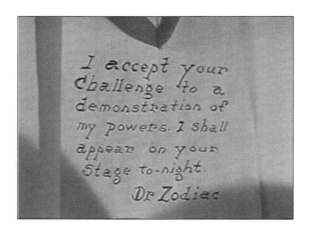

While there is no evidence for the *Treasure Island* connection, no one doubts that the cipher refers to "The Most Dangerous Game," and most people believe that it's a reference not to the short story but rather the 1932 film adaptation.

But Zodiac is writing in the 1960s. Films aren't available on VHS or DVD or BluRay or on-demand Internet streaming. If they aren't caught in their original theatrical run, the best chance is a revival movie house.

And, in the ten years preceding the cipher, there's zero evidence of a *Most Dangerous Game* revival.

In 1968, the Federal Communications Commission assigns licenses for new television channels. In San Francisco, KHBT-TV starts broadcasting on Channel 44 on 2 January 1968. In Sacramento, KTXL starts broadcasting on Channel 40 on 26 October 1968.

These new channels are independently operated. They're desperate for content. They license old movies. On Sunday 23 March 1969 at 11PM, KTXL broadcasts *A Game of Death*. And, earlier that month, on Saturday 1 March, KHBT broadcasts *Charlie Chan at Treasure Island*.

KHBT's transmitting antenna is on San Bruno Mountain, just south of San Francisco. KTXL's antenna is near Snodgrass Slough in Walnut Creek. If you map out both stations' broadcast zones, there's a dead center of overlap.

And it's the Vallejo and North Bay area.

†

News of the Harden's solution breaks on 9 August 1969, makes Page 2 of the *Chronicle*. There are a few more articles over the next week, but these focus almost exclusively on the Hardens. It will be noted that Zodiac made errors in his encoding. The final 18 letters are nonsense. He forgets text between the 2ⁿᵈ and 3ʳᵈ parts. When he arrives at the end, he discovers that he's screwed up his cipher's symmetry. So he plugs in nonsense.

EBEORIETEMETHHPITI.

As the furor dies down, the *Chronicle* reports on amateur cryptographers convinced that **EBEORIETEMETHHPITI** can be rearranged to spell **ROBERT EMMET THE HIPPIE.** When the reporter points out that there's not enough letters in the original to arrive at this conclusion, the amateur code breakers suggest that this was intentional. Zodiac wanted to make things more difficult. It's the first public instance of people examining the scant details and forcing what's available into a predetermined pattern while ignoring contradictory detail. A template is established.

After 12 August, there are no more articles about the Cipher Killer. Not until the end of September. The case came and went. The Zodiac period is remembered, retrospectively, as one of total hysteria. But here we have forty-six days of silence.

In his encrypted communiqué, Zodiac states that he's not going to tell anyone his name. Which he promised to the *Chronicle*. He's a liar and murderer, yes, but he's also a joker.

But, this time, the joke's on Zodiac.

The solution to his cipher isn't the big news on 9 August. The papers also say that Sharon Tate's butchered body was found in the hills above Los Angeles.

†

Everything in 1960s California comes back to Charles Manson. He and his Family of middle class acid drop-outs are the logical terminal point of the beautiful people living new beautiful lives and practicing that New American Spirituality. And while nothing is more tedious than the Family, there's no way to understand the Zodiac era without Manson.

Sharon Tate, Hollywood B-list actress, frosted blonde beautiful, wife of film director Roman Polanski. Husband coming off the massive commercial and critical success of *Rosemary's Baby,* which is about the devil impregnating a house wife who lives in New York City.

During the late hours of 8 August or the early morning of 9 August, Tate and three friends are killed in a bucolic Benedict Canyon house overlooking Los Angeles. The killers also kill a kid in the driveway. No one cares about the kid because he's nobody. He's not rich, he's not famous. He's there to see someone who lives in another house at the back of the property. The kid is named Steven Parent. Before he gets killed, he uses the back house's telephone. He talks to David Gerrold, the Science Fiction writer who penned "The Trouble with Tribbles" episode of *Star Trek*. In a few years, Gerrold will write an alternate history short story about the Tate-Polanski people killing the Manson family. The kid gets attacked while he's in his car. The Family slash his hand and shoot him four times with a .22. Then the killers go into the main house and butcher fabulous people. It's overkill. Sharon Tate is stabbed and stabbed and stabbed and stabbed and stabbed and stabbed and stabbed. Victims are bound with ropes. One gets a black hood over his head. The killers use Tate's blood to write the word **PIG** on her front door. The next night, Manson and the Family drive to the Los Feliz neighborhood and do it all over again. This time the victims aren't fabulous. They're a boring old couple. The LaBiancas. They get butchered. Their hands are bound, their heads covered with pillow cases. The male LaBianca gets the word **WAR** cut into his stomach with a carving fork. When the police find his body, the utensil is sticking out of his middle aged gut. LaBianca blood is used to write on the walls. **RISE. DEATH TO PIGS. HEALTER SKELTER.**

In about a year, the prosecutors of Los Angeles County will present a theory of the crimes. Manson was trying to bring down what he called *Helter Skelter,* named copped off the Beatles' White Album LP. *Helter Skelter* is code-name for race war. White versus Black. *Helter Skelter* is used to mask Los Angeles's complicity in the creation of Manson and destruction of Tate. Powerful people have had insane sex. It's not exactly a cover-up, it's more like a combination of expediency and the maintenance of civic cohesion. The prosecution theory is a polite fiction used to put the killers in prison while causing the smallest collateral damage.

Over the following decades, it emerges that the killings were in response to the 6 August 1969 arrest of Family member Bobby Beausoleil. He'd killed a guy named Gary Hinman. On Manson's orders. Drug deal gone bad. Beausoleil uses Hinman's blood to write **POLITICAL PIGGY** on the wall, and, in a genius attempt to deflect blame, tries to draw a Black Panther emblem. When Bobby is arrested, the Family's LSD braintrust decide to stage copycat murders. If these new murders look like Bobby's, then the cops will think that Black Radicals were responsible for Hinman. Bobby's not Black. Bobby will be freed. The Family butchers seven people. Paints the walls with their blood. Just like Bobby. But the cops don't let Bobby go.

When the case breaks and the killers are revealed, everyone is shocked. Manson and his Family live in hellish borderline acid poverty that seems like a bad parody of The Hippie. They're total scum and somehow networked into the avenues of Los Angeles power. There's a disconnect between what everyone thinks that they know about Los Angeles, which is that it's full of glamour and wealth, and these filthy freaks. Manson is right there in the entertainment-industrial complex. He used to live with a Beach Boy!

Before Manson became an acid guru, he was a cheap pimp. He knew what every pimp knows. If you have girls who'll fuck on your command, their flesh can help you accrue power. Not power over the girls. That comes through violence interspersed with affection. Power over the clientele. People in Los Angeles kept hearing stories about wild libertine San Francisco. And thought that they were missing out. And there was Charlie, just down from the Bay Area, and Charlie can get anyone what they want. An orgy with some groovy hippie girls? Boy, girl, boy, girl, boy, boy, girl, girl? What do you want to fuck? Name your choice, jack, and Charlie'll find your hole.

Bobby Beausoleil is the undisputed star of Kenneth Anger's short film *Invocation of My Demon Brother*. It's a masterpiece. The majority of footage is shot in San Francisco during the year 1966, part of an effort to make a film called *Lucifer Rising*. Bobby plays Lucifer. But those are difficult days. The individuals involved are not stable. The film gets put on hold, the footage moves with Anger to London. Somehow, as if by a miracle, Anger begins editing again in early August 1969. Right after Bobby gets arrested. Now the title is changed. A demon brother is being invoked. The film opens on 11 October 1969 in Los Angeles at the Cinema Theatre on Western Avenue and then moves to the Cinematheque 16 on Sunset Boulevard. Dead smack in the middle of the Sunset Strip. Where Bobby is a well-known figure. He was a guitarist in Love, the best band to emerge from Los Angeles.

Invocation premieres when California knows that Sharon Tate and her friends and the LaBiancas have been brutally murdered. But California and America have no idea why it happened or who did it. Manson has become such an unfortunate touchstone that it's hard to imagine a moment before he existed. This is that moment.

Cinematheque 16 is a mile from the entrance to Laurel Canyon. Where Bobby Beausoleil is also known. And where it's common knowledge that he associates with Manson. *Invocation* gets serious press coverage. Amongst the freaks and the squares. Anger is one of American underground cinema's two high priests. The other is Andy Warhol, recovering from the bullets. *Invocation* is considered. Seen by the scene. No one mentions that it stars someone who's been arrested for murder. Or his connections to Manson. But people know. They aren't saying. If they talked about Bobby, they'd also have to talk about what they did.

There are four months in which America knows Sharon Tate is dead but has not heard of Charles Manson. The moment begins on the same day that the press announces the cracking of Zodiac's cipher. Demonic diabolical murder is like anything else in the newspapers. There's only ever room for one big story. And the competition killed a celebrity.

Throughout August and September, when the Golden State should be thinking ZODIAC, all anyone can do is speculate about Sharon Tate. Much of this is informed by her marital relation to *Rosemary's Baby*. The murders are presented, almost daily, as the byproduct of black magic gone wrong.

Or drug rituals. Or drug black magic rituals. The hoods, the binding, the stabbings. The writing on the doors and wall. The media's fixated on the counterculture, on the mores of California's wild children, and the slayings transform that fixation into yellow journalism. Other than the Salem witch trials and the 1980s Satanic Panic, the American people will never be so deluged with fevered voodoo fantasies. There's a black cat around every corner.

It's worse in California. California is where it happened. California is where it had to happen. California is where it was always going to happen. The American people are hearing about stabbings and hoods and bindings and writing on the door.

And so is Zodiac.

He's doing what he always does.

Zodiac is learning.

chapter four

the sabbath is saturday

THERE ARE TWO HISTORIES OF AMERICA. 1969 is around when they split apart. It might happen a few years before, it might happen a few years after, but it happens. The first history is as old as the country's formation. It goes like: this is a glorious nation inspired by God and founded by people who came to a new land and braved hardship to establish a freedom of worship and belief. These founders are all White. If establishing the country involved moral compromises made from expediency, things like enslaving people from Africa and wiping out the indigenous peoples, well, that was God's plan. Everything is predestined. This is a country for those who fear God, for the individuals unchained by the Pope or any worldly authority. They have no king but Christ. The government is for and by these people and its purpose is to allow its citizens to live and worship as they choose.

The second history goes like this: the people of the first history set in motion a process more righteous than they imagined. They thought they built a country for White Protestants but they created a sacred place with ideals that superseded their creators. America is a land for all. Its government is for the children of slaves, for the descendants of the enslavers, for immigrants from Europe and from Africa and Asia and South America. Its people are unified in their differences. What brings them together is not adherence to creed but the higher ideals which animate the nation.

In the Twenty-First Century, the first history has receded and the second is the official story. But the first history people, the ones whose ancestors founded a nation on God and rapine, have never gone away. They abide. Sometimes they are burlesqued by media representations of their degenerate cousins and renegade children. The opiod addicts and speed freaks with bad politics and poor relationships to criminal justice. These examples are not broadly representative. The first history people are no longer a majority of the country's population but they are here and will never go away. This country was established to serve their needs. If they keep their heads down and lead quiet lives, if they work hard and maintain a covenant with God, they will thrive.

On 27 September 1969, two first history kids are in Napa County.

Which should not be mistaken for Napa, California.

The latter is the county seat of the former, administrative headquarters of the surrounding land. Napa County is rugged, beautiful. It's above the North Bay, sitting atop Solano County. The city of Napa is a fifteen mile straight shot north of Vallejo. To make things even more confusing, there's also the Napa Valley. It cuts through the county's western side like the slash of a Manson family member's knife. The Valley is where most of the cities and towns are located. It's also where wine is made.

In the town of Angwin, slight northwest of St. Helena, there is the Pacific Union College. It's the county's only four year school. Its students receive a better than average education. And while anyone can attend, the college is aligned with the Seventh Day Adventists. These two kids, the ones from the old American history, are themselves Seventh Day Adventists.

One kid is named Bryan Hartnell. He's 20-years old and from Troutville on the outskirts of Portland, Oregon. He's the son of Calvin Hartnell, chaplain at Portland Adventist Medical Center. There's one thing that's never made explicit in police reports. Hartnell's a giant. It's unclear how tall. Online, it's said that he's 6'7".

The other kid is Cecelia Ann Shepard. She was born in India in 1947 on New Year's Day. Her father, also a chaplain, went to the subcontinent for missionary work. She's 22 and from Loma Linda, California. Her father attended Pacific Union. She graduates high school in 1965 and then enrolls in La Sierra College as a political science major. In the summer of 1967,

La Sierra College merges with Loma Linda University. Both schools are Seventh Day Adventist. Cecelia transfers to Pacific Union College, where she majors in music. After two years, she transfers to the University of Riverside, where, now, in late 1969, she is a senior and a music major.

Cecelia's name has appeared in the newspapers. Not for anything sinister. She's singing at Pacific Union concerts and attending weddings. Including her sister's. Her father administers the ceremony. There's also appearances in *The Criterion*, the campus newspaper of La Sierra College. Asked in 1966 about the relationship between the Seventh-Day Adventist, the church, and politics, Cecelia says: "As a denomination which believes in separation of church and state, I think we should take a neutral stand. As individuals it is our own choice. We should take advantage of every opportunity we have to better ourselves as citizens, and a good citizen has a right to take every opportunity to challenge and better his government by participation."

Hartnell and Shepard are the opposite of Darlene Ferrin. They don't stick out. They do what they know, they keep their heads down. They dated a while back but haven't for some time. The only unique thing is their religion. The Seventh Day Adventists are a sect from what Greil Marcus called The Old Weird America. The group dates to the 1840s, when a New York state Baptist divined that Jesus Christ would return to Earth on 22 October 1844.

To the surprise of no one other than the Baptist and his followers, J.C. misses the return engagement. The followers do the same thing as every millenarian cult after the failure of prophecy. They adapt. They develop their own doctrines. These are too complex to recount in their entirety, but, essentially, the group believes that immortality is conditional on any individual's faith in Christ. When you die, you fall asleep until the apocalypse. That's when time ends. If you lived in virtue, you go to Heaven. If you didn't, you disappear. There is no Hell. Just non-existence.

Annihilation.

The Adventists get their name from a specific belief. Through Biblical analysis, they determine that the Sabbath is not Sunday.

The Sabbath is Saturday.

†

Cecelia spends Summer '69 in Loma Linda. Then, on the weekend of 26–28 September 1969, she and her friend Lori drive north. Cecelia returns to Angwin and Pacific Union. Not as a student. As a visitor. Cecelia wants to pick up stuff that she's left in a dorm and catch up with old friends.

On Saturday 27 September, she sees her friend Judy and her former beau Bryan Hartnell. Around 1PM, the trio hit a rummage sale in St. Helena. Bryan buys a television set. He's driving a 1956 Karmann-Ghia, a two door sportscar frame built atop the internals of a Volkswagen Beetle. The car is too small for Bryan to bring both the television and Cecelia back to campus. Bryan leaves the girls at the rummage sale and then comes back and gets Cecelia. They say goodbye to Judy. She has the impression that Bryan and Cecelia are going to San Francisco.

They decide, instead, to go out to Lake Berryessa. It isn't that far from school, maybe a fifty minute drive. When they were dating, Bryan and Cecelia used to go there all the time. Lake Berryessa is man-made, built in the 1950s. The crops in Solano County weren't getting enough water for proper irrigation. The government created a reservoir by flooding the Berryessa Valley. At the far east of Napa County. If a few communities were eradicated in the process, that was the price of progress and commerce.

Now, over ten years later, the Lake is a popular destination. It's artificial but feels like nature in extreme. It's utterly beautiful, the California that everyone imagines when they think of the Golden State.

†

In the available files of the Napa County Sheriff's Department, there exists a transcription of an interview with Bryan Hartnell. In the whole Zodiac era, this is the only primary source. It is the recording of someone who was there, who met and spoke with Zodiac. The interview happened within 24 hours of the event. It offers more than any other document.

It is now reproduced in full:

INTERVIEW OF JOHN ROBERSTON, DET/SGT., NAPA COUNTY SHERIFF'S DEPARTMENT, WITH BRYAN CALVIN HARTNELL (NSO CASE #105907) AT QUEEN OF THE VALLEY HOSPITAL ON SUNDAY, SEPTEMBER 28, 1969 (TRANSCRIBED FROM TAPE RECORDING BY M. FEURLE):

J.R. Can you give me this fellow's description and tell me what happened?

B.H. So many people have been asking me... I hope...

J.R. Well sometimes when we're repetitious, - I know it happens to me, I tell the same thing over and over and over, and sometimes I might vary a little, and if you do...

B.H. Shall I just start out and tell you what happened?

J.R. I don't want to tire you out.

B.H. I just don't want this to happen again to anybody else... Of course he might have his reasons, - I don't know...

J.R. Okay. Go right ahead. Start right from the beginning. What happened?

B.H. Okay. This girl came out from school, - I used to go with her two years ago, and she's now going to another school, and she came up to visit some friends and we were having dinner at the school cafeteria, and I said, "Well, are you doing anything special this afternoon?" and she said, "Why?", and I said, "I don't know. We could go out and either go for a walk, go to San Francisco, or, you know, just...", 'cause we used to be good friends. We used to have a good friendship. And so it got too late by the time we got around to what we were going to do. We had to stop in St. Helena for a couple items and then we had to cart a couple kids home and stuff, and by the time we finally got around to it, it was getting late, and I thought going to San Francisco'd rush you, you know, because by the time we got back for worship...

And so we went out to Berryessa, and there was this one place I used to go out... we used to all the time, you know... and I couldn't find it. And so I figured Ah, forget it, and this looks like as good a place as any. So I parked the car, - there were no other cars there. I had a Kharman Ghia, '56, white, with a black vinyl top, and it's in pretty good-looking shape. But we parked there on the road's edge and we walked Oh it must be about a quarter of a mile to down to the place where we went. We had... (unintelligible) ...peninsula, it's an an island I guess during the wetter season. You can see where it was levee... And so that looked like a lot... there was a big spreading tree up there. There were two of them, really, - one was a little bigger than the other. We took the one that was out on the point.

It was really beautiful out there. We were sitting on top... I lay down on my back and she lay down on her stomach beside me, you know, kind of resting her head on my shoulder, and we were talking, you know, kind of reminiscing about old times, and stuff. And I heard these rustling leaves, and I said, "You have your specs on. Why don't you see what the deal is over there?" And she says, "Oh, it's some man." And I said, "Is he alone?" And she said, "Yeah... (unintelligible) ... and she says, "Well he just stepped behind the tree." And I said, "What's the idea of that? To take a leak?" You know, 'cause that's the only thing I could think of, - just step behind a tree. And so I says, "Well, keep looking and tell me what happens," - and she squeezed my arm and says, "Oh my God, he's got a gun!"

And so he came out, and of course still actually I wasn't... There's some things you really wouldn't mind having happen, just for the experience of it. You know I thought,

Well I only got fifty cents on me. It's worth all of that having it happen. I didn't think about another angle. So I talked to him, you know. I said, "Well listen, Mac," (you know I'm in the sociologist field, you know, I'm pre-law, with history and psych.) You know I've read about the criminal mind and everything, you know. I thought well maybe the guy really does need help, you know. I says, "There's no strings attached." I says, "I don't have any money right now but if you need help that badly I can help you out in another way maybe." And he says, "Nah.. time's running short," he says, "'cause I just got out of... " - some prison in Montana, I don't know what the name of it is. Feathers? Do you know what the name of it is? I'll see if it sounds familiar. Fern or Feathers? It's some double name, like Fern Lock or something...

J.R. It's Lodge..

B.H. Oh yeah, yeah, - Lodge. At least we know we're together on that.

J.R. Mountain Lodge Prison, or something of that nature...

B.H. Yeah. You know he said he broke out and had to kill a guard getting out. And I said, "Well, man, I mean actually I don't mean to call your bluff or anything, but wouldn't you rather be stuck on a stealing charge than a threat of homicide? You know? And he says, "Well just don't start playing hero on me." You know, "Don't try to grab the gun," 'cause I didn't really figure the gun was loaded. I always thought it would be empty. I've heard a lot of times that this is what they do just as a bluff, but I decided not to call his bluff after he really, you know... I told him, "You know you're really wasting your time with me. I've got a billfold and this much change and that's it." And he said, he told the girl, "Go tie him up. I'd feel much better if you were tied up."

And she tied a couple of loose knots on me, so I made it look kind of tight... (unintelligible)... you know, just for a second, and he said, "Go ahead." And I whispered to her, "You know I think I can get that gun." And I said, "Do you mind?" And she got kind of fearful about it, so I figured since there's two lives involved, not just mine, I won't do it.

So I let her tie me up on the wrists again, and he tied her up, - terribly tight, you know, real... (unintelligible) ... put his gun away, and we were talking and all, - bantering, you know, basically. I was thinking, anything I can do to help, by the way just to keep the conversation going... Suddenly he was taking it all seriously, you know... So I was starting out and finally he said, "Okay, lay down. I've got her tied up", you know... He strung a rope between our ankles in the rear, so we were like this, you know, on our stomachs, tied...

J.R. You both facing the ground...

B.H. Right. And, oh, this was before. I got sort of ahead. So anyway, he said, "Get down," and I said, "Oh come on! Don't make me lay down! We could be here all night! We could freeze to death!" I said that a couple, three times, and he said, "GET DOWN! RIGHT NOW!" He got a little pushed off at me. So I got down and then he finished tying her up and clonked her down, - and then he goes... Sssswhoosh (a sound with his mouth)... (unintelligible)

And so I said, "Do you have bullets in there?" And so he pulled out the clip and showed me that he did. The bullets were about this long, I can remember, and about this fat, and they had the regular red cap on it, about this long. Maybe that doesn't give you any better description of the gun or not. I don't know. And it came out of the heel, the grip, you know. It slipped out from the bottom.

And now, to backtrack a bit. I was really trying to see what he looked like, you know. He had on pleated pants, these old type of suit pants, you know, and they were either black or dark blue, I can't remember now. And I can't remember what he was wearing for shoes. But he had on this cotton coat. You've seen the kind, that you just turn the collar up once, there's a zipper down the front, you know. They're real light, super-thin, you know...

J.R. Kind of a windbreaker...

B.H. Yeah, like a windbreaker. And it's got this blue, this little collar, sometimes the guys wear them standing up, you know.

J.R. What color was that?

B.H. That was dark blue. And I don't know. Maybe he had something in his pouch. I just took it as being a... as being a... you know, he was stout 'cause he looked kind of heavy. I think he was weighing two and a quarter, two fifty, somewhere in there. And I got kind of a look at his hair.

His voice... I can remember... almost like I'd heard it before. You know there's some drawls that a lot of people have similar. And... almost as if I'd heard it before... couldn't think where.

I gave that one up, I just gave it up on that angle. I looked through his hair. I kind of looked like it was combed, you know, like this... it was a brownish, you know, dark brown hair.

And this mask he had on. It was ingeniously devised. It was... he had four corners at the top, like the top of a paper sack... black. It came down, came down, with the front panel about to here, and a kind of a thing that came over the shoulders, you know, and then the same thing down the back, straight down. And in the front he had a circle with a symmetrical cross in the middle. You know what I mean by a symmetrical cross?

J.R. Um hum (affirmative).

B.H. The ends of the cross hung out about this far on each of the... you know, where it came out. The circle was this much... like this... and then it was like this, you see... hung out on the end, over the edge of the circle.

And he had clip-on sunglasses... it was hand to tell. You know, the sunglasses you clip on when you're wearing glasses, eyeglasses. He had those clipped on. I'm pretty sure... I don't think he had glasses, though. I think he just had these clipped on to his suit... you know, that little mask.

And I don't know how tall he was. Maybe 5-8 or maybe 5-10, 6 feet, somewhere in there. I'm a very poor judge of height because of my height. I have no meaning, you know. It's always down, you know. It can never be up...

And so I saw him put away his gun, and I was turning to say something to Celia, and all of a sudden I felt my back... just... no, I think I saw him pull it out... I don't remember... I think I saw him whip out his knife and just start stabbing me in the back... CHOMP, CHOMP, CHOMP, CHOMP! I was just (makes a guttural sound)... you know that kind of a sound... and Celia turned to see why I was (repeats guttural sound), you know, and she just about fainted. She went hysterical... (unintelligible) ... and when he finally stopped... I mean he went over and...

The doctor says there's six in the back, six wounds on my back. You ought to confirm that. One I've got went clean through the lung. I've got it draining. I did drain a couple pints of blood out as soon as I got here. I lost an awful lot of blood, I guess.

We were down... I mean it was absolutely no question in my mind... when a person gets stabbed as many times as we did... we were going to die. I mean there'd be no reason to question it. But somehow I, you know, started (unintelligible)... I just knew there was too much I had to live for. I mean really it does happen... about getting depressed and everything... when you're young you always think about these things... you know you think about it... and when you've got someone forcing your hand, - oh well, there was a lot of things I had to do. And what really kept me going... you know my parents are pretty Christian. I haven't been too much of a Christian myself... but if you believe in the principle you ask God to help you. Another thing,- What was my only strength was knowing two things. One, that I did not want to die, and two, that I felt that whatever was going to be was going to be, but I was going to try my damnedest to stay alive. And so, like I say, - before I left her I kissed her, and I said, "Well," I says, "I'm gonna try to get help."

There was a boat kept circling around out there in the lake and we started yelling at it and it finally came within about 100 yards of the shore and turned off its motor and stayed there watching us for about fifteen minutes, and we were just screaming hysterically, trying to get their attention, you know, to come over here. Oh, I don't know, I guess they were afraid that the guy might be there in the bushes and they were liable to get choked or something. So finally he came up a little closer. I didn't have my glasses on... I was just swaying, you know... and I had gotten one of her hands free before they came, and so I kept trying to get her to untie me, and she couldn't, she was too week, she said.

So finally I just kept hollering and hollering, and she said, "Turn around and let's see if I can do it again." She finally got it. My hands and my feet were just pure numbness... they're still numb but I'm sure that will go 'way. But I finally got... (unintelligible)... untie her so she could kind of relax out. 'Cause it was a terrible position, you know, upon our stomachs... (unintelligible)...

And so I started to go for help. I finally got myself fairly reconciled. I wasn't too worried about dying, if that was what was going to happen, but I knew I had to keep pushing on. I had to force myself into staying alive because it was... I could just see myself... you know, all sort of waves would come over... I just (coughing sound)... (unintelligible)... "Well, you're not gonna give up this easy", you know. And, like I say, I just kept believing that God would do everything the best, if the thing was gonna happen, but I couldn't see any reason why my dying would be the best good. So I just played along with that.

I just started to walk toward the road... everything blacked out on me... my visual... my mind was never blacked out, but my visual was. So I lay down... My eyes started to come open... I just saw a haze of trees, you know. In a little while I got up and went another twenty feet, and then the same thing happened... (unintelligible)... and sat down. Next thing I went clear... (unintelligible)... the road, and by that time I just fell... I just... I was trying so hard to go far I just went too far. Finally I heard this pickup coming... I was just laying alongside the road, and that's where this guy picked me up.

They weren't in any hurry at all, it didn't seem like, you know, but they finally called an ambulance. About fifteen minutes later it came... (unintelligible)... but I still believe... I've got feeling... starting to get a little pain to come through. But from the minute that knife blade went in, it was nothing but pure shock from there on. I mean I just did not expect it. I didn't expect that he would do that. That was a variable I had completely left out. And I guess he just took off running after we started running. I don't know. I never saw him before and hope not to see him again... at least outside of a courtroom.

It's hard for me to explain much more. I'm trying to give you a kind of example of his technique. He had some rope cut up in his back pocket. And he had a... well, I thought it was a police automatic because it was in one of these black leather cases, you know...

J.R. Was it in a smooth case, or did it have a basket weave like...

B.H. Can I have my glasses? Oh, they're not here. It was a smooth one, though.

J.R. Did he have this hood down to about the middle of his chest?

B.H. No, about like... well, I'll show you... Here... his stomach... You know I could see his... (voice fades away)

J.R. Okay. You said his hair looked dark brown. How could you see his hair?

B.H. 'Cause I saw it from where those goggles fit. I looked so closely to find out. And when he turned you know they kind of flittered... I could see his hair. It looked kind of greasy.

J.R. Now was he as heavy as I am?

B.H. Well I can't say 'cause he wasn't wearing those type of clothes. They were sloppy clothes, you know. And he just had on this old pair of pleated pants. I don't know... How tall are you?

J.R. I'm about five eleven.

B.H. Well, like I say, he was dressed kind of sloppily, you know. His pants real tight up here and his stomach kind of pouched a bit, you know. I don't know... it's hard to say 'cause I can't judge you with being in a suit and all, you know, and him not being professional-looking at all.

He could be about the same. It's hard to say. He was so sloppily dressed.

J.R. Bryan, you also mentioned a drawl. Well not a drawl, an accent.

B.H. It was just something... I guess his way of talking. It was something I couldn't repeat. It's like a song. Sometimes you know what you're going to say but you just can't sing the melody worth a darn.

J.R. Did he have a throaty voice or a high pitched?

B.H. In between. But it was just a unique way of talking.

J.R. Did he sound like an educated man?

B.H. Heck no! I don't think so.

J.R. Did he sound illiterate?

B.H. No. He didn't sound that way either. He just impressed me as being rather low class. The reason was because of his clothes, you know.

J.R. Did you lose consciousness when he stabbed you at any time? Did you observe him stab Cecelia?

B.H. Yeah...

J.R. What did he say after...

B.H. He stabbed her a bunch of times in the back. After she turned around, he got her once in the groin and one in the arm I think. He kind of went a little more hog-wild with her than with me, I faked dead... like that... I didn't want him to come back and give me some more.

J.R. So you were pretty sure he thought you were dead when he finished working on you?

B.H. I think he kind of thought that. Of course I don't know because we started talking right after he left. It's hard to say... (unintelligible)... 1 don't think she fainted either.

J.R. Was she in a lot of pain, did she tell you?

B.H. Oh yeah. She was more weak at the time... (unintelligible)... from the religious angle. I told her I sure as heck wasn't going to have any deathbed conversion. "No," she says... (unintelligible)... I mean it was just like you were gonna die and had a few things to say. But I felt more and more I wasn't losing strength as much... (unintelligible)... that I thought I could cope with...

J.R. What you did was a courageous thing. It was a terrible thing to have happen to anyone.

B.H. Well there was nothing we could do. We were kind of at the mercy of him. I mean I wanted to get that gun... (unintelligible)... There was a time I think I could have gotten it...

J.R. Did it appear to be a .45 to you? An automatic?

B.H. It was about this long... along the stock... and had a wood edge on it, you know.. on either side...

J.R. Handles.

B.H. Yeah... yeah..

J.R. Did the bullet look anything like that?

B.H. No. It was kind of like this, only it was gold, and this part here came out along with this and then round the gold, round the blunt end. Not quite that blunt-ended, though.

J.R. Was it fat? Fatter than this?

B.H. Yeah, I think it was a little fatter. But it was gold, you know. And I didn't see any of this here. There was a part where it crimped... Well, almost like that .22, short, only a lot bigger. It was about like this length, maybe more stubby.

J.R. Well I'll get a .45 a little later and we can bring it up and let you observe it.

Let's take the suspect. His hands...

B.H. I don't remember if they had gloves on or not. I can't remember now. I keep thinking that he had gloves on. I can't figure how he tied us... Let's ask Celia, she probably knows about that.

J.R. Did he swear? Did he use any profane language or obscenity?

B.H. I don't think so. If he did it was no more than 1 was using at the time. I don't think he used any obscenity. He might have used a swear word or something, you know. That wasn't striking to me...

J.R. Do you have any idea what his motive might have been? Money?

B.H. Money. He said he was going to go to Mexico and he was flat broke.

J.R. Did he search you after he...

B.H. Heck no! Very unprofessional. He didn't even end up taking that loose change and didn't even take my billfold.

J.R. Why did he stab you when you weren't fighting him off or anything?

B.H. I couldn't! Even if I'd have wanted to. I was laying on my stomach...

J.R. So what would have been the purpose of him to stab you, do you think?

B.H. Well I (unintelligible)... but I think he got rattled... (unintelligible)... very, very nervous. His hands were shaking... (unintelligible)... Are you nervous?

J.R. I'm just curious. If you could write me that symbol you were telling me about. Do you think you could draw me a picture of that even without your glasses?

B.H. Um hum (affirmative). (Draws)... kind of like that. I can't see very well...

J.R. Yes, I see. Okay...

B.H. (unintelligible)... that I could really die...

J.R. Does this ring a bell?

B.H. This one here. This is more like it, but I'm not sure. It was distinctly that design. It was thick. More thick marks.

J.R. Okay. What color was this? Do you recall?

B.H. Black. And that was white.

J.R. This was black.

B.H. No, that was white. It was about this tall.

J.R. Two and a half, three inches?

B.H. About four by four... three by three...

J.R. How do you feel? Am I tiring you out too much?

B.H. No, I've had a couple shots. It's not hurting me at all.

J.R. Do you think Cecelia could tell me any more than you have already told me? Add anything?

B.H. (unintelligible)

J.R. Did he slap you around? Slap her?

B.H. No.

J.R. He was a much smaller man than you?

B.H. Not much. About your height I guess. I don't know.

J.R. Well you're getting kind of sleepy. I'll ease up on you.

B.H. Have you gotten any clues at all?

J.R. Yes, we've got some good clues. Before we get this guy it's going to take a lot of work.

B.H. Remember he said he was headed for Mexico.

J.R. He's headed for Mexico?

B.H. That's what he said.

J.R. I'll leave you my card. let's right up here. I'm going to go down and talk to your mom and dad.

B.H. Have the news heard about this at all?

J.R. Yes.

B.H. Was there anything in the paper today?

J.R. No, it wasn't in...

B.H. The Napa paper?

J.R. Well there's no Napa paper on Sundays. It's been on the news media...

B.H. Names? Did they name my name?

J.R. I don't know, to tell you the truth.

B.H. The reason I asked is my girl friend lives in Portland and I've got to talk to her before it gets to her...

J.R. Okay.

B.H. What time is it now?

J.R. It's one o'clock.

B.H. What are the rates now?

J.R. Don't you worry about the rates.

B.H. Well I should probably give her a call...

J.R. You're looking real good. You've got some color...

B.H. Is there a phone real close by?

J.R. I'll get the nurse...

B.H. 'Cause I'd like to call her now...

J.R. Now if you think of anything that you want to see me about, my card's here. You can have the nurse call me. I'm gonna be up here quite a bit.

B.H. You say you have a guard out here?

J.R. Yes.

(END OF INTERVIEW)

chapter five

loose change

IF ANYTHING'S FUNNY in the Zodiac era, it's the end of Hartnell's interview. Less than 24 hours have passed since he and Cecelia were stabbed, he's doped to the gills on painkillers, he's in a strange hospital, and he's suffering from shock. And what's Bryan concerned about?

These are real people with concerns beyond the violence. Their lives are complex tapestries. The attack might be over but Bryan's still got to deal with the disasters of the day-to-day.

He's got six holes in his back and what makes him worry?

Catching hell from his lady.

Being put in the doghouse.

The interview contains so much information that its nuances are lost on the first read. Hartnell can't judge Zodiac's height. Everyone looks small to Hartnell. His gargantuan physicality is an unspoken subtext in so much of what he says. When you're that tall, you live in a different world, one where nothing fits, where people treat you different, but also one with an altered sense of what's plausible. Normal physical threats do not apply. A gun can still kill you. So can a knife. But if the reach of your arms is double that of normal men, it diminishes the likelihood of an ass-kicking. No one picks a fight with the person who can pound them into the dust. And if some stupid drunk does pick that fight, well, they get what's coming. Hartnell says that he didn't mind the idea of being robbed. Just for the experience. He doesn't have that much money of him, so what's going to happen, really? It's the thought of someone who's never experienced true physical peril.

Hartnell thinks that he could've gotten Zodiac's gun. This isn't someone puffing themselves up. The man is a giant. He's almost a foot taller than Zodiac. His reach is enormous. This is a realistic assessment. But he doesn't grab the gun. Because he doesn't want to imperil Cecelia.

Throughout the interview, Hartnell reads as offended by his attacker's class origins. This dialogue is recorded in the hospital, Hartnell is in shock, the worst thing has happened to him. So one can't judge the words. But he's bothered by Zodiac's socioeconomic origins. The shabby clothes, the sloppiness. Low class. It's one thing to get stabbed. It's another to be stabbed by someone beneath you in the social hierarchy.

The snobbery is useful. It confirms something. A gun bought from Sears and stationary purchased at Woolworth's. Zodiac is poor. Or lower middle class.

The most important thing that Hartnell says, an idea that surfaces several times, is that Zodiac is nervous. His hands are tremorous. There's not a robust data set on the behavior of people who kill in serial. Most victims don't survive. We can't compare and contrast. What does it mean that Zodiac's hands shook? It could be the excitement of the event. But this is a man who has only killed with a gun. The gun makes it easy. The gun only asks for the pull of a trigger. The knife demands commitment, dedication, decisive action and resolution. It's not easy to stab someone. A distaste can be inferred from what Zodiac does after Lake Berryessa. He goes back to the gun. This is a person in over his head. He stabs because it's a necessary component. Like everyone else in America, he's been reading about Sharon Tate. He's seen the blueprint, knows how to ensure maximum media coverage.

†

Before Bryan and Cecelia arrive at the site of their doom, three young women drive towards Lake Berryessa. They come in through the north via Pope Valley on Knoxville Road, which runs along the western side of the Lake. They drive south and park.

They're not far from where Bryan and Cecelia will have their picnic. As the women are parking, another car pulls in behind them. It's a blue two-door Chevrolet sedan with California plates. It gets so close that its bumper almost touches their car. There's a third car in the parking lot, one with Arizona plates, and it's got a man and a woman in it. The occupant of the blue car is a White male adult. He does not leave his vehicle.

The women go down to the beach and sunbathe in their bikinis. Thirty minutes pass. They notice that they're being watched by the man from the blue car. He's standing about 40 to 50 feet distant. He stares at them. When they stare back, he looks away. All three women offer a similar description. Six feet tall, maybe 200 pounds, stocky or muscular, nice looking, about 30-years old. He's wearing dark pants and a black pull-over or a short sleeved sweater. One woman says that the shirt was bunched up in front with a white t-shirt hanging out of the back. Another says that she thinks it was either a t-shirt or a white belt. Thirty more minutes pass. The man walks north. He comes within 20 feet of the women and disappears out of sight. The women return to their car at 4:30PM. The blue Chevrolet is not there. They did not see the man get into his car.

Was it Zodiac?

The description is similar to the one offered by Bryan Hartnell. But there are differences. Hartnell describes Zodiac as low-class. He doesn't say that Zodiac is muscular. He says that he's paunchy. Is a personal appearance that the women consider nice looking what Bryan Hartnell finds low-class? Hartnell identifies Zodiac as wearing a blue wind-breaker. Which is very different than a short sleeved sweater.

If the man is Zodiac, why didn't he kill the women? Did he decide that three victims were too complicated? Or does he always need a male victim?

We only know about Zodiac's successful crimes. How many times did he fail? How many times did he look for victims and find nothing?

The attacks that happened imply the ones that did not. The man from the blue Chevrolet might as well be Zodiac. The Zodiac that no one knows. A Zodiac who seeks his chance and has circumstance conspire against him. It happens more times than the successes.

†

There's another sighting. Around 6:30PM, just after Cecelia and Bryan have been stabbed, Dr. David Rayfield and his son are near the crime scene. They're down at the beach. They see a White male adult. He's about 5'10", heavy build, wearing dark trousers. He's got a dark shirt on. Rayfield says that the shirt has "red in it." It's long-sleeved.

The White male adult realizes that he is being observed. The White male adult turns around and walks south. The Rayfields only see the White male adult at a distance of about 100 yards. The cops think that this is probably not Zodiac. There's about four coves between Rayfield and the crime scene. It's a long way to walk. But that shirt has enough red in it to be visible at 100 yards. If this is Zodiac, it's a large volume of human blood.

†

When Zodiac leaves them to die, Bryan and Cecelia free themselves. There's a boat out on the water and, after much screaming, they flag it down. The man on the boat is fishing. He's staying at the Rancho Monticello Resort, located a few miles north on Knoxville Road. The fisherman speaks with Bryan but won't come off the water. He's terrified by the blood. He navigates back to the resort. He speaks with the owner, who calls the Park Rangers.

Two Rangers are up near Pope Valley. Around 7PM, they receive a radio call about an attack. They drive down Knoxville Road and arrive at the resort. They speak with the fisherman, they speak with the owners. One of the Rangers decides to travel by water with the owners and the fisherman. The boat arrives at the peninsula. Cecelia is bleeding under a tree. The other Ranger arrives in his truck and finds Bryan by the side of Knoxville Road. He's covered in blood and screaming, "HELP ME! HELP ME!"

The Ranger tries to talk with Hartnell. Bryan's worried about Cecelia. The Ranger gets Bryan into the truck and then walks down to the picnic peninsula. His partner and the fisherman and the resort owners are there. So is stabbed girl. When the Ranger gets back to his truck, Bryan's collapsed. He lays Hartnell on a blanket. Then it's radio calls for an ambulance.

Lake Berryessa is the middle of nowhere. There aren't any emergency services. The call goes out around 7:20PM. Bryan and Cecelia don't get into an ambulance until after 7:45PM.

They arrive at Napa's Queen of the Valley Hospital around 8:50PM. Bleeding for over two hours. Bryan has six stab wounds. Cecelia has ten. The medical examiner thinks that the blade was nine-to-eleven inches in length and one inch in width. Possibly sharpened on both sides like a bayonet. Cecelia is still capable of speech, but she's not going to make it.

She'll die in two days.

†

When Bryan and Cecelia are in the ambulance, the investigation begins. The Napa County Sheriff's Department is on the scene. They find Bryan's car three-fourths of a mile away. They don't see the important thing at first but then it becomes apparent. Someone has used a black felt-tip pen to write a message on the passenger side door.

It reads:

Vallejo
12-20-68
7-4-69
Sept 27-69-6:30
by knife

There's a footprint near the vehicle. Impressions from the same footwear are discovered near the crime scene. Plaster casts are taken. The footwear will be identified as military issue. Civilian size 10 1/2. This particular shoe is from the International Shoe Company. The uppers are manufactured by the Weinbrenner Shoe Company of Merill, Wisconsin. The sole by Avon company of Avon, Massachusetts. Over one million were manufactured in 1966. 103,700 were shipped to military installations on the West Coast.

Around 7:40PM, a phone call comes into the Napa Police Department switchboard. This is in Napa, California. The city that is the county seat. The Napa PD is not the Napa Sheriff's Department, who are on-scene and investigating. David Slaight answers, saying, "Napa Police Department, Officer Slaight." The response comes from a young male voice, possibly early twenties. The voice says: "I want to report a murder, no, a double murder. They are two miles North of Park Headquarters. They were in a white Volkswagen Karmann-Ghia." There is a pause. Slaight asks, "Where are you now?" In a barely audible response, the voice says, "I'm the one who did it."

Slaight hears the phone being put down but not hung up. If Zodiac's account in his 4 August letter is true, if the Vallejo payphone rang as soon as he hung up and drew someone's attention, then the killer is learning.

The connection remains open. Slaight can hear, or thinks that he can hear, voices in the background. It's difficult to tell because he's also using another line to telephone the Napa Sheriff's Office and there's transmissions blaring from the police radio. Slaight informs his superior officer and then phones the operator to see if the call can be traced. The operator says that the call originates from a payphone. The man spoke with the operator before speaking with Slaight, asked to be connected to the police, but refused to give his name. The operator says that she will hold the line open until the phone can be found.

Police files state that the call is traced to a phonebooth beside the Napa Car Wash near Clinton & Main Streets. Later, another story circulates. The cops put out a general call for help. It's heard by the news director at a local radio station. He drives through town, looking for every payphone until he finds one hanging off the hook. He shouts CAN YOU HEAR ME? This is not detailed in available files.

When they arrive, the police lift fingerprints off the telephone. They're fresh enough that moisture is visible. On 10 October, the Napa Sheriff will forward these prints to the FBI and ask if they match latent prints taken from the 31 July letters. The FBI writes back on 23 October. To the degree that they can be compared, the prints don't match.

†

Let's go back in time. The killer has just stabbed Hartnell and Cecelia. Maybe he encounters Dr. Rayfield and son. Maybe he does not. Zodiac needs to do two things. He needs to write a message on the side of Hartnell's Karmann-Ghia and he needs to get away. Maybe his car is a blue Chevrolet. Maybe it's not.

How does Zodiac know which car belongs to Bryan Hartnell? There are enough people at Lake Berryessa that a random guess can go wrong. If the Karmann-Ghia is parked some distance from the crime scene, Zodiac didn't just come upon his victims. He had to see them with the car. Or follow them as they drove on Knoxville Road.

All of the people involved—the Doctor and his son, the young women, Zodiac, Hartnell and Shepard—are in an area known as Bum's Beach. It's publicly accessible and there's parking lots, but there's little extant data about the topography of 1969. In the early 1980s, Bum's Beach was transformed and upgraded into the Oak Shores Day Use Area. The roads changed and new parking lots added. Police reports are not helpful. Most of the area doesn't have a name and this is aeons before global satellite positioning. The earliest files estimate the distance between the crime and the car is 3/4ths of a mile. A later report issued by the California Bureau of Investigation will include a PERT chart. PERT is an acronym for Program Evaluation and Review. It's the mid-century precursor to the PowerPoint Slide. This chart states that Hartnell's car was 3/10ths of a mile from the site of the attack.

Assume that Zodiac's car door estimate is correct. He stabs Hartnell and Shepard at 6:30PM. He then has walk to Hartnell's car, write on it, and walk to his own car. Or he's got to walk to his own car, then drive to Hartnell's, write on its door, and leave. We know where he goes next. He goes to the city of Napa. To call the police.

The shortest route to Napa is south on Knoxville Road to the CA-128 and then the CA-121. If we assume that after making the phone call,

Zodiac's final stop is either Vallejo or San Francisco, there's a difficulty with the southern route. It requires the phonebooth to be a certain destination, something planned in advance. There is no way to go south on Knoxville Road and happen, by chance, upon a phone booth at the intersection of Main & Clinton Streets. He'd either have to know the exact location or travel around Napa until he finds a phone.

There's another plausible route. Zodiac escapes Lake Berryessa by traveling north on Knoxville Road, drives through Pope Valley and Angwin, comes out the other side and heads south on the Silverado Trail, which will bring him several blocks from the telephone. It's a longer drive, but not by much. The time frame is doable. This route also saves him from driving past the Ranger Station on Knoxville Road, slightly south of the crime scene, and keeps him on back roads until the very last minute.

†

Almost no one has accused Zodiac of knowing Bryan Hartnell or Cecelia Shepard. It is accepted, widely, that they had bad luck. They could have been anybody. Like the hood and the ropes and the knives and the writing on the wall, they were props on a set dressed by Charles Manson.

Zodiac arrives with a gun, just like the weapon that the Family used to kill nobody Steven Parent who'd just gotten off the phone with the man who wrote "The Trouble with Tribbles." Then he ties up his victims. He does it while wearing a hood. Admittedly, in the Tate case, the hood was found over the face of one of the victims. But it's still a hood. Then he stabs them multiple times. Then he writes a message on a door.

Other people have noticed the correspondence. The most powerful manifestation is Howard A. Davis's book *The Zodiac / Manson Connection*. It's an attempt to link Zodiac with the Family, to suggest that the crimes had the same origins. It isn't a huge stretch. Before Charles Manson went to Los Angeles, he spent time with the beautiful Haight-Ashbury people. He interacted with the counterculture's more unsavory elements. The freaks amongst freaks. Bobby Beausoleil was a fixture of the Haight, lived with Kenneth Anger, starred in *Invocation of My Demon Brother*.

Zodiac / Manson has raw fevered pulp power.

But it is based in a fundamental misunderstanding.

Zodiac is not a product of the counterculture. Zodiac is a byproduct. The killer was one of the people in California, generally found amongst its less economically empowered classes, who spent the 1960s being pelted with media stories about the wild children of Berkeley and San Francisco. Student radicals. Hippies. Student radical hippies. Kids who rejected everything the lower orders had achieved during California's post-World War Two prosperity. Worse yet, the kids wanted the lower orders to feel bad about what they'd achieved. The message from Berkeley was the same message that always comes from Berkeley: if you are enjoying life, you are evil. You are complicit in war crimes and butchery and you're too ignorant to recognize the blood on your hands. The norms which you value are gears in a machine that manufactures death. We reject these norms. We will fuck anyone we want, we dispute the church and the institution of marriage, and we will get as high as kites.

The people around places like Vallejo and Benicia were paying attention. And they were furious. Their fury is a key component in Ronald Reagan's electoral victory in 1966. They made a Hollywood has-been their state's Governor. He'd campaigned on a promise. He said that he'd lower the long arm of the law upon Berkeley. He'd bring the radicals to heel. He would teach the wild children the difference between right and wrong. Reagan crushed the incumbent. 57.5% vs 42.3%.

While Vallejo and Benicia people looked at the hippies and felt revulsion and loathing, there was also a kind of envy. The wild children were the most American of Americans. They said that they stood in opposition to the greed and malice of the war machine, but two central planks of their ethos floated in heavy U$A waters. Free love is a euphemism for collecting, about fucking as many people as possible. Acquisition at all costs. When you wear out the old car, you buy a new one. And the hippies offered enlightenment at $2 a pop. Undisguised drug capitalism. A holy sacrament that only requires you pay the preacher. Like every other sham church. The Vallejo and Benicia people, bred in a consumerist society that taught its citizens to envy the biggest consumers, couldn't help but want to get in on the action. But also knew that they couldn't. They had children, they had marriages.

Zodiac resents the freaks but he wants to be a freak. But he can't join the club. He's either too old or too square or from the wrong socioeconomic background or doesn't have the right education or lacks the social graces to acquire the freak lingua franca. The tradename is the dead giveaway. No real freak would call themselves Zodiac. It's the most debased currency. At the least, they'd go for their star-sign. Zodiac is a square's idea of the counterculture.

To imagine a connection between Manson and Zodiac is to identify the accident while ignoring its substance. Zodiac didn't work for Manson. But Zodiac took inspiration from Manson. Or from the media depictions of the crimes.

Zodiac is staging a public relations campaign. It's faltering. The tradename didn't take. The cipher got solved in a week. But every single day, newspapers and the television are telling Zodiac what works. Knives, rope, writing on a door.

Bryan Hartnell and Cecelia Shepard could have been anyone. They had the bad luck to be in the worst place at the wrong time. They had the bad luck to be Seventh Day Adventists. They were thinking about going into San Francisco but then the day grew long and Bryan realized that it'd be a tight squeeze because they were supposed to come back to Pacific Union College and worship on the Sabbath. Which is a Saturday. It's not their fault. They're like any victim of any crime. No one arrives at the scene of brutalization without the story of their life pushing them towards that unholy place. There's a web of actions and choices and pathways that bring the victim to the attacker. In the case of Bryan and Cecelia, they were people from the first American history. They believed that the Sabbath was Saturday. That's what got them to Lake Berryessa.

Zodiac didn't go to Lake Berryessa in the hopes of leaving survivors. The phone call proves it. He thought that Hartnell and Cecelia were both dead. At the moment that he spoke with the dispatcher, both victims were alive. But Zodiac thought they were dead. Unable to bear witness.

Which asks a question. Why go through the effort of making a hood? Why adorn it with the Zodiac symbol? Why bother?

As this was the first and only of his attacks in daylight hours, maybe it's a simple question of disguise. But if disguise is the object, why not do what everyone else does? Why not wear a ski-mask? Maybe Zodiac wore the costume to gauge the success of the public relations campaign. The symbol was reported upon, but not reproduced, by the *Examiner*. The visual only showed up in one August article in a Vallejo newspaper. The campaign is faltering. The evidence is in Bryan Hartnell's testimony. When he recounts the symbol, it's clear that he has zero concept of its intended meaning. He has no idea that he's been done by the Cipher Killer.

There's been a long-standing theory that this hood has some ritualistic significance. But again, the evidence is in Bryan Hartnell's testimony. The killer isn't an occult maniac. He's a nervous low class dude who says that he just escaped from prison. And there's not a hint of witchcraft.

Maybe it's something else. Maybe Zodiac likes dressing up. Maybe there's some aspect of his civilian life that allows him this pleasure. Maybe he's got familiarity with elaborate costuming and this is spill-over, the first thing that he grabs. Maybe this is the killer's equivalent of pantyhose pulled over the face, the spare object in the backseat.

†

The stabbings happen in Napa. Zodiac happens in the press. There's the thing and then there is its mediated representation. The thing is a fact. Immovable and inviolable. The representation is a story. The story can change, get better, get bigger. It's the real action.

News doesn't break until 29 September 1969, Monday after the Saturday black Sabbath. An article runs in the *Chronicle:* STABBINGS LINKED TO 'CODE' KILLER. It makes Page 31. Either it's seen as unimportant or the edition was typeset and this was the only available space. Later that evening, Zodiac makes the *Examiner*: KNIFE ATTACKS POINT TO 'CIPHER KILLER.' Page 10. The next day, with Cecelia Shepard dead, Zodiac makes Page 2 of the *Chronicle*. Each of these stories recount the basic details of the attack and previous crimes and the ciphers. None refer to the killer as Zodiac. The tradename hasn't taken. But details are accruing. The Manson formula worked.

And, then, finally, he gets what he wants. He's the front page headline of the 30 September *Examiner*. Bold type, huge point lead. POLICE DARE

CIPHER KILLER. It's the same. The dead kids, the dead waitress, the dead student, the notes, the cipher, the knife, the ropes, the car door, the hood. The only new detail is Napa County Sheriff Captain Don Townsend asking that the Cipher Killer write or make a phone call. The cops need more information. Zodiac is directing his own police investigations. His underlings need new orders.

The Cipher Killer lingers for a few days in San Francisco's newspapers, but these articles offer diminishing returns. There's nothing to report. There are no leads other than scant forensic evidence. Behind the scenes, the fingerprints are checked against potential suspects. They turn up nothing. The story gets about a full week and then disappears. The killer has sent no letter, taken no credit. Townsend asked. Zodiac did not answer. By 5 October, the Cipher Killer is gone from the *Chronicle* and the *Examiner*.

The story lives in the *Napa Valley Register*. It's more of a local crime, anyway, and almost every day there's something new. An interview with Hartnell. Pictures of the ropes. Pictures of Hartnell's belongings. Pictures of Hartnell in his hospital bed. On 10 October, the *Register* publishes a story about Hartnell being released from the hospital and returning to classes at Pacific Union.

On 8 October, the *Register* runs BABY BRUTALLY SLAIN AT "HIPPY" FARM CAMP. A 26-year old grapepicker named Leonard John Cirino is accused of slamming a long sharp weapon into the head of his 10-month old daughter. Other people jump into a pickup truck and drive the infant, head sliced open, to a grocery store. They summon help. The paper runs a picture of the truck's tailgate. Dripping with a child's blood.

The Cipher Killer burns out.

His last burst is front page of the 9 October *Oakland Tribune*. TRACING THE MAD KILLER'S FOOTSTEPS. It focuses almost exclusively on Lake Berryessa, recounts all the pertinent details, vaguely hints at the Vallejo killings. Doesn't mention the ciphers or the tradename.

And then, for a second, the story is gone.

†

But Zodiac is getting there.

Zodiac just needs that final push, the performance that really makes it, the one that achieves madness.

And he's got an idea.

chapter six

ann lacks motor spirit, haight-ashbury is innsmouth, blackie's a moron

IF YOU WANT TO MAKE IT, go to the city. Hit the biggest place around. Kill all you want in Vallejo, in Napa, but that's not real headlines. The idea is embedded in the beginning. Two 31 July letters are addressed to San Francisco newspapers. The city is the real score. Zodiac can terrorize the people of the North Bay until the end of time and won't get what he wants.

San Francisco has been a worldwide story since 1967's Summer of Love in the Haight-Ashbury district. All the acid-eyed beautiful people took an also-ran in American life and transformed it into a national fixation.

1967 was two years ago.

Now it's 1969.

And this ain't the Summer of Love.

On 27 September 1969, the day that Zodiac's at Lake Berryessa, a verdict is returned. A jury finds David Hinkle, 18, Larry "Blackie" Garrett, 26, Joseph "Skinny" Henderson, 24, and Clyde "Scavenger" Safley, 24, not guilty of murdering Ann Jiminez.

Ann's from Bellingham, Washington. Ann's 19-years old. Ann grew up with a father who suffered post-traumatic stress disorder. Ann's father spent four years in Japanese prisoner of war camps. Ann's father drinks. Ann's father screams with night terrors. Ann's father abandons Ann and her mother and her two sisters. Ann gets into drugs. Ann gets put in a correctional center. Ann has a glandular disorder that makes her obese. Ann is 5'5" and tops out at 270 pounds. Ann undergoes months of psychotherapy. Ann takes up with a boy from Los Angeles. Ann marries the boy. The boy gets hooked on dope. The boy gets Ann pregnant. Ann loses the baby in labor. Ann goes back to Bellingham. Ann lives with her mother. On the day before Thanksgiving 1968, Ann runs away to Haight-Ashbury. Ann lands in an apartment at 1480 Waller Street. Ann's in a building that is full of freaks. Ann knows the freaks. The freaks knows Ann. Ann has a boyfriend named Jesus. As in Christ. Ann and Jesus live in an apartment with Cass Thomas and her boyfriend. It's 28 December 1968. One month and one day since Ann came to Haight-Ashbury. One of the freaks, a girl whom everyone calls Sunny, thinks that Ann stole Sunny's boots. Ann didn't steal Sunny's boots. Sunny thinks that Ann stole Sunny's boots and now all the freaks think that Ann stole Sunny's boots. Ann is brought into another apartment in 1480 Waller Street.

Sunny.

thinks.

that.

Ann. doesn't. have.

quote, ***motor spirit***, unquote.

Ann's, quote, too passive. Ann's not aggressive, offensive, or dominant, unquote. In other words, Ann doesn't have amphetamine psychosis. The freaks stage a turn-out. They've got motor spirit. Sunny uses a knife to slit Ann's bra straps and underpants. Skinny's married to Sunny. Skinny puts a knife to Ann's throat and punctures Ann's skin. Ann doesn't want to be turned-out. There's about fifteen to twenty people in the apartment. Hippies and bikers. Everyone's watching. It's like a movie. Or a really groovy late night show from Televisionland. They say that Jesus saves. But not here, not now. Jesus just lets it happen. A girl named Chris beats and kicks Ann. Scavenger is a hustler, a male prostitute. Scavenger's smoked two joints of Acapulco Gold, drank a bottle of wine, and shot a dimebag of speed. Scavenger's got motor spirit. Scavenger shaves off Ann's pubic hair with an electric razor. The freaks beat Ann. Ann's in love with Blackie. Blackie forces Ann into oral copulation and sodomy. He doesn't stop when Ann screams.

Someone looks out the window and sees eight plainclothes cops. The freaks stop the turn-out. The cops go away. The freaks get back to turning-out Ann. The freaks have motor spirit. The freaks cut off Ann's hair. The freaks write on Ann's body with lipstick. Someone kicks Ann in the head. The kick causes a massive blood clot. Three of Ann's friends drag Ann back to Ann's apartment. Ann's friends try to revive Ann with smelling salts and a homemade respirator fashioned from a garden hose. Ann won't come back to life. Ann's friends call the police. The cops see dead Ann. The cops arrest the freaks. At trial, the prosecution is unable to establish who delivered the kick that killed Ann. Blackie's lawyers have a defense. They call Blackie a moron. That's the word they use. In court. Moron. It's a novel defense strategy. Blackie is border-line psychotic with paranoid and schizophrenic tendencies. Blackie's got an IQ between 50 and 60. Blackie's mom was a drunk. Blackie's dad was brutal. Blackie spent ten years in Iowa mental institutions where he learned, quote, cruelty and perverse sex, unquote. Blackie can't read or write. Skinny's lawyers have a defense. Skinny stopped Blackie from using a broom handle on Ann. Skinny's lawyers say that Ron Pogue killed Ann. Ron Pogue was 17-years old and pleaded guilty in juvenile court to forcible oral copulation. Ron Pogue was deported to Canada. Ron Pogue kicked Ann in the head after Ann bit Ron Pogue's penis. David Hinkle's lawyers have a defense. David Hinkle is a ninth grade drop-out from Detroit. David Hinkle's mother has been in a mental institution for seventeen years. David Hinkle says that Ann consented to having sex with David Hinkle after she agreed to have sex with Thomas "Hercules" Longfellow. Hercules pleaded out on a rape charge. Hercules is awaiting sentence. Scavenger's lawyers have a defense. Scavenger called himself David Coddington. Scavenger used the alias because he's an Oregon parole violator. Scavenger only got an education as far as seventh grade. Back in Arkansas. Scavenger served three years for auto theft in Arkansas. The prisoners turned-out Scavenger. Scavenger's lawyers say that Scavenger had too much motor spirit to do anything other than shave off Ann's public hair. The papers call Ann a fat, lonely misfit. The prosecution calls Ann a fat, lonely misfit. The cops call Ann a fat, lonely misfit. The defendants call Ann a fat, lonely misfit. The defendants' lawyers call Ann a fat, lonely misfit. No one goes down for murder. No one faces the death penalty. Blackie gets two counts of oral copulation and one of sodomy. Skinny gets two counts of oral copulation. David Hinkle is set free. Scavenger is set free.

San Francisco.

1969.

Motor spirit.

The hippies and their acid and free love haven't taken over. It doesn't matter. There's the thing and there's the media representation of the thing and media representation is what matters. Nothing else is of import. Other cities in America have radical reputations—there's New York and Los Angeles and the university kids in Madison are as wild as any—but San Francisco is the byword. If you're old, San Francisco means degeneracy. If you're young, it means a new way of living. No surprise that when Zodiac becomes Scorpio in *Dirty Harry,* the action moves to San Francisco. Vallejo means nothing. Napa means nothing. San Francisco can't be escaped. It's this insane place, the most beautiful city in America and full of the country's biggest freaks. It's been like this from the beginning. Back in the gold rush days, people didn't have motor spirit. They had tertiary syphilis. The freaks are in the hills and the valleys and now they're in Victorian houses and Golden Gate Park and you can't go five hundred yards without encountering a drug casualty. America's children have broken free of their parents. First they were wild. Now they have motor spirit. Ten bucks of enlightenment in a needle full of speed. Do enough enlightenment and you'll go insane. Nothing says motor spirit like walking down Market Street while talking to the voices and punching the side of your own head. Sometimes maybe the voices tell you to kill. If you're selling motor spirit, you've got to deal with the competition. Mergers, acquisitions, capital. Your motor spirit must be the only motor spirit. The Mafia is in the motor spirit business. So are the Hells Angels. So are other motorcycle gangs. Drugs are money and violence. Bobby Beausoleil killing Gary Hinman sets its all off, another motor spirit murder, drug deal gone bad, gives Zodiac an idea for ropes and knives and writing on the door. Bobby and Manson both lived in the Haight-Ashbury. Bobby and Manson got motor spirit.

San Francisco is the epicenter.

San Francisco is where you get motor spirit.

†

11 October 1969.

Invocation of My Demon Brother is premiering in Los Angeles. By the end of the night, a man named Paul L. Stine will be dead. He will be shot in the back of his head. A 4cm long and 2cm wide hole will be blasted into his skull. The bullet will travel from the right temporal lobe into the left anterior. The path of the bullet will measure between 1.5-to-2.1cms. His skull will fracture. The copper leaded bullet will fragment and lodge in Stine's left temporalis muscle. There will be extensive subarachnoid and epiarachnoid hemorrhages throughout the cerebral hemispheres. Death sentence from pull of trigger.

Paul Stine is like Bryan Hartnell and Cecelia Shepard. He's a person who leaves no real traces. All he did was make good. But Paul Stine is different than Bryan Hartnell or Cecelia Shepard. Paul Stine is not raised in the warm bosom of the first American history. He comes from the God people's degenerate cousins. The relatives whom they never mention, the ones put in jail to maintain social order, the ones who come to Haight-Ashbury and get motor spirit.

Paul Stine's father is born Milford Stine. But everyone calls him Teddie. He's from Arkansas. By 2 June 1928, Teddie's in Hubert, Oklahoma. That's the day that Teddie marries Audra Busby. The marriage license says little but implies much. Teddie signs his own name even if his literacy skills aren't the strongest. Audra can't sign. She's too young. Teddie's 24. Audra's 16. Her father signs, consents to the marriage. Teddie and Audra stay in Hubert for another eight years. Until 1936 or thereabouts. They have two daughters and a son. But the economy gets bad, it's the Great Depression, and they're in the Dust Bowl. All of those farmers who'd gone out to the middle of the country and didn't know jack about sustainable agriculture. They screwed up their own soil. When a drought came followed by winds, their debased land blew across over America. Sometimes the dirt made it to New York City. Hubert isn't one of Oklahoma's hardest hit counties, but it's close enough. People start going West. They drive out in old junked cars. California does what California always does. It promises a new life for people brave enough to make the journey. Teddie hears the promise. He uproots his family and moves to a town called Exeter.

About a year later, Paul is born.

Some folks come to California and it fashions them into the person that they always knew they were. Other folks come out and California turns them mean. Teddie got mean. In 1941, Teddie uses brass knuckles on a son-of-a-bitch. The cops come to Teddie's home but he runs across a field and everyone forgets about Teddie. In 1943, when Teddie's 38-years old, he's arrested on disturbance of the peace. His fingerprints get forwarded to Sacramento. The cops arrest him again. On the brass knuckles beef. He gets dragged to Visalia. In 1947, Audra has Teddie arrested and brought to court for not supporting their five children. He gets two years' probation. The judge orders him to pay $60 a month. In 1948, in Sacramento, Teddie is arrested between I and J Streets. He's with a bunch of drunks and transients. One of them gets a fractured skull. Teddie didn't do it. Teddie was watching. Teddie's gone to seed, Teddie's got no hope and no future. Teddie's abandoned the family. In 1968, Sacramento buries Teddie in a pauper's grave.

Audra manages. She's in the California that no one thinks about, the one that's not on the coast, the California of the east. It's inhabited by people of no particular importance. It's where the strip-mall is being born. It's where tract homes erupt like cystic acne on the greasy face of a teenager. Audra and the kids move to Modesto. Just about the state's least glamorous place. This isn't Vallejo with its waterfront and nearby mountains and old Victorian homes. This is the California where everything is the color of dirt. Paul attends Hughson High School and graduates in 1956. Paul ends up at Fresno State College. California still believes that its economic dominance can be established by access to higher education. There is no tuition for state residents. Only small usage fees. This won't change until the squares hire Ronald Reagan to punish Berkeley's wild children.

At Fresno State, Paul gets an internship via the Citizenship Clearinghouse. He's assigned to the Democratic County Central Committee to aid in the campaigns of Bert DeLotto and Charles B. Garrigus. Paul's learning politics, how they turn blood and offal into sausage, and he's getting paid to do it. $10 a week. For ten weeks. It's no fortune but for Paul it's real money.

He supports himself as a dishwasher at a drive-in restaurant and as a kennel man at a pet hospital.

About when Paul graduates Fresno, Audra remarries. She gets hitched to Roy James Harrison. He's 65 to Audra's 49. Harrison's got something of Teddie. Or he did. Back on 1 July 1919, Harrison, then 23, is married to the first of at least three wives. Mabelle West. That was her maiden name. The marriage has been on the rocks for a few months, ever since Mabelle's father died and left an inheritance. Harrison and Mabelle live at separate addresses. Early on the morning of 1 July, Harrison breaks into Mabelle's mother's house on Laidley Street. That's where Mabell's living. Harrison's wearing a mask and handkerchief. He stumbles upon Mabell's mother, Agnes West. She's the whole problem. Harrison shoots and beats his mother-in-law. Harrison crashes into Mabelle's bedroom. "I have just killed your mother," he says. "Now I am going to kill you and myself." Mabelle's cool as ice. She talks Harrison down, gets him to leave the apartment and promises to tell the cops that it was burglars. Mabelle finds her mother. Mabelle calls the cops. Harrison is arrested. Agnes West doesn't die. Interviewed in city prison, Harrison blames booze. He's sentenced to two years in county jail.

Paul graduates Fresno. He becomes an anonymous person leading an anonymous life. When he's murdered, it's reported that he used to work for the *Turlock Journal*, a small newspaper outside of Modesto, and that he lives with his wife at 1842 Fell Street, five blocks due north of where motor spirit turned-out Ann Jiminez. Paul's a graduate student at San Francisco State University, working towards a PhD in Philosophy. By day, he's a salesman with the Northern Life Insurance Company. By night, he drives a cab. He's working his way. Making it in the world.

Paul is the most American of Zodiac victims. He's like the vast majority of the country's two hundred million citizens. The ones who never make the newspapers. Paul has no reason to be good. No reason to expect anything other than cruelty. No reason to get a Doctorate of Philosophy. No reason to play by the rules. And yet he persists.

Until he gets shot.

†

Stine's murder bakes Zodiac into the fabric of San Francisco. But it's the crime about which we know the least. The San Francisco Police Department has only released the tiniest amount of documents. The murder exists in outline and rumor. Everything is speculative.

On 11 October 1969, at around 8:45PM, Stine shows up for work. Yellow Cab Company at 695 8th Street. He takes out a car. He picks up a fare. It's at Pier 64, down in the southeast of the city, looking out over the Bay at Oakland. The fare needs a ride to the airport in South San Francisco. It's a short drive, maybe twenty minutes on the US-101. Stine drops off the fare and heads back to the city. He must have a beer somewhere along the line, maybe before he showed up for work or maybe around the airport. When the medical examiners do Stine's autopsy, his blood alcohol level is 0.02%. Way below the 0.10% legal limit.

Back in the city, Stine gets a call from dispatch at 9:45PM. Someone wants a cab at 500 9th Avenue. Along the way, and no one knows how, he picks up another fare. The best guess is that Stine gets flagged down. Stine asks the man where he's going. The man tells Stine the destination. It's on the way to 500 9th Avenue. Stine says, "Get in." He wants to double his money.

When Stine is next seen, it's at the corner of Washington & Cherry Streets in Presidio Heights. Washington runs east-west. Cherry runs north-south. Presidio Heights is an upper class neighborhood, quiet. It gets its name from the Presidio, an expanse of trees and dirt trails two blocks north of Washington Street. Parts of the Presidio are a public park, part is an Army base with barracks and officer's quarters. There's a public golf course, too. The Presidio is the northernmost tip of San Francisco's peninsula. It's what you drive through on the way to the Golden Gate Bridge.

Three teenagers see Stine at Washington & Cherry. They're in the house at the intersection's northeast corner. They're up on the third floor. One of them looks down at the street. Parked at the southeast corner is Stine's cab. A man is slumped in the cab's front seat, sort of in the middle. His head rests in another man's lap. It's almost tender. Except the other man looks as if he's going through the slumping man's pockets. The teenagers think that the slumping man is being robbed. They never hear a gunshot. The cab is pointed west. The teenagers are looking down from the third floor windows.

They're facing the driver's side. The robber is on the passenger's side. It helps that someone's turned on the overhead dome light.

When the robber finishes with the slumping man, he gets out through the passenger side door. He uses a rag to wipe down the passenger side and then he walks over to the driver's side and wipes that down too. He walks north on Cherry Street towards the Presidio.

One of the teenagers calls the cops. It hits police radio at 9:58PM. The teenagers describe the robber as a White male adult, early forties, heavy build, reddish-blonde crew cut. Wearing eyeglasses, dark brown trousers, a dark navy or black Parka jacket, dark shoes.

But the call that goes out over the radio isn't for a White male adult.

It's for a Negro male adult.

†

One can see it as systemic police bias. Which it is. But it's also a tragedy beyond the normal tragedies of law enforcement. This moment, which is about two minutes long, max, is the very best chance of catching Zodiac. He's committed one of the fuck-ups that let the cops get their man, a stupidity that allows society to tell itself the story of criminal justice. He let himself be seen.

Two police cruisers are in the immediate area. One is traveling east on Washington Street, occupied by officers Frank Peda and Armond Pelissetti. They're a few blocks away. The other cruiser is occupied by Donald Fouke and Eric A. Zelms. Both cruisers get the call, hear that the suspect is a Negro male.

Fouke's driving north on Presidio Street, six blocks east of the cab. Fouke drives up to Jackson Street, one block north of Washington, and turns west. He's headed towards Cherry. In the meantime, Peda and Pelissetti are arriving at the crime scene.

Driving west on Jackson, Fouke observes a White male adult, 35-45 years of age, about 5'10", 180-200lbs, medium heavy build, barrel chested, medium complexion, with light colored hair that might be greying in the back (this effect might be due to lighting), crew cut, wearing glasses. The man is dressed in a blue waist-length zipper type jacket (Navy or Royal blue), elastic cuffs and waistband, zipped part way up. Brown wool pleated type pants, baggy in the rear. (Rust brown.) Might have been wearing low cut shoes.

Fouke sees the man on what must be the northern side of Jackson Street. He watches the man turn north onto Maple and head towards the Presidio. In a memorandum that Fouke issues on 12 November 1969, he writes that the man walked with no hurry and a shuffling lope. His head is slightly bent towards the ground. Fouke thinks that the man was of Welsh extraction.

For now, let's assume that these details are true. The description matches almost every detail of Bryan Hartnell's interview. Down to the jacket and old style pleated trousers. Zodiac is within several feet of the cops. He's here, right now.

The solution is before them.

And they let him go.

Because he's not Black.

†

11 October 1969 is an unusually windy night. It was bad the night before, too, downing trees and plunging parts of the city into darkness and setting off wildfires in the greater Bay Area. If the reports of 12 October are to be believed, 11 October is worse than 10 October. In some places, the gusts reach over 100mph. Everything that's happening, right now, these actions that have been scrutinized for decades, occur in an environment where it's difficult to hear anything. Gales are raging. Washington & Cherry is at the crest of a hill. The winds are coming from the north, blocked only by trees in the Presidio.

It might explain why the teenagers didn't hear a gun shot. It might also explain why Fouke and his partner didn't stop the pedestrian.

The cops discover dead Paul Stine on the front seat, head down by the passenger side floorboard. Blood everywhere. Photos end up on the Internet. Two are of Stine, hanging out of the passenger seat of the car after the police move his body. In one, just after the corpse is repositioned, there's no blood beneath him. In another, taken not much later, the pool on the pavement is large and black. Before and after.

Homicide detectives show up. One is Dave Toschi. The other is his partner Bill Armstrong. They were lead investigators on the Ann Jiminez motor spirit gang bang.

There's a hard-on myth about Toschi. The story is that when he pulls the Stine killing, he's established as the city's Supercop, that he's known around town for his bow-ties, that he's the inspiration for Steve McQueen's character in *Bullit*. The fourth best film about San Francisco. There's no contemporary evidence for this myth. It's a made-up factoid that gets copied and repeated until it becomes true, until it's something that everyone accepts because everyone accepts it. When McQueen filmed *Bullit,* Toschi had only been on homicide for about a year. There are enough extant 1968 photographs to prove that Toschi wasn't dressing like a wild maverick. As the 1970s progress, Toschi becomes increasingly flamboyant, a man with a big brash San Francisco personality. That's not who he is at Washington & Cherry. Right now, he's one of the better detectives in the homicide department. But they're all pretty good. Even if criminal justice is inadequate.

Toschi and Armstrong investigate. They discover multiple bloody fingerprints in and on the cab. Presumably no one has touched the car since Zodiac walked away. The prints belong to Zodiac. He tried to wipe them away but didn't get all of them. It was all so rushed. Zodiac took Stine's wallet and the keys to the cab. There are a pair of small bloody gloves under the dash.

The cops discover what Zodiac was doing to Stine. He wasn't robbing the driver. Not in the way that the teenagers thought. He was removing pieces of Stine's striped shirt.

There's ambiguity about whether or not the removal is done by hand or with a bladed instrument. Photographs of the shirt circulate on the Internet. The lines of detachment are almost straight. Even in ideal circumstances, it's difficult to rip fabric in symmetrical lines. Let alone in the front seat of a car, the fabric wet with blood and wrapped around a corpse. The dead weight and body contours work against the hand. So the killer uses a blade. Other than the fingerprints, this is the most important physical evidence. It tells us that the killing wasn't an impulse crime, that this was a planned attack. The point here isn't just the killing but also the retrieval of an unholy relic.

The assailant's description is corrected. The Negro male becomes a White male adult. A police search is mounted near and in the Presidio. It's unclear when this occurred. The scope of the operation suggests that it happened some time after the three teenagers watch Zodiac walk north on Cherry Street. Military police and bloodhounds and spotlights. Nothing is found. Zodiac is gone, gone, gone. The cops had their chance. But the cops were doing what the cops always do. Looking for a Negro male.

They blew it.

†

The cab's meter is running. At 10:45PM, it reads $6.25. It allows the cops to estimate Stine's point of origin. Where he picked up his fare. The best guesses are either Mason & Geary or the Fairmont Hotel in Union Square. The three teenagers did not hear a gunshot. But it was windy. So it could have happened at the corner of Washington & Cherry. Given the available information, the best guess is that Zodiac was a passenger in the back seat. He tells Stine where he wants to go. Stine drives towards the location. The police establish an official story that Stine was driving to Washington & Maple, one block east of Cherry. But their first public pronouncement says that the fare was to Washington & Laurel, four blocks east of Cherry. The story goes like this: Zodiac gets picked up, says he wants to go to Washington & Maple. When the cab arrives, Zodiac tells Stine to drive west for another block and shoots the cabbie at Washington & Cherry. But the shooting can't happen when the ride is over. The meter is still running. Zodiac must kill Stine at a stop that is not the final stop. There's another complication. Zodiac took Stine's cab keys. The teenagers saw Zodiac wiping down the driver's side door. Zodiac could have been a passenger in the back seat of the cab. Or could have been in the front. In either scenario, why would he come into contact with the driver's side door handle? The most plausible answer is that Zodiac kills Stine at a stop sign, probably Washington & Maple, gets into the driver's front seat, pushes Stine over, and drives to Washington & Cherry.

Tonight, Zodiac is nowhere near Vallejo. He's off his home patch. He can't cruise around and wait for victims to present themselves. This isn't

Lake Berryessa when there's always schismatic Christians on a Sabbath picnic. For the first time, Zodiac is on a schedule. The hood and the ropes and the writing on the door have created a circumstance, a moment of possibility. A window is open. If Zodiac is going to crawl through, he's got to do it now.

He must go to San Francisco.

But maybe he doesn't know the city that well. If you're in a strange place, how do you ensure a victim and enough privacy to remove part of that victim's clothing?

Hail a cab.

Why Washington & Cherry or Laurel or Maple?

There's a chance that it's a stupid joke. On his envelopes, Zodiac uses stamps bearing the visages of US Presidents. There's that story about the first US President George Washington and a cherry tree.

A better answer comes from the map. It looks like this:

1. Washington and Cherry Streets
2. Washington and Maple Streets
3. Jackson and Maple Streets
4. Julius Kahn Playground
5. Lyon Street steps
6. Maple Street footpath

If you're going north, like, say to Vallejo, there's two quick routes out of San Francisco. The Golden Gate Bridge, at the top of the Presidio, or the Bay Bridge to Oakland. Someone on the east side of the Presidio can get on the 101 and drive over the Golden Gate Bridge and be out of the city in five minutes. Why kill south of the park? If you murder and jump into your car, maybe someone'll hear the noise and make your license plate. But if you use the Presidio as your escape route, in darkness, they'll lose you in a minute. Even if the cops bring out searchlights and dogs, you'll be impossible to find, you'll be on the park's eastern border. You'll be on Lyon Street, rushing down its stairs. There's a unique feature on Maple, one that suggests this has been planned out. Go north on Cherry and it ends in a cul-de-sac, there's no way through to Pacific Avenue, the street that borders the Presidio. But Zodiac goes north on Maple. Which terminates in a cul-de-sac, but also has a very small footpath to Pacific Avenue. A person can walk through, jump down to the street. Someone in a car can't follow. It subverts pursuit. Just like the Lyon Street steps.

Maybe it's all a coincidence, maybe none of this is what happens.

If it is, Zodiac's chosen the best possible escape route. San Francisco is dominated by topography. Go two flights down on Lyon and you're in another world. In this place, a pedestrian moves faster than a car. It's the perfect spot to lose the cops. Which is exactly what Zodiac does.

†

Throughout 1969, the *Examiner* and the *Chronicle* run stories about cab drivers who are tired of being victimized. They're striking back. They're packing heat.

4 January: HAS GUN, WILL TRAVEL—CABBIE FOILS STICKUP.

12 Feb: CABBIE KILLS THUG AFTER $21 ROBBERY.

5 April: A LITTLE COP WHO SHOOTS BIG SUSPECTS.

24 April: AN S.F. CABBIE OUTWITS GUNMEN.

13 May: A CABBIE CAPTURES ROBBER.

19 August: 2-GUN CABBIE WINGS BANDITS.

Paul Stine might not have a chance. Zodiac doesn't know it. This is the first time he's picked on someone who might fight back. But Paul Stine isn't carrying. He's a graduate student trying to make some bread. He lives with his wife on Fell Street. He spent most of his life escaping from circumstances. He's trying to make good. He's studying Philosophy. But all the epistemology and ontology and inquiries into the nature of reality aren't worth much when you pick up the wrong fare. All the words in the world put together still aren't thick enough to stop a bullet.

chapter seven

benighted

THE SMARTEST MOVE ZODIAC EVER MADE was killing someone in San Francisco. Until 11 October, the investigations are handled by small town police and sheriff's departments. They do shoeleather work. Talk to victims' friends and family. Find out if victims have enemies. Interview potential enemies. Exclude on basis of alibis. Check ballistics.

Vallejo and Napa and Benicia are close, geographically, to San Francisco. But they're a million psychic miles away. They're as far as the Earth is from the Pleiades. Excluding slain babies at hippie camps, North Bay crime is the normal litany of human jealousy and greed and mental illness. The standard formula for violence and theft. San Francisco is different. The hippies and freaks have motor spirit. The motivating factors remain the same, it's always money or sex, but filtered through acid and speed and grass and half a decade of New American Spirituality. SFPD homicide detectives Dave Toschi and Bill Armstrong waded into the aftermath of Ann Jiminez's turn-out. Toschi saw the beaten body, lipstick swears written on flesh, and then went upstairs to where the turn-out happened. He held the shorn hair of a fat misfit in his own hands. Toschi knows that anything is possible. Hippies who kill because they think that they are Jesus Christ. Hearts hacked out of rival drug dealers. Toschi and Armstrong are no different than anyone else in America. They've been reading about Sharon Tate. Ritualistic murder and black masses. Zodiac saw the same news reports. Zodiac restaged the Tate slaying. Knives, ropes, writing on the door. SFPD has the organizational and financial heft to sway the investigation. The adults are now in the room and they think that they're dealing with an occult crime. Because they are always dealing with occult crime. From the moment that the killing of Stine is linked to Zodiac, the investigation is lost in a labyrinth of bizarre speculation. Common sense is gone. Zodiac can be anybody. Zodiac is an astrologer. Zodiac is a ritual slayer. Zodiac is a sex maniac. Zodiac is everything.

†

No one knows anything. It's like the time between Sharon Tate's slaying and the apprehension of Charles Manson. A crime has been committed. The cops think that it's a cab robbery gone wrong. The killing makes the *Examiner*. A short blurb about a man named "T.L. Stine" shot in Presidio Heights. The witnesses, the victim, the running meter. On 13 October, the SFPD releases a suspect sketch. It resembles half of California's middle aged White men.

On 15 October, *The Los Angeles Times* runs a front page article by staff writer Dave Smith. Its appearance is unprovoked by the murder of Paul Stine. Smith writes before anyone knows that Zodiac shot the cab driver.

The piece is exceptionally long, runs off the front page onto two more. One page is the entire of side of broadsheet. Advertisements excluded. Smith brings forth Zodiac. It's all here in outline. The killings, the letters, the cipher. Smith interviews experts, or at least the people who call themselves experts, and goes past the attacks to the motivation.

The Los Angeles Times is the best regarded media outlet on the West Coast. This is a time before the Internet transforms the Bay Area into the stalking grounds of international overlords. Before San Francisco becomes the money zone. Before San Francisco ruins the world. Los Angeles has the glitz of showbiz and it's got the filthy lucre of the Cold War aerospace industry. Southern California is the glory and the power. Coverage in San Francisco papers won't make Zodiac. No one takes San Francisco seriously. It's an also-ran that fascinates because of motor spirit.

Los Angeles has the real juice. Its most prestigious media organ says that the killer is real. He must be considered. Smith does what no one else has. He uses the tradename that the killer gave himself. This is the true birth of Zodiac.

One must be kind to this era's writers. They didn't have five decades of wheat sorted from chaff. Even so, Smith's article is a particularly bad example of Zodiac writing. It isn't just the factual errors about David Faraday and Betty Lou Jensen and Darlene Ferrin. It's the conclusions, the opinions of the experts. Zodiac's poor spelling indicates that Zodiac doesn't have a good job. Zodiac is a sexual inadequate. Zodiac times his killings to the phases of planets. Zodiac's crosshairs are rich in symbolic meanings. Zodiac uses the symbol X, representing water in the alphabet of the legendary continent of Mu, which is why Zodiac always kills near water. Zodiac stabbed Cecelia Shepard in a pattern that resembles the Zodiac symbol. Zodiac hates women because he always kills the women. Zodiac switched to knives because gun violence lost its thrill. Zodiac is a paranoid schizophrenic.

The Cipher Killer is dead.

Long live Zodiac.

†

On Monday 13 October 1969, an unknown individual goes to an unknown destination in San Francisco. He deposits a letter that he's written. It's addressed to the *San Francisco Chronicle*. Inside the envelope, he's included part of Paul Stine's bloodstained shirt. The letter reads:

> This is the Zodiac speaking.
>
> I am the murderer of the taxi driver over by Washington St & Maple St last night, to prove this here is a blood stained piece of his shirt. I am the same man who did in the people in the north bay area.
>
> The S.F. Police could have caught me last night if they had searched the park properly instead of holding road races with their motorcicles seeing who could make the most noise. The car drivers should have just parked their cars and sat there quietly waiting for me to come out of cover.

School children make nice targets, I think I shall wipe out a school bus some morning. Just shoot out the front tire & then pick off the kiddies as they come bouncing out.

The letter arrives on 14 October. There's no record of what happens when it is opened by *Chronicle* staff.

On 15 October, the same day as Smith's *Times* article, the letter hits Page 1. THE BOASTFUL SLAYER / LETTER CLAIMS WRITER KILLED CABBIE, OTHERS. The *Chronicle* reprints the first part of the letter and includes a reproduction of its initial lines. It does not run the threat against school children.

The article specifies that the letter was written in blue ink with a felt-tip pen. The article is an instruction manual. If anyone wants to write their own Zodiac letter, they now have every required detail. Blue ink. Felt-tip pen. Crosshairs. Enough penmanship that any halfway decent copycat can become The Zodiac.

In the early morning of 15 October, Dave Smith's article hasn't made its way to San Francisco. The *Chronicle* mentions "Zodiac" but it's buried deep. Hours later, when the afternoon *Examiner* reports on the letter, it's clear that people have seen the *Los Angeles Times*. The *Examiner* puts the letter on Page 3. Now the paper calls the Cipher Killer by his chosen tradename.

Now the killer is The Zodiac. And he's speaking.

The *Times* and its prestige would have launched the killer into the stratosphere. But to have Smith's article appear on the same day as the *Chronicle* running the bloody shirt? It's overload. It's the beginning of an era.

†

The letter has one phrase that accounts: "I am the murderer of the taxi driver over by Washington St & Maple last night..."

The SFPD's first description of the Stine murderer appears on a wanted poster released 13 October. It describes the killer's presumed M.O.: "Suspect takes cab in downtown area at 9.30 pm and sits in front seat with driver. Tells driver destination is Washington and Laurel area or area near Park or Presidio. Upon reaching destination, suspect orders driver to continue on at gunpoint into or near Park where he perpetrates robbery. In one case victim was shot in head at contact. Victim's wallet and ID in name of Paul L. Stine and Taxi Cab keys missing."

The SFPD think that Stine's murder is linked to two previous robberies. The wanted posted contains the following information: "Refer Homicide Case No. 696314 / Robbery Cases No. 692895 and 687697." The homicide case is Stine. In the organizational schemata of the SFPD, the first two numbers of any case refer to the year. The files on 692895 and 687697 have been destroyed. So we can't check. But in the 24 April 1968 edition of the *Examiner,* there's an article on Page 13. PASSENGER TAKES CABBIE'S MONEY, LOCKS HIM UP. Robert Williams, a cab driver, picks up a fare at 279 5th Avenue. About a three minute drive from Washington and Cherry Streets. Williams drives the fare to Oakland. The passenger pulls a gun, robs Williams, and locks the driver in the cab's trunk.

Zodiac writes that he killed Stine "last night." It suggests a letter written on 12 October, a date of composition that predates the wanted poster. When Zodiac specifies Washington & Maple, he's not issuing a correction and there's no reason to invent details. It's a statement of fact. Zodiac shot Stine at that intersection. Then drove the body to Washington & Cherry.

"Last night." The postmark is San Francisco 13 October PM. Why didn't Zodiac mail the letter on 12 October? Like all the circumstantial details, "last night" points to someone who doesn't live in the city. If his home is in San Francisco, all he'd need do is walk until he found a mail box. But if he lives or works in the North Bay? This is a man with a job and a civilian life. Each of his attacks occurs on a weekend. Lake Herman Road and Blue Rock Springs happen on Friday nights. Lake Berryessa and Paul Stine happen on Saturdays. A Friday night killing can be done after work and requires no travel. But if you're going out of town, one waits for Saturday.

12 October is a Sunday. It's more than a Sunday. It's Columbus Day. In 1968, legislation fixes Columbus Day as a federal holiday on the second Monday of every October. But the legislation does not go into effect until 1971. 12 October is the holiday.

The delay allows us to infer something about the killer. When he shoots Darlene Ferrin and Michael Mageau, it's 4 July. It's a federal holiday. No one works on 4 July. Zodiac writes a letter on Columbus Day, a Sunday, and can't mail it until a day later.

On 4 July, he could have traveled anywhere. He could have killed at any hour. This isn't a man who only operates at night. Yet on a day when he should have all the time in the world, he does it darkness.

Something beyond work restricted him.

What keeps you from doing what you want? What keeps you busy on Independence Day and a holiday Sunday?

Could Zodiac be a man with family?

†

On 17 October, the *Chronicle* publishes ASTROLOGER JOINS HUNT FOR ZODIAC. The SFPD have been talking to an expert on the stars. They need to understand Zodiac's motivation. Buried several paragraphs down is the news that the SFPD has publicized the threat against school children. Now everyone in the Bay Area knows that Zodiac is going to pick off the kiddies. In the case of emergency, school bus drivers in San Francisco are instructed to keep moving. At all costs. Protect the kids. Unmarked cars tail school buses. Up in Napa, cop cars follow buses and have shotgun wielding ride-a-longs.

A climate of fear destroys civil society. The creation of this climate requires a demonstration of violence. Something bloody enough to draw attention. Once the deed has been done, subsequent threats of violence are given undue gravity.

On 29 October 2004, three years after the attacks of 11 September 2001, Osama bin Laden articulates a new idea. The big moves are over. al-Qaeda is going to bleed America with a thousand small cuts. Osama bin Laden has realized that an overreaction is more powerful than an explosion. On September 11, he helped kill 2,977 American people. In response, the country embroiled itself in war that will claim the lives of over 4,400 of its troops and physically wound another 32,000. There is no accurate count of the PTSD head cases. A million Iraqis will die. The United States will waste over one trillion dollars on a conflict that serves no purpose or function. Osama bin Laden knows that if you threaten the weak people in government, terrify them into believing that a disaster will occur on their watch, they will respond by poisoning their own society.

This is what bin Laden says:

> All that we have to do is to send two Mujahedin to the farthest point East to raise a piece of cloth on which is written al-Qaeda in order to make the generals race there to cause America to suffer human economic and political losses without their achieving for it anything of note other than some benefits for their private companies. This is in addition to our having experience in using guerrilla warfare and the war of attrition to fight tyrannical superpowers as we alongside the Mujahedin bled Russia for 10 years until it went bankrupt and was forced to withdraw in defeat.

The piece of cloth needn't say al-Qaeda. It can be a bloody relic taken from a cab driver. Zodiac has killed five, wounded two. He's demonstrated the capacity for violence. The new threat is issued. The weak men in government respond. Bay Area communities adopt policies that sour the lives of every school child within their jurisdictions. Armed guards on a bus? Some kids must find it fun. But other children must have their dreams invaded.

Now the civil authorities work for Zodiac. They do his dirty work. They're poisoning the psychic landscape. They're creating the terror.

†

As the climate of fear is boiling hot, the *Chronicle* publishes its first Zodiac article attributed to staff writer Paul Avery. ZODIAC—PORTRAIT OF A KILLER. We need only quote the opening line: "The killer of five who calls himself 'Zodiac' is a clumsy criminal, a liar, and, possibly, a latent homosexual." It's a smear piece, contains no new information other than the SFPD denying Zodiac's claims about evading cops in the Presidio. Chief of Inspectors Martin Lee says it's impossible that Zodiac could have escaped detection. Lee does not mention that the search took place late in the game. The article recycles the myth about Zodiac's knife pattern on Shepard, suggests the knifework indicates that Zodiac is unsure of his manhood. Somehow the stab pattern makes him queer.

Paul Avery will become an important part of the Zodiac story. Right now, he's just a reporter on a new beat. But this is as good place as any to say that Avery has been done a serious injustice. In David Fincher's *Zodiac,* Avery is portrayed by Robert Downey Jr. as a degenerate alcoholic who fails out of journalism. In reality, Avery remains a writer for most of his life. He covers the Patty Hearst kidnapping. He and Vin McLellan co-write a book about Hearst. *The Voices of Guns.* It's a masterpiece, one of the very best works of American True Crime, vastly superior to anything else on its chosen topic. Hearst was kidnapped by the Symbionese Liberation Army, a Maoist group from the East Bay. Avery and McLellan are the only people to write about Hearst and the SLA with any sense of the radical milieus of Berkeley and Oakland. They're the only people who take the Maoism seriously. Maoism is half the story. The book is a phenomenon. And one of its authors was burlesqued as a drunk and dope fiend.

On 20 October, police from relevant jurisdictions descend on San Francisco. A Zodiac seminar. They share hints, tips, clues, and hunches. They come away with nothing. Despite headlines about a gun license angle, they know nothing but what Zodiac has written. The SFPD's credulity, its capacity to believe anything because it's seen everything, infects the other municipalities. Now all cops are thinking motor spirit.

News circulates that a 2-year old girl's body has been found in Los Gatos. It's reported that she's found stabbed in the throat. This is in the fog of discovery. Later, it's revealed that she was attacked by wild dogs.

The police and the press link the toddler's death to the unsolved 3 August 1969 slayings of Deborah Gay Furlong, 14, and Kathy Snoozy, 15. Down in the Alameda Valley, near San Jose, Deborah and Kathy go for a picnic in a wooden grove. Deborah is stabbed over 200 times. Kathy more than 100. The case is resolved in April 1971. A college student named Karl Werner, 18, is charged and convicted. Right now, all three deaths are potential Zodiac crimes.

On 21 October, the *Examiner* runs ZODIAC'S GRAPH: IMPOTENT, SHREWD, PARANOID. It's an interview with handwriting expert William F. Baker. From Zodiac's pen strokes and letter forms, Baker deduces personality defects. Baker practices Graphology. A person's mental state can be apprehended, in microdetail, from how they wield the pen. Certain strokes are signs of schizophrenia. It's the first public utterance that anyone, police included, are analyzing the letters beyond their words.

Graphology is like almost all pre-DNA forensics. It's junk. Criminal justice is a story that society tells itself. Everywhere in America, people are convicted on evidence that is garbage. It's hair analysis, it's bite marks, it's blood-type matching, it's hypnosis, it's fiber evidence, it's coerced confessions, it's lie-detector tests. It's pseudoscience. There are no better tools. Graphology and handwriting analysis will play a large role in the Zodiac investigation. All the cops have is the letters. There is almost no evidence other than what the killer has written.

†

On 22 October around 2AM, the Oakland Police Department receives two phone calls. The caller announces himself. "This is the Zodiac." He demands that the police get in touch with F. Lee Bailey, one of the super-lawyers who dominate mass media. Decades in the future, Bailey will be infamous for his drunken defense of O.J. Simpson. In 1969, he's the guy that you want if you're facing the gas chamber. Bailey pulled a not-guilty verdict for Sam Shepard, a neurosurgeon who might have killed his wife and who might be the inspiration for TV's *The Fugitive*. Bailey worked with

Albert DeSalvo, the Boston Strangler. If the police can't get Bailey, the caller says that he'll settle for Melvin Belli.

Belli is like Bailey. Another superlawyer. He punishes the fat cats with tortious victory. He was counsel for Jack Ruby, the man who assassinated the man who assassinated President John F. Kennedy.

Bailey is famous throughout America. As is Belli. But Belli's local. Indisputably the most famous man in San Francisco. Everyone in town knows Melvin. As omnipresent as the Golden Gate Bridge or Coit Tower. He's a big brash San Francisco personality. He's got that flair for flamboyance. He owns a skeleton that he brings into the courtroom to demonstrate human anatomy. He poses with the skeleton for press photographs. He's named the skeleton. The skeleton is Elmer. On 11 October 1968, exactly one year before the murder of Paul Stine and the Los Angeles premiere of *Invocation of my Demon Brother*, Belli appears in an episode of *Star Trek*. Belli plays Gorgan, a mystical space entity who controls the minds of children. Gorgan dresses in elaborate hippie space robes. The episode is a travesty. In a media mega-franchise that has recycled almost every piece of intellectual property into plastic tat, there's never been a Gorgan toy. It's better to pretend as if the episode never happened.

The caller wants a superlawyer to appear on KGO-TV Channel 7's morning show. Hosted by Jim Dunbar. The caller will phone in and speak with a superlawyer. The cops call Channel 7. The cops call Belli. The cops discover that the news media and Belli have something in common with Zodiac. Melvin and Televisionland never turn down publicity.

The show goes on air at 6:30AM. For its first 49 minutes, Zodiac does not telephone. At 7:14AM, while the show is in commercial, the phone rings. The caller says that he's Zodiac. He hangs up immediately. Belli pleads on air. Another call comes in. The caller tells Belli and Dunbar that his name is Sam. Sam says that he has headaches. Sam says that he killed a kid. Sam says that he wants to meet Belli on the rooftop of the Fairmont Hotel. Alone. Belli gives Sam advice. Belli suffered headaches until he visited a chiropractor. Sam should try it. Sam hangs up and calls back several times. Sam says that he needs to kill kids. Sam speaks in monosyllables, leaving Dunbar and Belli to do most of the talking. The show runs for three hours, well past its normal airtime. Sam and Belli get on a private line and arrange to meet in front of the St. Vincent de Paul Thrift Store on the 6200 Block of Mission Street in Daly City. About three blocks south of San Francisco city limits. The meeting is set for 10:30AM.

Belli shows up. The news media shows up. Sam does not.

The cops tape the KGO broadcast and play the audio for Bryan Hartnell and Vallejo dispatcher Nancy Slover and Napa dispatcher David Slaight. The three people who've heard Zodiac's voice. They play it for the Oakland dispatcher. No one thinks that Sam is Zodiac. The cops think that Zodiac made the original calls to Oakland. He offered details about the crimes.

Sam's appearance on Televisionland is such a comedy of errors that it breaks the fever. It's hard to be afraid of a menace that causes this much stupidity. Zodiac starts to disappear from the newspapers. Not completely. There's an *Examiner* Page 1 about how the cops have nothing to go on. For the next two weeks, the articles are ancillary. They're about people arrested on suspicion of being Zodiac but who aren't Zodiac. They're about Napa trying to establish emergency services at Lake Berryessa. Everyone agrees that Cecelia Shepard might have lived if she didn't bleed out for two hours before receiving medical attention. The *Chronicle* reports that foreign reporters have descended on San Francisco. The Germans are represented by *Stern*, the Italians by *L'Europeo*, the French by *Paris Match*.

Zodiac has gone international. The formula worked. Dead Paul Stine worked. The terror threat worked.

chapter eight

one can't spell CALIGULA
without C-A-L-I

ON 7 NOVEMBER, the *Examiner* runs ZODIAC CALLER TRIES TO KILL TEACHER WITH ARSENIC. Page 4. The *Chronicle* covers it the next day. ARSENIC IN SOFT DRINK—ZODIAC? Page 3.

Daniel Williams, 24, lives at 1234 Bush Street in Martinez, across the Carquinez Straight from Benicia and Vallejo. Williams is a school teacher. Starting on 23 October, the day after Sam appears on the Jim Dunbar show, Williams receives anonymous phone calls from an individual who says he's "The Zodiac." Sometimes, the individual sobs over the phone and complains of headaches. Sometimes, the individual says that he has to kill. One time, the individual tells Williams that he went to a Martinez school with murderous intent but turned back when he saw the police. The individual tells Williams, repeatedly, that he is going to "kill the lady of the house." The last call came on Sunday 2 November 1969. In the early afternoon. The individual says that Williams is a dead duck. Williams goes out and comes home around 9PM. Someone has pried the screen from his back door. Williams calls the cops. They search the house. Nothing is missing. The cops leave. Williams goes to his refrigerator. He takes out a bottle of 7-Up. He's drunk from this bottle before. He drinks from the bottle again. There's an unusual metallic taste. Williams spits the liquid out and calls the police. The police perform a content analysis. They discover enough arsenic to kill a human being. The analysis doesn't come back until 7 November. The news breaks the same day.

Someone is reading about Williams. His tradename is Zodiac. This is the actual Zodiac. Not the one who called Jim Dunbar. Not The Zodiac who put arsenic in 7-Up. Genuine issue original. On 8 November, an unknown man goes to an unknown location and deposits a letter that he has written. It could be at a post box. It could be at a post office.

The seven page letter, known as the "Bus Bomb" letter, is one of the two longest Zodiac correspondences. Like the 13 October letter, its envelope contains a piece of Paul Stine's bloody shirt. It reads:

> This is the Zodiac speaking
>
> Up to the end of Oct I have killed 7 people. I have grown rather angry with the police for their telling lies about me. So I shall change the way the collecting of slaves. I shall no longer announce to anyone. When I comitt my murders, they shall look like routine robberies, killings of anger, & a few fake accidents, etc.
>
> ———————————————————————————
>
> The police shall never catch me, because I have been too clever for them.
>
> 1   I look like the description passed out only when I do my thing, the rest of the time I look entirle different. I shall not tell you what my descise consists of when I kill
>
> 2   As of yet I have left no fingerprints behind me contrary to what the police say in my killings I wear transparent finger tip guards. All it is is 2 coats of airplane cement coated on my finger tips—quite unnoticible & very efective
>
> 3   my killing tools have been boughten through the mail order outfits before the ban went into efect. Except one & it was bought out of the state.
>
> So as you can see the police don't have much to work on. If you wonder why I was wipeing the cab down I was leaving fake clews for the police to run all over town with, as one might say, I gave the cops som bussy work to do to keep them happy. I enjoy needling the blue pigs. Hey blue pig I was in the park—you were useing fire trucks to mask the sound of your cruzeing prowl cars. The dogs never came with in 2 blocks of me & they were to the west & there was only 2

groups of parking about 10 min apart then the motor cicles went by about 150 ft away going from south to north west.

ps. 2 cops pulled a goof abot 3 min after I left the cab. I was walking down the hill to the park when this cop car pulled up & one of them called me over & asked if I saw anyone acting suspicious or strange in the last 5 to 10 min & I said yes there was this man who was runnig by waveing a gun & the cops peeled rubber & went around the corner as I directed them & I disappeared into the park a block & a half away never to be seen again.

Hey pig doesnt it rile you up to have your noze rubed in your booboos?

If you cops think I'm going to take on a bus the way I stated I was, you deserve to have holes in your heads.

Take one bag of ammonium nitrate fertilizer & 1 gal of stove oil & dump a few bags of gravel on top & then set the shit off & will positivily ventalate any thing that should be in the way of the blast.

The death machine is all ready made. I would have sent you pictures but you would be nasty enough to trace them back to developer & then to me, so I shall describe my masterpiece to you. The nice part of it is all the parts can be bought on the open market with no questions asked.

1   bat. pow clock—will run for aprox 1 year
1   photoelectric switch
2   copper leaf springs
2   6V car bat
1   flash light bulb & reflector
1   mirror
2   18" cardboard tubes black with shoe polish in side & oute

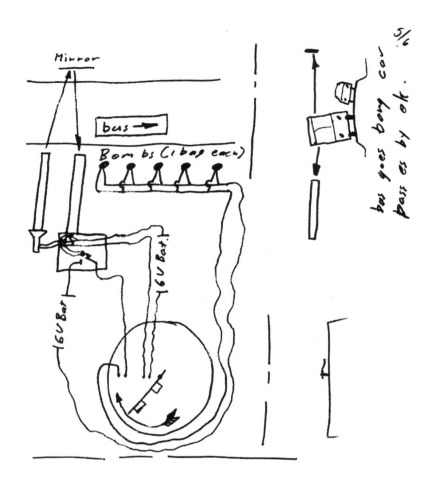

the system checks out from one end to the other in my tests. What you do not know is whether the death machine is at the sight or whether it is being stored in my basement for future use. I think you do not have the manpower to stop this one by continually searching the road sides looking for this thing. & it wont do to re roat & re schedule the busses because the bomb can be adapted to new conditions.

Have fun!! By the way it could be rather messy if you try to bluff me.

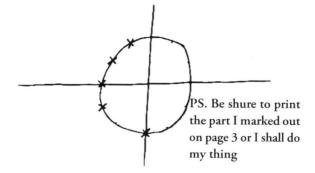

PS. Be shure to print the part I marked out on page 3 or I shall do my thing

To prove that I am the Zodiac, Ask the Vallejo cop about my electric gun sight which I used to start my collecting of slaves.

A claim of 7 dead but with no specification of the unknown two victims. But don't forget: the media attributed Zodiac as author of the Deborah Gay Furlong and Kathy Snoozy killings.

And he's changing his method of collecting slaves. In the moment, the threat is credible. No one expected him to stab college kids at Lake Berryessa or shoot a cab driver in San Francisco. The cops will never again be able to tell the difference between his killings and random crimes. Fifty years later, it's possible to see this statement as an acknowledgment that he's done killing and an attempt to establish a framework. Now he'll be able to claim every random death that makes its way into the media. It's a perfect scheme. The reign of terror doesn't need any more blood. This is bin Laden territory. Zodiac's hoping that when he waves a cloth that reads ZODIAC, the whole world will jump in terror.

After he establishes the framework, he spends two-and-a-half pages attempting to discredit statements that the police have made to the press. He doesn't look like the description, he doesn't leave fingerprints. He bought his guns mail order. He was wiping down the cab to leave fake clues.

In years to come, the press will ask, WHAT HAPPENED TO ZODIAC? Here's the answer. The police got his fingerprints. It's there in the statement about fake clues. Zodiac didn't know that he was being observed. He had no idea that there were witnesses. If the teenagers hadn't seen him, how would anyone know that he wiped down the cab? Why leave clues if no one's watching?

Something happened in Stine's cab. A mistake was made. Maybe the gloves came off. Evidence was left. The prints aren't perfect but they're good enough to exclude suspects. Zodiac doesn't know this. Zodiac fucked up.

Given the press of 15 October, he doesn't need to kill again. His fame is assured. He'll always have a dynamite Wikipedia entry. Zodiac is California myth. Bryan Hartnell said that Zodiac was really nervous. This isn't a man who likes killing. This is a man who likes media coverage. Now that media coverage is guaranteed, there's no need to kill. He will always be known. Take this book as evidence. It's being written almost 52 years after the events. The formula worked. He could change his method of collecting slaves. He could take credit for everything. And he wouldn't risk getting caught. In the meantime, if he could confuse the police investigation by discrediting its key evidence, well, why not?

Then there's the paragraph labeled MUST RUN IN PAPER. Which the newspapers do. The press are like the police. They're taking orders from the killer.

Unlike the three points of discreditation, this section is not a negative statement. It's a positive assertion, and it's not responsive to anything in the press. If his account of misdirecting two cops is correct, then the officers in question are Donald Fouke and Eric A. Zelms. Fouke is interviewed in later decades. His recollections shift and change with the years. They're never entirely satisfactory.

On 12 November 1969, the *Chronicle* breaks the news about this letter and Zodiac's claims of a police encounter. The very same day, Fouke writes a memorandum about Zodiac on Jackson Street. This memo is so exacting in its description, and so closely matches Hartnell's, that it's hard to imagine how Fouke saw, comprehended, and remembered these details if he only witnessed someone walking on Jackson Street.

Given the memorandum's date, it's impossible to see it as anything but ass-covering. But whose ass is being covered? Is it Fouke's? Or is it the SFPD's? Some version of this encounter happened. Maybe Fouke's memorandum is an accurate recounting. Even so, it's a disaster. The SFPD could have caught Zodiac. They had the best chance. They let him go because the system thought that Paul Stine's killer was a Black man. If Zodiac's account is correct, then the disaster is spectacular. It means that two cops stopped, talked with, and released Zodiac. Because he wasn't Black. The memorandum is issued on the same day as the seven page letter hits the media. This is one instance where we have to consider that Zodiac is telling the truth.

Then there's four pages of bombs and death machines and basements and electric sights. The drawing looks as if it were done by a child. Unless the drawing is a gag, unless it's another joke, then it's fashioned by someone who lacks the training to produce a professional schematic.

Zodiac is an autodidact.

If the Woolworth's stationary and the gun from Sears indicate his socioeconomic status, Zodiac is working class. He's someone who believes, with some justification, that he can master the world if only he sits down and reads enough books, that he can substitute a library card for a formal education. He's got a quality that's common amongst working class autodidacts. He has the resentment of the person who knows the same things that the big shots learn at fancy schools and who also knows that he'll never get any credit for this knowledge.

The newspapers have theorized about him. He's impotent, he's ineffectual, he doesn't have a good job, he's not a highly intelligent individual. In all likelihood, some of these perceptions are not new. He's probably dealt with them in his civilian life. They may be the defining features of that life.

Zodiac always wants credit. The ciphers and the bombs are a different way of earning a new kind of credit. This is a man who wants people to know that he is significantly smarter than the average guy.

†

The greeting card doesn't arrive with a piece of Paul Stine's shirt. It comes with another cipher. The card's exterior looks like this:

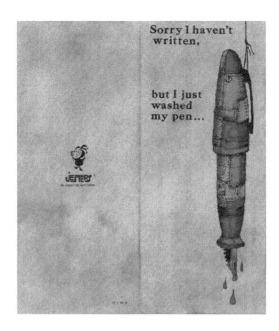

The card's interior looks like this:

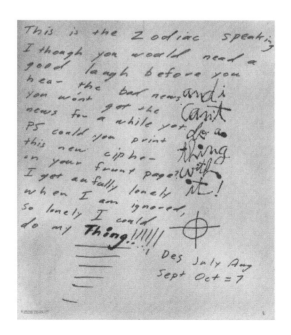

The cipher looks like this:

The short message echoes the letter. Zodiac's on about doing his thing. This is a square echoing the counterculture, the outsider's idea of the insider's lingo. On 30 October 1969, the *Chronicle* runs an installment of *Dear Abby*, a venerable advice column. This one is headlined: HOW CAN ONE TELL A TRUE HIPPIE?

In a previous installment, Abby asks her readers for a definition of the word hippie. The 30 October column prints the responses. One of them reads like this:

DEAR ABBY: A hippie is a runaway, a cop-out, an escapist. He has nothing to contribute to society and hangs around with people like himself, sharing that nothing. He gives the appearance of being unwashed and his hair is long and wild. He dresses in a manner to attract attention while insisting that all he wants is to be left alone to do his "thing." (His "thing" is doing nothing.) He shouts about his "right to discover his own identity" and to be "himself." Then he turns on with marijuana and LSD, and can't remember where he's been or who he is. A hippie is anti-establishment, anti-church, anti-conformist, and anti-everything.

A 23-YEAR-"OLD FOGEY"

The greeting card list of months and victims. It includes "AUG." The extra two victims are indeed Deborah Gay Furlong and Kathy Snoozy. Zodiac didn't kill them. But the media said that he might have. Zodiac takes the credit. Otherwise, the card's just a delivery mechanism for the big score.

The second cipher.

More than any other document, this slip of paper kept the mystery alive and lent itself to more interpretations than can be counted. Graysmith's *Zodiac* includes a pseudo-solution. Other people post pseudo-solutions for decades. In letters to the FBI and SFPD and on the Internet. This one document generates a thousand mysteries. And offers a million solutions. None of them are true. Some folks speculate that the cipher can't be solved because it's nonsense, that it's a joke, there's no actual text. But in the sixth row, Zodiac makes a correction. He replaces one symbol with another, scratches out the first, writes the second on top. Which you don't do unless there's a message. And which tells us something about Zodiac. He's not flawless. He makes mistakes.

On 11 December 2020, the *San Francisco Chronicle* breaks the news. Three men cracked the code. David Oranchak, Sam Blake and Jarl Van Eycke. Confirmed by the FBI and the simplicity of their solution. In marked contrast to the pseudo-solutions, this one reads like a Zodiac letter, requires no leaps of logic, and responds to contemporary events. Correcting for mistakes that Zodiac makes in his encryption, the solution reads like this:

> I HOPE YOU ARE HAVING LOTS OF FUN IN TRYING TO CATCH ME THAT WASNT ME ON THE TV SHOW WHICH BRINGS UP A POINT ABOUT ME I AM NOT AFRAID OF THE GAS CHAMBER BECAUSE IT WILL SEND ME TO PARADICE ALL THE SOONER BECAUSE I NOW HAVE ENOUGH SLAVES TO WORK FOR ME WHERE EVERYONE ELSE HAS NOTHING WHEN THEY REACH PARADICE SO THEY ARE AFRAID OF DEATH I AM NOT AFRAID BECAUSE I KNOW THAT MY NEW LIFE WILL BE AN EASY ONE IN PARADICE LIFE IS DEATH

The three men work from deductions made on Zodiac message boards and use software written by Van Eycke that is forked from other decryption software written by another Zodiac researcher. From the beginning of the publicly accessible Internet, people have been dumped thoughts about Zodiac into the vast surveillance network. They've offered suspects and suspicions and hunches. It's tens of millions of words. This is the only the second time that anyone solves something major.

Zodiac splits the encryption into three sections. Like the 31 July cipher, this one employs a homophonic substitution scheme. Multiple characters are assigned to individual letters. But Zodiac also uses a transposition scheme. Start with the first character in the cipher. Then move two spaces right and one space down. Like the knight on a chessboard. That's how it works. Each letter followed by its successor nineteen characters later. When the text hits the end of a line in the first two sections, it wraps around to the left.

The third section is two lines, doesn't use transposition. It's homophonic substitution. Some words are out of place. Others are spelled backwards. It's not unreasonable to assume that this section is offered as a key to the first two sections. Solve the last two lines and you can solve the rest if you find the pattern. But for a homophonically substituted message to be cracked, there has to be a minimum number of characters. This idea is called the unicity distance. And Zodiac comes up short for anything like an easily solvable cipher.

The major takeaway is that Zodiac didn't call Jim Dunbar. The cipher can't predate the television program, which aired on 22 October. It's a labor intensive process. Maybe it took two weeks to complete.

In 1969, no one knows this.

All they've got is the two letters and a new mystery.

†

On 12 November 1969, the *Chronicle* breaks the news. Article by Paul Avery. An avalanche of coverage follows, but the air's out of the balloon. Zodiac's underestimated how easy it is to bore the press. He promised and didn't deliver. No kids are dead. The story goes nowhere. The *Chronicle* doesn't mention the new bomb threat. It's as if a lesson has been learned. Or the city's calculated overtime pay for cops following buses.

More articles appear. But say nothing. There's a memorial concert at Pacific Union for Cecelia Shepard. The resort owners around Lake Berryessa have agreed to provide emergency services.

On 1 December 1969, Charles Manson and the Family are arrested for the Tate-LaBianca slayings. Even if Zodiac hadn't been losing steam, this would have pushed him from the front pages. The story from Los Angeles is crazier than anyone could imagine. Acid hippies fascist White Supremacists kill Hollywood sexpot. That's fifty years worth of headlines. Manson becomes a fixed icon of American life. He's the blood stained Statute of Liberty.

On 14 and 15 December, Zodiac's dragged into the story. There's a summit in Los Angeles. Bill Armstrong attends. Someone from Napa attends. They're checking to see if Manson is Zodiac. Or Zodiac is Manson.

One day before the first anniversary of the murders of David Faraday and Betty Lou Jensen, someone calls the highway patrol station in San Jose. The caller says that he's The Zodiac. He threatens to kill five patrolmen and a family of five. There's been countless fake Zodiacs. This one is blown off and forgotten.

Except.

The next day, on the anniversary, on 20 December 1969, an unknown man goes to an unknown destination and deposits a letter. The letter is addressed to the home of Melvin Belli.

Belli's in Europe. He's in Munich for a conference. But that's not why Belli is in Europe. He's in Europe because he's the attorney who helped the Rolling Stones set up a free concert at the Altamont Speedway. It happens on 6 December. It's going to show Americans that there are new ways to get together and be beautiful in peace and harmony. The Stones use the Hells Angels as security. The Hells Angels are a fearsome motorcycle gang. The living embodiment of motor spirit. They don't just have motor spirit. They also sell it. There's no barrier between the stage and the audience. The Hells Angels are there to keep people from getting on the stage. They're paid $500's worth of beer. They get drunk. People in the crowd fight each other. They fight the Hells Angels. One of the Hells Angels knocks out Marty Balin of the Jefferson Airplane, the band most associated with Haight-Ashbury. The Jefferson Airplane live together in a twenty-room mansion overlooking Golden Gate Park at 2400 Fulton Street. Mick Jagger of the Rolling Stones is on stage and says, "Hey, hey people, sisters, brothers and sisters, brothers and sisters, come on now! That means everybody just cool out!" As the Stones play a song derived from African-American music, the Hells Angels kill a Black man named Meredith Hunter. Knife in the back. Hunter's drawn a .22. And then he's dead. Coming so soon after Manson, the knife is seen as a stake driven through the collective heart of the beautiful people.

The Age of Aquarius is over. And Belli helped stage the execution.

Belli does what a rogue always does. He fucks off out of town.

The letter arrives at his house on 23 December. Delayed by seasonal traffic. His housekeeper forwards it to his office. A secretary opens it. Presumably the day before Christmas. News of the letter doesn't appear in the papers until Sunday 28 December. Zodiac has sent a letter to the only person in San Francisco more publicity hungry than Zodiac. It allows Belli to change the conversation. Altamont is a distant memory. Now Melvin is the Zodiac whisperer. Inside the envelope, the secretary finds a third piece of Paul Stine's shirt.

The letter reads like this:

Dear Melvin

This is the Zodiac speaking. I wish you a happy Christmass. The one thing I ask of you is this, please help me. I cannot reach out for help because of this thing in me wont let me. I am finding it extreamly difficult to hold it in check I am afraid I will loose control again and take my nineth & possibly tenth victom. Please help me I am drownding. At the moment the children are safe from the bomb because it is so massive to dig in & the triger mech requires much work to get it adjusted just right. But if I hold back too long from no nine I will loose complet all controol of my self & set the bomb up. Please help me I can not remain in control for much longer.

Belli's departure from San Francisco is announced by Herb Caen, the world famous gossip. It's there on Page 29 of the 18 December 1969 *Chronicle*: "**SCOOPS DU JOUR**: The search for Zodiac is suddenly hot again—this time in the Seattle area... Around New Year's Eve, Mel Belli will be in Algiers for a session with Eldridge Cleaver on a nonlegal matter that may make them both richer..."

A template is established with the 4 August letter, made obvious with the 8 and 9 November mailings. If the papers write about Zodiac, then Zodiac writes to the papers. After this letter of 20 December, there are eight subsequent communications. Five are sent after the media invokes Zodiac. In most cases, the connection is so clear as to be indisputable. Look at Herb Caen's article of 18 December, with the two names together, and it's hard to think that this communication isn't part of the pattern.

Back in October, after the Jim Dunbar show, news articles report that Sam's been calling Belli's home. Belli accepts that the caller is not Zodiac but believes the man needs psychiatric and legal help. Belli offers to help Sam. He also extends his hand of friendship and assistance to Zodiac.

This letter is the response.

Zodiac says he's going to take his ninth and tenth victims. Who's number eight? Someone who doesn't exist. Someone whom Zodiac didn't murder.

This letter has been read as serious, as if Zodiac is asking for help. But it's a joke. It's how Zodiac closes out his year. On the anniversary of its beginning. By making fun of Belli. Please help me Melvin I am sick I can't stop killing.

Except that he can stop. He has stopped.

The killer is a joker.

And so ends the year of Zodiac.

chapter nine

today cats, tomorrow kids

BUT THAT'S NOT THE END.

There's the killer who murders in San Francisco and Vallejo and Napa. And then there's Zodiac, who lives in the press. And then there's The Zodiac, who creeps out of the newsprint and radio and television coverage into the imaginations of the citizenry. Some are children, delighted or terrified by the bus fiasco. Some are people with motor spirit. Some are mentally ill. Some have made themselves mentally ill with motor spirit. Some are normal folks, terrified and captivated.

The killing has stopped.

Eventually, Zodiac will cease sending letters.

But.

The Zodiac lives forever. He's the bogeyman. The Zodiac can be anybody.

†

The Zodiac is conceived on 31 July with ciphers sent to three newspapers. People don't have the tradename but they flood the police with tips and telephone calls. People think that the killer is their unpleasant neighbor or the weird kid from school. It's the start of labor pains. But The Zodiac isn't born until 15 October. *Los Angeles Times* and bloody shirt. What comes out of the womb is a homunculus made of metastatic cells, spreads to every brain. *If anybody can be The Zodiac, then why can't I?*

It really begins on 22 October, the same day that Sam appears on the Jim Dunbar show. Someone calls the Palo Alto police and threatens to "pick off the kids as they get on the school bus." The article about this threat is poorly written, makes it sound as though the call arrived before the SFPD circulates news of the bus threat. But it comes after. Zodiac might like to use the telephone system but this is not Zodiac. This is The Zodiac. On the same day, the *Ukiah Daily-Journal* publishes an article about tips that've come in since 17 October. Most are from people who think that they saw Zodiac down at the park. They didn't. They saw The Zodiac. One tip is from 21 October. An 8-year old girl is walking on Lake-Mendocino Drive, east of the train tracks. A light colored car drives past. Its driver throws a note at the girl. The note says: YOU'RE NEXT—Z.

The same day, Joe Stine issues a challenge. Joe is Paul Stine's brother. Joe wants to be Zodiac's next victim. If Zodiac's such a tough guy, why not pick on Joe? Why not try and kill this former Korean War Veteran? Joe's plenty tough too. Come on, come and get me, Zodiac. See what happens. No one reports that it's a suicide attempt. Death by Zodiac. There's television coverage of Joe issuing his challenge. He looks destroyed. He and his brother weren't that far in age and Paul was there for the bad times, Paul was someone who knew, really knew, where Joe came from. Now Paul is gone. Joe wants to be next. Joe wants Zodiac to save Joe from the feelings that Joe can't express. Every single thing that a person goes through, no matter how hard, will be of some use. You always learn something. Every single thing except death. Death don't have no mercy. Death is the endless absence of another. It's the full stop. You learn nothing but how to co-exist with an empty space. Death's the one vacuum that nature does not abhor, a thing that time cannot fill. Paul is gone. Joe's got to keep living. Joe asks the press to print the address of the car garage where Joe works.

A Virginia state assemblyman is an amateur astrologer. He thinks that Zodiac plans his murders according to the waxing and waning of the moon. He thinks that the next killing will occur on the 24-26 October weekend.

Five citizens in Los Angeles call the LAPD and say that Zodiac sounds just like someone they know. Someone brings a Zodiac wanted poster into the San Francisco Hall of Justice. The Hall is seven-storeys and occupies a full block on Bryant Street. Opened in 1961, it contains most of the city's law enforcement. It's got the police department, the district attorney, the medical examiner, the public defender, courtrooms, the sheriff's department, and the probation department. It's Zodiac central. Someone brings a wanted poster into the Hall. They've drawn on the poster. With lipstick. Just like the motor spirit freaks who drew on Ann Jiminez. "See," says the person, "this proves that Zodiac is a woman!"

This says nothing of Sam on the Jim Dunbar show. Sam is 29-year old Eric Weill. He grew up in Berkeley. His father's name is Sam. He was born on 10 January. He'll call Belli in January 1970 and say, "I can't wait, it's my birthday." In November 1949, when Weill is 9-years old, he makes the newswires. He brings a bloody sheet to his mother and shows her that he's lost a tooth. He says that his babysitter and his babysitter's father beat him. The cops investigate, discover that Eric was thrown out of the sitter's house for acting like a brat. When the cops question young Eric, he admits that he pulled the tooth himself.

Somehow this gets nationwide coverage.

Eric never escapes the Bay Area. He graduates from Berkeley High and becomes a counterculture photographer. In December 1965, he's at a press conference starring Bob Dylan, who meets the cream of the Bay Area journalistic and youth elite. He answers their questions for just under an hour. The conference is taped and broadcast. Watch the video, now, and it's apparent that this is the exact moment before the old America surrendered to the new. Half of Dylan's interrogators are from a world where you could be a two-piece suited company man and determine the country's intellectual and aesthetic future. The other half are proto-freaks, the people who are about to supply a sparkling new culture that will be legitimated when it is processed into filthy lucre. Right now, no one's figured out how to make mass market money from the freaks. Not yet. But they will.

Every single person in the room—square, freak, gay, lesbian, bi, straight—wants to fuck Bob Dylan. The lust is visible. What they need is for Dylan to explain this moment, explain what's coming and what's being lost, and guide them into their uncertain destiny. They want a righteous shag and some pillow talk. And Dylan himself? He's bored, ten years beyond everything that these people are about to experience. He says that he doesn't care. He means it. Which no one can believe.

In this moment, Eric Weill is another Californian who stopped cutting his hair, sucked on a Thai stick, went to the record store, and thought that he purchased the Voice of God. He asks Dylan the first questions.

WEILL: I'd like to know about the cover of your, of your, forthcoming, er, your, uh, uh, album. The, uh, the one with "Subterranean Homesick Blues" in it. I'd like to know about the meaning of the photograph with you and the wearing the Triumph t-shirt. [1]

DYLAN: What'dja want to know about it?

WEILL: Well I'd like to know—that's an equivalent photograph, it means something it, it's got a philosophy in it. *[Dylan and crowd laugh.]* I'd like to know, visually what it represents to you because you're a part of that.

DYLAN: Um. I haven't really looked at it that much. I don't really...

WEILL: I'VE THOUGHT ABOUT IT A GREAT DEAL.

DYLAN: It was just taken one day when I was sitting on the steps, you know. I don't, uh, I don't really remember I mean very too much about it.

WEILL: Well, what about the motorcycle as an image in your, in your songwriting? You seem to like that.

DYLAN: Well, we all like motorcycles to some degree.

WEILL: I do.

---

1   "Subterranean Homesick Blues" appears on *Bringing it All Back Home*. The image in question appears on *Highway 61 Revisited*. By December 1965, both had been available for months.

Eric's got problems. Eric's got motor spirit. He fixates on Zodiac. He calls Jim Dunbar. He calls Belli. In March 1970, Eric goes to a Black Panther rally and threatens to blow people up with a stick of dynamite. He waves a knife at reporters. He makes newswires. A photo of Eric being menaced by a cop with a truncheon. The photo looks like this:

When he's arrested, Eric gives his name as Clifford Heinz III. A long dead ketchup heir. Eric gets sent to Napa State Mental Hospital. He apparently calls Belli from the hospital. The calls are traced. Sam is identified as Eric.

Other than a marriage later in the same year and a divorce in 1972, Eric disappears until the 1980s. He resurfaces as a Berkeley eccentric. He haunts the campus and lives in an ancient 1930s milk van. He dresses as Abraham Lincoln and seems to have legally changed his name to Abraham Lincoln IV. On 30 April 1980, Eric is arrested for going into the University of California Art Museum and defacing a Richard Avedon portrait of Andy Warhol and Andy Warhol's friends. The portrait includes the fully nude Candy Darling. Eric's disturbed by Darling's dingle. Eric is photographed in court. He's dressed like Abraham Lincoln. A few months later, Eric is arrested on campus. The school newspaper *The Daily Californian* is sponsoring a student Fun Run. Eric shouts at the fun runners. He throws chairs around.

Eric hangs around for decades, lives in squalor. Eric's not from nowhere. His parents are educated. His sister is Rita Weill. She was an editor for *Broadside!* magazine, the house bible of the folk music set.

In 1971, Takoma Records releases *Rita Weill Sings Ballads and Folksongs*. It's a lovely record. If slightly mannered.

Eric's got problems. Eric's got motor spirit. Eric hangs on for decades until he kills himself in 2006.

Eric's mind is The Zodiac's home. The underground early warning network of the unwell and the motor spirited and the crazy and the mad and degenerate cousins of people from the first American history. Their brains are the soil in which The Zodiac grows. Hoods and ropes and letters and ciphers. This is The Zodiac speaking.

†

An anonymous person mails a letter to the Santa Rosa Police Department. It gets misdelivered to KRON-TV. The station reads the note on air and then turns it over to the cops. The note threatens to kill a kid in Santa Rosa.

On 24 October, Robert Gorman gets a letter published in *The Examiner.* He thinks that the paper's Zodiac coverage is hypocritical. Why are the *Examiner*'s journalists and editors so upset about five dead people? Aren't these the same folks who support America's military conflict in Vietnam? Why pretend to care about five people when America has maimed and murdered hundreds of thousands of Vietnamese?

A day later, the sentiment is echoed in the *Berkeley Tribe*. The *Tribe* is an underground newspaper, an off-shoot of the venerable *Berkeley Barb*. There was a labor dispute at the *Barb*. Its radical writers left and founded the *Tribe*. On 19 October, the *Examiner* publishes a message to Zodiac. It offers to help with legal representation if the killer turns himself in. On Page 10 of its 24-30 October edition, a day after Gorman's letter, the *Tribe* publishes its own message to the Zodiac. This message is authored by a person named Blaine.

Blaine suggests that Zodiac, if he has indeed killed, is animated by the spirit of an America that used murder and rapine to establish its hold over stolen territory. Blaine asks that Zodiac consider the arbitrary nature of a criminal justice system that does not punish its police when they kill. Blaine lists several citizens murdered by police. If Zodiac has killed, Blaine doesn't think that Zodiac should turn himself in. Zodiac must walk the Earth and find peace within himself and become a penitent pilgrim. Throw his weapons into the sea. Burn his past. Go to a land where hate & war & violence are not the main energy.

Then there's Paul Alvarez, 33, who drives a school bus in Palo Alto. He's chauffeuring kids across a Bayshore Freeway overpass when he hears a gun shot. He keeps driving. As he's been instructed. When he gets to school, Alvarez discovers a bullet hole in molding above the emergency door exit. A criminalist examines the bus. There's no bullet hole. The bus is dented and has paint transfer marks. The criminalist thinks that something came off a truck and hit the bus.

A reporter from the *Dayton Daily News* in Ohio runs a classified addressed to The Zodiac. In the *Examiner* and the *Chronicle:*

> ZODIAC Please send me your diary and other biographical information. Give yourself up and I will assist in legal and medical help. Will write novel on your life and series of articles for widespread publication. Please get in touch for everyone's sake. Dale Huffman. Reporter.

A chalk note is discovered on a slate board at North Avenue School in Sacramento. It threatens the lives of children. It concludes: "My name is Zodiac."

A Hollywood film producer is in the Vallejo-Napa area. Don Allison. He's shooting footage for a project called *The Zodiac Case.* He plans to give

The Zodiac a common name like Ted Smith. Production is scheduled to start in December. The project never materializes.

A 22-year old hitchhiker says that she was raped by The Zodiac. She's visiting from Florida and hitching around 2PM. A man picks her up and drives her to Mount Tamalpais in Marin County. He says that it's a shortcut to San Francisco. He parks on a dirt road, tells her that he's The Zodiac and rapes her. He robs her of $100. The woman is found by a motorcyclist who brings her to safety. She tells her story and then refuses to go the hospital because it wouldn't be groovy to travel with a cop.

A 14-year old Crescent City high school student is revealed as the author of a letter to a local newspaper. In the letter, the student wrote that he was The Zodiac and was going to kill children on Halloween. The suspect is discovered after the examination of 2,640 handwriting samples. Asked why he wrote the letter, the 14-year old says that he didn't have anything better to do.

In Santa Rosa, a college student named Stephen Fain walks into the unfortunately named Sambo's Restaurant. A little old lady stares at Stephen. She gets up and calls the cops and tells them that The Zodiac is drinking coffee at Sambo's. The cops show up. They know Fain. They know he isn't Zodiac.

In San Mateo, a 25-year old man calls the operator and says, "I'm the Zodiac, you're next on my list, operator." He hangs up. The operator holds the line and traces the call. She reports the call to the police. The cops go to the man's house. He greets them with a .22 caliber rifle. He invites the cops in and hangs the rifle on a rack. He says that he'd been sleeping. When questioned, he admits making the call. But says that he'd only been joking.

On 20 November, a man named David Martin has serious motor spirit. He takes drugs and goes berserk. He's at home in the Ingleside section of San Francisco with his wife and their 11-year old daughter and 9-year old son. Martin cuts his wife. He grabs his daughter. His wife and son run to his wife's mother's house. Her mother calls the cops. The cops go to the Martin family home. The cops knock on the door. Martin comes outside. daughter clutched in his hands. He's got a saw against her throat. He goes on a tirade about his wife and tells the cops to go away or he'll kill his daughter. He shouts that he is The Zodiac. Other cops sneak into the house. Martin runs inside. His daughter's neck has cuts and abrasions. Martin pulls out chunks of his daughter's hair. Motor spirit. A cop lines up a shot and fatally wounds Martin. As Martin dies, he says, "Thank you officers. It's through. I'm the Zodiac."

Paul Avery writes an article linking an ambush shooting to Zodiac. But the suspect and victim are both African-American.

Out in Oklahoma, there's a Sunday radio talk show on KTOK 1000 AM. On 7 December, someone calls in and breaths heavily and speaks with great emotion. The caller asks if the host knows the caller's identity. The host says that the caller sounds like the person who called Jim Dunbar. The host and the caller know about Sam on Dunbar because clips were broadcast coast-to-coast on major television networks. Sam was national nightly news, biopsied into two minute segments. "Oh," says the caller. "I left California because it got too hot for me." "Are you trying to tell me that you're the Zodiac killer?" asks the host. "I could be," says the caller. He adds that Oklahoma is better for him because so many people kill themselves on the highway. Which makes it legal. The host says that the station is tracing the call. The caller says that he had better hang up. He says that there will be more killings before his capture. "There are plenty of parking lots."

On 17 December, down in Pacifica, south of San Francisco along the Pacific Coast Highway, a wave of cat murders is solved. At least 15 felines are dead. There's a gang of youths, between 11 and 16-years of age, who call themselves the Cat Assassins and Cat Killers Club. Initiation requires that new recruits capture and murder two cats. Most feline victims have their heads wrung off. The killers leave notes on the bodies. One reads: "Today Cats, Tomorrow Kids." Another says: "Zodiac Killer."

On 21 December, a classified runs in the *Chronicle*. "'Zodiac' Information or opinions wanted regarding him. Send to: Research Study Group, 205 School of Journalism, Communications Center, University of Iowa, Iowa City, Iowa 52240."

†

The year ends with North Hollywood's *Valley Times*. Front page story. ANOTHER ZODIAC? It's about the murders of two young women. One case won't close until decades later. Cold case DNA. The other won't be solved. The cops lose the genetic material. The article is by Jim Newson. The opening paragraph: "Though it isn't discussed 'officially,' police admitted today the possibility that Los Angeles may have its own 'Zodiac' murderer. The L.A. version's target: pretty Jewish girls in their early 20s."

This is before the media and law enforcement develop the concept of the serial killer. Everyone knows that there are patterns in multiple murders. But the sociopathic sexual predator compelled to murder over and over again does not exist as a categorical profile. The idea's time is now but there's no name. Jim Newson borrows another. He calls it ZODIAC. Cipher Killer as stand-in for the men who go around killing the same woman who is all women. Evolution has made the human brain very good at pattern matching. The human brain takes disparate elements and fashions them into an idea, into the semblance of a pattern. Zodiac isn't like Manson. Manson is a loathsome person caricatured by the press and law enforcement. But Manson is defined. Whatever they say about Manson, Charlie will then say something about himself. Manson is news footage. We know Manson. He's the acid hippie fascist killer. Zodiac is different. There are no definitions. There are only letters. Which say so much while saying almost nothing. Anything can fit the pattern. Zodiac can be molded into any shape or form.

Some people put themselves into Zodiac. They become The Zodiac. They make a phone call. They write a letter. Some put others into Zodiac. They call and say that their wretched son-in-law is The Zodiac. The neighbor who parks too close to the property line. The mentally ill person who hangs around in front of city hall.

Every grudge and resentment is manifested. The cops investigate, clear the fingered. The flood of names becomes a trickle and then, for a while, it runs dry. The impulse has to go somewhere. Law enforcement is part of this. They've being paid to put a name on the crimes.

Then it goes beyond law enforcement.

It's amateur sleuths. It's Robert Graysmith.

Zodiac is Arthur Leigh Allen.

Zodiac is Rick Marshall.

Zodiac is Berkeley professor Michael O'Hare.

Zodiac is William Joseph Grant.

These names don't pan out. These men are not Zodiac. The best guesses of law enforcement and authors and Internet sleuths come to nothing. But everyone's got the same habit as every other citizen in our mediated society. Everyone's addicted to gossip. Everyone's jonesing, everyone's fixing for new entertainment. The maw gapes.

New names arrive.

Zodiac is Lawrence Kane.

Zodiac is Ross Sullivan.

Zodiac is Jack Tarrance.

Everyone can be The Zodiac.

Anyone can be The Zodiac.

part two

DECADENCE

chapter ten

satan saves zodiac

IT'S 1970. ZODIAC IS A GHOST. No one'll hear a peep for four months. Zodiac is nowhere but The Zodiac is everywhere. Charles Manson was a dud. The months after Tate were a moment, a thing, a panic. Then the monster was revealed. And it was Charlie, unwashed denim with desert dust. A bozo, a loser, so much smaller than anticipation. But the window can't be closed. The new model has a name. The Zodiac. He's behind every corner.

Take, for example, 1 January.

The previous decade is done. Everyone's glad to watch it go. It's the most exhausting of times, begins when Norman Mailer stabs his wife and ends with the writer running for Mayor of New York City. 1969 isn't quite the hell of 1968. But it's bad enough. Good luck and good riddance.

At the flick of midnight, when 31 December becomes 1 January, a social revolution explodes. California's Family Law Act of 1969, signed by Governor Ronald Reagan in September, goes into effect. California gets rid of a blame-based system and institutes No Fault Divorce. Now, here, in this new decade and forevermore, a first in America, either party can initiate the proceedings and free themselves from the prison and no one has to go to Reno or perjure themselves in the process. This isn't to say that, by the end of the jail break, most people won't end up hating their spouses. That's a given. But the law takes away the hypocrisy. The prison is the major divide between the wild children of San Francisco and Berkeley and their parents in Benicia and Martinez. What separates freaks from squares is nothing more than bad timing. The squares come of age when there is no birth control pill. Barring the pleasures of homosexual assignations, the biological imperative has one destination. The creation of new life. It means that marriage, a legalized scheme of property rights, takes on a special and oppressive significance. The freaks choose free love as a rejoinder. They can't articulate it as such, but what do you think they mean they're droning on about suburban conformity and the stifling atmosphere of home? It's punks bitching about the warden's rules. There's no escape other than to run away with the beautiful people, to drop acid and listen as Charlie raps about race war and how there is no time and how if there is no time then there is, ipso facto, no morality. On 1 January, something happens. And it's monumental. It unlocks the gates. It's an easy way out. It transforms California into the Land of Permission. Three years earlier, the squares hate the freaks so much that they cast a Hollywood actor as Berkeley campus sheriff. But the Family Law Act redefines the squares. The 1970s are a decade in which Reagan voters become swingers and casual dope smokers. The promised land is wide open and everyone's invited to pillage. The California people, the ones who benefit from that post-World War Two prosperity boom, are the new residents. They think they have everything. But they look at the wild children and realize they can have a little more. And here it is. The division is erased.

Zodiac reveals something his letters. It's there in 1969 and achingly visible in the future communications. Zodiac is a man who can't join the freaks, who's trapped by the square world. No matter how hard he tries. No matter what he does. But now Ronald Reagan has removed those strictures, this is his true gift to voters, the manifestation of societal change through unexpected vessels. The squares hated the wild children so much that they needed a Hollywood actor, a man made of fantasy and permission, to turn them into the wild children. The Family Law Act creates a generation of latchkey kids with boozy moms who keep the tract house and perved-out dads who move to North Hollywood apartments. In 1969, this option was not available. Zodiac couldn't join the freaks. So Zodiac goes out and murders.

If only he'd waited.

†

1 January is forty-five minutes old. SFPD patrolman Eric A. Zelms is on special assignment. Night beat in the Tenderloin. He's working with a new partner, Richard G. Bodisco. Before this evening, the two have never met. They walk their rounds, wander the city, and then, around midnight, grab something to eat. Oresete's restaurant at 118 Jones Street. They're there for a while, shoot the shit and chew the fat. Bodisco gets up and walks to the restroom. Whilst he answers nature's call, there's noise from the street, the shattering of glass. Someone runs into the restaurant and says that people are breaking into a pawn shop.

Zelms rushes outside and sees 20-year old Michael Webster standing with 29-year old Vincent Fredericks. The two men are African-American. They don't know each other well, not really, they meet up at a party and get drunk and, in that way when you're drunk at a party and talking with someone you don't know very well but whom the alcohol makes your very best friend, the two men decide that their best course of action is to go the Tenderloin and find one of Fredericks's lady acquaintances. She'll be throwing another party. They get to Jones Street. Fredericks, a student hairdresser, sees a pawn shop called the Trading Post and drives a curling iron through its plate glass window. He wants a watch that's on display.

Zelms gets onto Jones Street. He's drunk. This fact only emerges at trial. He gets into a confrontation with the two men. Or, anyway, that's the story offered by newspapers and the prosecution. In reality, it appears that Zelms only gets into it with Fredericks. Based on eyewitness statements, it's not impossible that Zelms is the aggressor, that he attacks Fredericks and not vice versa, and then it all goes haywire. Zelms fumbles his service pistol, and then Fredericks has the gun in his hands and he's firing three bullets into Zelms. Two are killing shots.

Webster and Fredericks run. Five minutes later, they're caught by another pair of cops. Fredericks gets into a shoot-out with the new cops.

Zelms is a goner. He's 22-years old, he's got a wife, he's starting a family. And his story is done.

Webster didn't break a window, didn't shoot Zelms. He doesn't get into a gun battle. Webster runs from the guns and is caught a block later. He didn't flee to escape the cops. He just didn't want to get shot. Both men will be charged with voluntary manslaughter, both men will go on trial, both men will be convicted.

Criminal justice is a story that society tells itself. And if you're in America and you kill a cop, you're nothing, you're scum, you're less than dirt. Lee Harvey Oswald could have been the greatest anti-hero of American life but forty-five minutes after he killed the President, he shot a cop. And became another loser, a nobody.

Even if you don't kill a cop, even if you're just standing with someone whom you don't know very well and who told you about a girl in the Tenderloin, well, so what? You're going down. Evidence will be fashioned to demonstrate your guilt. Contrary material will be ignored. By judge and jury. And if you're Black? They don't invent new rules. They use the standard playbook.

There's a discordant note in early news reports of Zelms's death. It disappears in subsequent days, the narrative transforms into the good cop serving the city. In the first appearances, there's a sense of Zelms's discomfort with the job. Articles state that he was thinking about leaving the force. The money isn't good, he's only been on the beat for less than a year. And then there's the drinking. And the apparent anger when he sees Fredericks and Webster. Something is here. Maybe it really is that a rookie policeman's salary isn't enough for a 22-year old trying to start a family and establish himself in the Land of Permission.

But.

Three months earlier, back on 11 October, Zodiac encounters a police cruiser on Jackson Street. Maybe the car drives past. Maybe the car stops and the patrolmen speak with the killer and let him go because they're looking for someone like Michael Webster and Vincent Fredericks.

The cruiser was driven by Donald Fouke.

His partner that night?

Eric A. Zelms.

Maybe Zodiac is why Zelms is working a special assignment in the Tenderloin on New Year's Eve. It's one of the shittiest things that a cop can be doing. Bad night, crummy neighborhood. Maybe this is soft discipline, the kind that leaves no paperwork. Maybe Zelms is sent to his death because Zodiac mails a letter that embarrasses the SFPD, exposes that two cops let a killer go free. And one of those cops is Zelms.

Zelms could be at the Trading Post because this is the exact job that you give to a rookie, to someone so low in the hierarchy that they lack any mechanism of objection. But maybe he's on Jones Street because of his small part in a major fuck-up. Even if he and Fouke didn't stop Zodiac, that's the stink that never washes off. There's always whispers. *That guy? You know about him? No? He let Zodiac go.* It's possible that Zelms is bleeding to death on Jones Street not because he was drunk and in the wrong place at the wrong time. It's possible that he's dying because he had the worst of luck. He saw the face of Zodiac.

Seven people have witnessed the visage, the flesh not covered by an executioner's hood.

Five are now dead.

†

On Saturday 17 January, a lovesick cab driver named Naji Srour is nowhere to be found. He drives for Yellow Cab in Pacifica, just south on the Pacific Coast Highway, the town where Cat Assassins wring the heads off their victims and leave Zodiac-themed notes on the bodies. Srour is driving on Friday night. When his shift ends at 2AM on Saturday, he doesn't return to dispatch. Time passes. Telephone calls come into Yellow Cab. The caller inquires about Srour. The caller knows the number of Srour's cab. Finally, the caller says that Srour will never return. The owner of Yellow Cab, a man named Milton Henke, gasps, "The Zodiac has him!" An all-points bulletin goes out. Everyone in copland and cabland thinks that Srour is as dead as Paul Stine. But he's not. Eventually, his cab is found outside his girlfriend's apartment. He's alive. The girlfriend has another beau. Who saw the cab. And wanted revenge on the competition.

It's a silly story, one that goes nowhere, but it shows that cabbies are like the police and the freaks in the Haight. They've got their own subculture, their own private mythologies, their own cabbie anecdotes and language and shared knowledge. Their own lore. Zodiac has joined the pantheon.

Ten days later, on 25 January, two SFPD patrolmen discover a cab in Presidio Heights. It's double parked. Its headlights are on. When the cops look inside, they find the driver, Charles Jarman, 28, shot through the head. He's still breathing. But he'll die in a day. When the news breaks, a question is asked in unison. IS IT ZODIAC?

Dave Toschi and Bill Armstrong work the case, go to the cab. In the backseat, someone's dropped an envelope. It's addressed to Robert Brommell. He's 20-years old, a White boy junky. He's from Oregon, abandons his wife and 6-month old daughter, ends up in the same place as every hopeless person in America's northwest. San Francisco. The envelope's from his lawyer. Two partial fingerprints embedded in the fiber. Armstrong and Toschi take the envelope to the Hall of Justice and run it through a system that analyzes partials. The prints belong to Brommell. He's arrested in a few days, found in bed with a girl named Anita. Within four hours of his apprehension, he admits responsibility.

SFPD has Zodiac's partial prints. These must be run through the same system. The cops come up with nothing. If Zodiac's ever been arrested, it wasn't in San Francisco.

One day before Brommell is arrested, Yellow Cab offers a reward for Zodiac. $1,000. That night, Gerald Clancey, 29, tries to rob a Yellow Cab driver at Fulton & McAllister. The driver is George A. Alexander. He's 41-years old and he's packing. He allows Clancey to take money at knife-point and then follows the robber into the street and shoots him dead. The cabbie mythology is working over time. Gerald Clancey decides to rob the wrong person. And takes a shot in the temple at twenty feet.

†

Eric Weill's back at it. On 5 February, he calls Jim Dunbar's television show, again refers to himself as Sam. Something goes wrong with the recording. Only Dunbar's voice is captured. Weill does the same thing that he did on his previous appearance, speaks in monosyllables and fragments, leaving

Dunbar to ask questions reminiscent of a freshman term paper. Restate the answer in the form of a question. If anyone thinks that Sam is Zodiac, Dunbar's questions set the issue to rest. Sam talks about the Hells Angels and their role at Altamont and the death of Meredith Hunter. Recent issues of *Rolling Stone* magazine have covered Altamont, making it a cause célèbre about our music and our lifestyle. Which sounds nothing like Zodiac.

†

In March, someone calls the cops in Redding, California, way up north near Mt. Shasta, and says that he's The Zodiac and he's going to pick off the high school kiddies. Nothing happens. When it's like this, when The Zodiac is a voice on the phone, nothing ever happens. Everyone is bored by the dynamic. These calls are so routine that they rarely make the newspaper. Zodiac's moment is over. He threatened. Nothing happened.

On 22 March, a woman shows up at the police station in Patterson. She says that she was driving from the Los Angeles area, headed to see her mother. Out on Highway 132, a car was behind her and flashing its headlights until she pulled over. A man comes out of the car and says that one of her wheels is loose. He offers to tighten her lug nuts. She agrees, lets him work on the tire. As she drives away, the wheel comes off. She nearly crashes. The man from the car stops and offers the woman a ride to the nearest service station. She agrees, takes her infant daughter from her own car. He drives them around for a few hours, passing several service stations. Finally, when the man comes to a rolling stop, the woman grabs her daughter and jumps from his car and hides in a field. A couple picks her up and drives her to the Patterson police station. When she gets there, the woman is in a state of hysteria that only worsens when she sees SFPD's Zodiac wanted poster. It's on the wall. She cries out that this is the man who abducted her.

It's pure myth, the stuff of legend, ends up in Graysmith's *Zodiac* and Fincher's adaptation. Read the police reports and it's impossible to believe that any of this happened. The cops find the car and it's been set on fire but all four wheels are attached. The bolts are loose on the right rear wheel. Only two are in place. But the wheel is on the car. If the story is true, Zodiac drove back to the car, found the wheel on the highway, hoisted the vehicle on a jack, reattached the wheel and then burned the car.

It's not clear that the woman was kidnapped. She says that the man never threatened her. Zodiac might change his killing tools and method, but he doesn't linger. He doesn't wait. Zodiac goes for the kill. At most, you've got twelve minutes. Bryan Hartnell says that Zodiac is nervous. He isn't good with killing. He wants to get it over with. In the moment, this woman's story receives almost no press coverage. A crucial aspect of the story, that the wheel came off the car, isn't true. It's possible that this a woman with so much motor spirit that she torches her own car and invents the easiest excuse, the name embedded in every imagination.

The Zodiac lives.

†

Months go by without word one from Zodiac. The last letter is sent to Melvin Belli on 20 December 1969. And now it's April 1970. More than anything, this tells us about Washington & Cherry. George Washington couldn't tell a lie. But Zodiac can. Why stop killing? Fingerprints, direct ineradicable forensic evidence that can't be changed or altered. Zodiac's not stupid, he's not a compulsion killer, the attacks have zero detectable sexual elements, and while they feature small fuck-ups and disasters, the mistakes are not defining features. Until Stine's murder. Something went wrong. Zodiac keeps writing letters but the air is out of the tire. Zodiac happens in the press. The killings happen at Lake Herman Road and Blue Rock Springs and Lake Berryessa and Presidio Heights. The killings are fuel for the fire. But now Zodiac can't kill. The fire only burns if there's fuel, the letters only work when energized by death. Zodiac is bored. Zodiac can't kill. Zodiac left evidence. Despite the learnéd opinions of experts and psychologists and psychics, Zodiac does not want to be caught. He will never be caught. If he can't kill, if there's no fuel, then there's no more fun. The game is up, the game is over. The tire is deflating. Zodiac won. Zodiac lost.

†

On the evening hours of 19 April, some friends of the lamp designer Robert Michael Salem get worried. They haven't heard from Bobby for a few days. And Bobby's a guy who you hear from. The friends go to Bobby's live/work space at 745 Stevenson Street, around the corner from City Hall and the main branch of the San Francisco Public Library. Bobby's door is locked but his friends smell the rank odor of death. Decay leaks out with all the pungency of adolescent bedroom marijuana. The friends break down the door. When they see what's inside, they call the police.

Bobby's pad is decorated in bleeding edge au courant fashion. It's a psychedelic wonderland. Everything is in its place. So is Bobby. He's on a couch. He's been stabbed in the chest and the back. His throat is cut. One of his ears is removed. He's nearly decapitated. A bloody Egyptian ankh has been drawn on his stomach. The throat looks so real that it's unreal but it's not the unreality of Televisionland. It's negative space that draws the eye, that rewrites the brain's knowledge of human anatomy. The psychedelic couch hides the dried browning blood but it's obvious that Bobby's been dead for some time. The killer stalked through the apartment, dripping Bobby's viscera. The killer empties Bobby's wallet. The killer takes Bobby's ear. The killer uses Bobby's shower.

The killer put his hands into Bobby's blood.

The killer wrote on the walls. With Bobby's Blood.

The killer wrote: SATAN SAVES ZODIAC.

And drew an Egyptian ankh.

It all looks like this:

The press plays it both ways. This is the first murderous Zodiac activity in a long time. So there's that angle. But a fingerprint is found in the apartment. This print does not match the partials taken from Paul Stine's cab or the phone booths or the letters. Skepticism is apparent from word one. This isn't Zodiac. This is The Zodiac.

The press drops hints that Bobby's a homosexual. Bobby's got immaculate taste and lives alone with a great number of cats. Bobby is found in a white jumpsuit. Bobby's friends have a standing invitation to drop by whenever they like. It's a gay murder, common enough of an occurrence to have its own cop slur. *Homocide.*

In normal circumstances, the papers would have ignored the killing. This is de facto policy for dead homosexuals. But this one can't be ignored. Bobby's killer uses the magic word. ZODIAC. Say it aloud, paint it on a wall, and it works like ˈˈˈ or مسمس اي حتفا. It opens the cave. Bobby gets smeared in the press, the sniffing disapproval of beat journalists who believe that the homosexual lifestyle has only one certain destination.

SATAN SAVES ZODIAC.

These articles are just about the only information regarding Robert Salem. His lamp business gets a few mentions in design catalogs and his birth certificate says that Bobby's baba was from Syria, but otherwise, there's nothing. He's not a Zodiac victim. He's a victim of The Zodiac. He's like the woman on Highway 132. But Bobby didn't live to tell the tale. There's no post-Graysmith tabloid appearances, no for-cash interviews, no $5,000 cheque for a 30-year old exclusive. There's just a few short notices that Bobby was queer and Bobby is dead. Death has erased his little pleasure zone filled with immaculate décor and the bodies of other men.

These scant notices are a bonanza compared to the coverage afforded other gay men. A large number of these individuals aren't named, exist only in the SFPD's homicide yearbooks.

†

Bobby gets column space and a half-solved homicide. In July 1970, two hippies are picked up after a traffic accident in Big Sur. One is named Stanley Dean Baker, the other's Harry Allen Stroup. Baker's 22-years old, Stroup is 20. They're from Wyoming. They're traveling in a foreign car registered to a man named James Schlosser. They crash Schlosser's car into a vehicle owned by Robert Parks of Ann Arbor, Michigan. There's the confusion of the automobile wreck, the sudden intimacy of parties in a situation for which they are unprepared. Baker asks Parks to borrow a screw driver. Baker is 6'2", hulking, a former athlete who got kicked out of the Navy, blonde beard, long hair. Parks gives Baker a screwdriver. The hirsute giant pries the license plates from Schlosser's car. Baker throws the plates off a cliff.

It's decided that Parks will drive them to civilization where they can figure out the next step. As they pass through a small town, Baker and Stroup beg Parks not to stop. They're convinced that the townies hates hippies. Parks pulls over and asks the men where they got the car. Baker tells Parks that Baker killed a man, whom he describes as a fag, on a beach and then stole his car. Parks says, okay, fine, and starts driving. Baker goes on about the murder. Stroup implores Parks not to listen. He says that Baker is a good person, he's just got problems. Too much acid can fuck you up, right? Don't take him seriously. Baker and Stroup get out of the car and run away. They disappear into the woods. Parks calls the police.

As Baker and Stroup walk along the Pacific Coast Highway, they're picked up by the cops. They're arrested and searched. Each man carries a bone in their respective pockets. Stroup says they're chicken bones and kept for good luck. This is contradicted by Baker who says something like this: "I have a problem. I am a cannibal." The bones are from human fingers. The flesh is gnawed off.

Baker tells his story.

He'd spent the earlier part of 1970 in California and headed back to Wyoming. He and Stroup hitched up to a rock festival in Canada, most likely the Calgary stop of the touring Festival Express 1970. The line-up includes The Band, Janis Joplin, Ian & Sylvia, Mountain, Grateful Dead. They hitch back to Montana. Baker and Stroup meet a man named Jim Huggins, who's promised Baker a timber industry job. But, as they drink beer, Huggins says it's a no go. Baker's got too many warrants for drug violations.

Here, the story gets blurry. It depends which scenario you want to believe. Baker's or the prosecution's. Baker says that he and Stroup have an argument and split up. Baker's furious and drunk and takes LSD and he's in a rage against The Establishment and he's hitching and gets picked up by a 22-year old social worker named James Schlosser. Whose car will later be crashed in Big Sur. Schlosser and Baker end up going to Yellowstone National Park and camping by the Yellowstone River. There's thunder and lighting and LSD and motor spirit and Baker butchers the social worker. He hacks off the limbs, cuts out the heart, removes the head, separates the body into six pieces. He eats the heart. Uncooked. He hacks off the finger bones. He gnaws the flesh from Schlosser's fingers. Baker says that he steals Schlosser's car and somehow meets up with Stroup, who has no idea what's happening. They drive to California. They crash Schlosser's car. That's Baker's story. The prosecution says that Stroup helps with the murder and the cannibalization.

Both versions emerge at Stroup's November 1970 trial. By this time, Baker has pleaded guilty to first degree murder, pulled a life sentence. He's the star witness, speaks with motor spirit. Baker says that he controls the weather, he's a member of the Church of Satan, and from the age of ten, he was in a psychic war with Jimi Hendrix. Hendrix dies in September 1970, choking on his own vomit about three blocks from the Portobello Road. Baker claims that he vanquished Hendrix with witchcraft. Hannibal Lecter made real, what True Crime writers refer to as an electrified courtroom, that moment when an idiot's babbling is supercharged by the human need to believe in ghosts.

The prosecution asks Baker if he knew Bobby Salem. The prosecution asks Baker if he killed Robert Michael Salem. The prosecution asks Baker if he ate any part of Robert Michael Salem's body. Baker invokes his Fifth Amendment right to not self-incriminate. It's not a guilty verdict. But it's not nothing. The prosecution does not ask about the fingerprint in Bobby's apartment.

If Bobby is a homosexual and Baker, when referring to Schlosser, says that he killed a fag, the easy assumption is that both murders are rough trade, the person who gets picked up and exchanges bodily fluids and then goes into a motor spirit spiral of shame and self-recrimination. The only option is kill the person who witnesses what you've done.

Goodbye, Bobby. Goodbye, Michael Schlosser.

San Francisco decides that there's no point extraditing Baker to California. He's locked up in Montana. He's got a life sentence.

Plus, he killed a queer.

Baker gets paroled in 1986.

†

In its 20 April morning edition, long before Baker crashes in Big Sur, the *Chronicle* runs BIZARRE 'ZODIAC' MURDER. The story's not much, a thousand words that start on Page 1 and continue on to Page 24.

It's a grotesquerie that spaces out advertisements.

But someone's reading. He must get the paper in the early morning.

In a few hours, he'll make his way to an unknown destination in San Francisco and post a letter. It's the first of two times that he sends a letter with an AM postmark.

chapter eleven

oh it was gorgeousness and gorgeosity made flesh

THE LETTER READS LIKE THIS:

> This is the Zodiac speaking
> By the way have you cracked the last cipher I sent you?
> My name is—

A E N ⊕ ⊗ K ⊘ M ⊘ ↓ N A M

I am mildly cerous as to how much money you have on my head now. I hope you do not think that I was the one who wiped out that blue meannie with a bomb at the cop station. Even though I talked about killing school children with one. It just wouldn't doo to move in on someone elses teritory. But there is more glory in killing a cop than a cid because a cop can shoot back. I have killed ten people to date. It would have been a lot more except that my bus bomb was a dud. I was swamped out by the rain we had a while back.

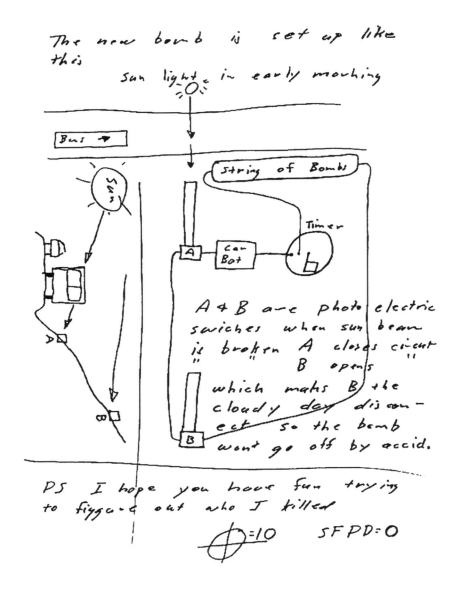

The new bomb is set up like this

Sun light in early morning

Bus →

String of Bombs

Sun

Timer

A

Car Bot

A & B are photo electric swiches when sun beam is broken A closes circut B opens which maks B the cloudy day discon- ect so the bomb wont go off by accid.

B

PS I hope you have fun trying to figure out who I killed

⊕=10   SFPD=0

News of the letter doesn't break until 22 April. Paul Avery makes Page 1 of the *Chronicle*. Zodiac won't get front page treatment for another six months. The air is out of the tire and the ride is almost over.

Zodiac inquires about his last cipher, the one that won't be cracked until 2020, and includes a new one. These thirteen characters are supposed to contain his real name. Given past claims, it's a sure bet that the glyphs offer nothing but a taunt or a lame joke.

Not that anyone will ever know. Zodiac creates a cipher that can never be solved. There's millions of plausible answers and millions beyond that. Barring a minor miracle, or some unknown aspect, no solution can be proven. Decrypting a cipher without its key demands a minimum threshold of characters. Repetition demonstrates solution. The new offering falls short of the requirement. Unicity distance is not met.

The letter references three recent events. Zodiac asks about the reward on his head, a nod to Yellow Cab's effort in January. Then he mentions the "Blue Meanie" wiped out at the police station, a direct reference to the 16 February 1970 bombing of the Park Police Station in San Francisco. This station is located near the southeast corner of Golden Gate Park, just beside Kezar Stadium.

Kezar Stadium is where the San Francisco 49ers play home games, it features in *Dirty Harry*, and it's where, on 23 March 1975, Bob Dylan and Neil Young play a benefit concert for San Francisco's public schools. The men duet on "Knockin' on Heaven's Door." The titular line is changed: "Knock, knock, knockin' on the dragon's door."

The Park Station bombing is never solved. One cop dies, eight other cops are injured. Zodiac's phraseology is important. Blue Meanie. These villainous creatures are found in the 1968 animated Beatles film *Yellow Submarine*. When the movie is released, the term experiences instant adoption as freak slang for the police, a phrase that breaks up the monotony of shouting PIG! Open any underground newspaper and the Blue Meanie is present. Here, again, Zodiac watches the circus that he can never join.

16 February 1970 is a day of madness. While someone's planting a bomb at the Park Police Station, there's a student riot in Berkeley. And someone's trying to blow up a factory in Oakland. And someone's using a sniper rifle to shoot at the Hall of Justice. The 17 February *Examiner* includes first notice of another famous American crime. It's Page 1. Headline: NEW TATE-TYPE FAMILY KILLING. It happens way out in North Carolina, on the Fort Bragg military base. Captain Jeffrey MacDonald claims that hippies broke into his house. The hippies chant: "Acid is great, kill the pigs, hit 'em again!" and then stab MacDonald and murder his wife and two young daughters

and use his wife's blood to write **PIG**. In time, the story proves to be bull-shit. MacDonald kills his family and inflicts a superficial wound upon himself. Like every one else in America, he's lived through headlines about Sharon Tate. He's got the message. Writing in blood, hippies, acid. The perfect disguise for an otherwise pathetic story of a small man so insulted by his own powerlessness that he kills the weak ones. Zodiac got there first. Then Jeffrey MacDonald. Then Stanley Dean Baker. The blueprint is ever present, media made.

The Berkeley protest is part of a wave of social unrest fueled by the trial of the Chicago Seven, the counterculture leaders accused of fomenting a riot during the 1968 Democratic National Convention. The defendants used to be the Chicago Eight, the extra digit being local star Bobby Seale, co-founder of the Black Panthers. Seale ends up literally bound and gagged in the courtroom. This leads to a mistrial, severing Seale's case from his co-defendants. The trial is unbelievable bullshit and sparks protests and riots from its September 1969 inception. Of great importance is a Chicago protest in October 1969. It happens as Zodiac murders Paul Stine. The protest is organized by the Students for a Democratic Society and The Weather Underground.

A/K/A The Weathermen.

The Weatherman are a gang of rich kid quasi-Maoists who decide that The Revolution will arrive through asynchronous violence. Street protests, violent assaults and bombings. The protest is called the Days of Rage. The Weatherman plant a bomb on a statue that commemorates policemen killed during Chicago's 1886 Haymarket affair, which starts out as a peaceful protest in support of workers and then someone throws a bomb that kills eight cops. The city puts unrelated anarchists on trial and hangs four. There are counterculture bombings before October 1969, but the Days of Rage are right around when the idea takes hold, when it becomes de facto policy of the most radicalized Leftists. There's almost too much symbolic resonance in the Days of Rage deriving from a riot at the Democratic National Convention. That doleful event in August 1968 is when the counterculture loses. It looks like they win, like they've finally demonstrated the basic nature of state repression. But that's just Televisionland. The reality is different. A few months after, Richard Milhous Nixon wins the Presidency, and it's clear, at last, that there's not going to be a socialist revolution lead by a vanguard of dope-addled college kids. The acid promises of a better future become motor spirit. The beautiful experiment fails. The mood has shifted, the country is no longer bemused by their antics, the permissive era is over. The new tactic is embraced. It'll become a dominant feature of the 1970s. Radicals bomb the living fucking shit out of America. Explosions go off everywhere. Police stations, state capitals, FBI offices, the US Capitol. The radicals set off so many bombs, literally in the thousands, that the American people accept these acts as inevitable. People can get used to anything. The Weatherman chose their name after a line in a Bob Dylan song—*you don't need a weatherman to know which way the wind blows*—that ends up more apt than they could imagine. The American people accept bombings with the same resignation as they do bad weather. Shit happens. The frequency makes the radical elements banal and achieves nothing other than priming the American people for fifty years of conservative governance. The bombs ensure Richard Mihous Nixon's massive 1972 electoral victory over George McGovern. And the bombs extend the Vietnam War. Nixon becomes obsessed with the idea that he can't win the war abroad if he loses the war at home. He believes that the North Vietnamese think they can wait until American opinion so sours that Nixon will have no choice but diplomatic capitulation. He identifies the radicals as the major factor driving public opinion. So he expands the war. To demonstrate that he won't give in to radicals. Two weeks after Zodiac's letter of 20 April 1970 arrives at the *Chronicle*, it's revealed that the United States has been bombing the living fucking shit out of Cambodia on the theory that the North Vietnamese hide materiel and troops in Cambodian territory. These military bombings are the necessary precondition for a genocide that claims the lives of at least one million. And the necessary precondition for the military bombings are the radical bombings in America. In a development that surprises no one of depth or conscience, it turns out that random violence achieves nothing but more violence. No one gets the message. No one will ever get the message. Everyone's in the dreamy thought process of motor spirit. In later decades, an idea takes hold. America convinces itself that the counterculture won. That all the beautiful people and the hippies and the freaks came together and made a better America. But that's not what happened. What happened is that Martin Luther King Jr. and Lyndon Baines Johnson transformed

America. And then women and homosexuals, mostly excluded from the counterculture unless they accepted terms defined by straight men, followed their example. No one cares. What happened is never what people remember. Social change was never the point of the Weatherman. The radical fringes are made up of sociopathic people with motor spirit. They attach themselves to whatever cultural trends serve as a pretext for violence. It happens in America, it happens in Germany with the Rote Armee Fraktion. It's mayhem dressed in revolutionary kitsch, just enough high fashion to distract the liberal elite. If you're part of that liberal elite, nothing is more haunting than your own uselessness and nothing is more appealing than the ones who lift up the Kalashnikov and Molotov, the ones whose courage and conviction cut through a polysyllabic dialogue that goes nowhere and changes nothing. For the people who plant the bombs, the message never matters. The message is the pretext. Only violence matters. If the Weatherman fell asleep and somehow woke up in the Germany of 1934, Rip Van Winkle in reverse, then these leftist radicals would have no problem joining the Schutzstaffel and kicking the shit out of Jews in Dachau. Monsters always find their niche. The message never matters. The point is violence and infamy. Which gets us back to Zodiac and his letter of 20 April.

The letter's third contemporary reference is the claim that Zodiac's first bomb was swamped out by rain. Between 9 January and 27 January, the heavens open up on the Bay Area. Torrential downpours. Half of the region floods, houses slide down hills, and there's rivers in the streets of San Francisco. If Zodiac did make his bomb, if he did bury it, there is no question that it would've been destroyed. Ammonium nitrate must be kept dry. But Zodiac didn't make a bomb. Something went wrong at Washington & Cherry. A bomb is harder than waving a piece of cloth that says ZODIAC.

It seems indisputable that this letter was sent in response to the news about Bobby Salem and SATAN SAVES ZODIAC. When The Zodiac tried to poison a school teacher in Martinez, Zodiac wrote in and took the credit. Zodiac always wants credit. But this letter is curious. Zodiac only claims ten dead. In his letter of 20 December to Melvin Belli, Zodiac writes that he's about to take his ninth and tenth victim. Following Paul Stine's murder, there's a progression of imaginary victims. At least one new slave each month. But this is four months later and Zodiac only claims ten in paradise. Given the letter's references to contemporary events, none of which extend past February 1970, a possible explanation is that the text was written months earlier.

Zodiac isn't making the news. He's chasing it. Maybe he wrote this letter in February and couldn't be bothered to mail it until circumstance forced his hand, until news of The Zodiac was too good. The air is out of the tire and the ride is almost over. This could explain the AM postmark. All he has to do is go to a post box in San Francisco. Drive into the city, drop the letter, head to work, wait for the response.

†

For a week, things are quiet. And, then, on 28 April, an unknown man goes to an unknown destination and deposits an envelope in a mail box. It looks and reads like this:

If you don't want me to have this blast you must do two things. 1 Tell everyone about the bus bomb with all the details. 2 I would like to see some nice Zodiac butons wandering about town. Every one else has these buttons like, , black power, melvin eats bluber, etc. Well it would cheer me up considerably if I saw a lot of people wearing my buton. Please no nasty ones like melvin's

Thank you

As with the dripping pen mailing of 9 November 1969, this greeting card is humorous. Supposedly. The joke here is a little more explicable—sorry your ass is a dragon is a terrible pun. "Sorry your ass is dragging." *Sorry you haven't found me.* Zodiac's a joker.

The dripping pen card is copyrighted 1965. The dragon card is copyrighted 1967. The greeting card industry is one of constant turn-over and new product. Cards sit on the shelves for a limited time. Unsold stock is shipped back to the supplier, and even if a handful are kept by retailers and sold at discount, it's unlikely that either of these cards were bought with the intention of sending them to the *Chronicle.* They're too old. This is junk that Zodiac purchased before he started killing, before he emerged as a writer. Murder is an expression of the murderer's personality, the small details reflect the individual. This is a man with some abiding interest in the postal mail. It predates the letters. The cards are only sinister because of their recipients.

There's a shift here, a subtle one. Zodiac is no longer dictating the terms. He's not giving orders. He's asking that details of the bomb be published. He's begging for more coverage. That's what happens when the killings stop, when there's no more fuel for the fire. It's an admission of defeat. The second bus bomb is never going to be built.

The *Chronicle* covers the 20 April letter on 22 April. Zodiac mails the dragon card on 28 April. Eight days. In that time, the *Chronicle* and *Examiner* report on the following: (1) A firebomb in San Rafael. (2) Two young men arrested in Isla Vista, California, home to the University of California's Santa Barbara campus. The men are accused of planting a bomb at a local Bank of America branch. (3) Bomb threats at Pennsylvania State University. (4) General Electric's annual shareholder meeting held under heightened security because of a bomb threat. (5) 52 bombs found in Puerto Rico. (6) Two bombs going off in Lawrence, Kansas. One at a chemical plant, one at the University of Kansas. (7) Two arsonist fires at Stanford University's Center for Advanced Study in the Behavioral Sciences. (8) A bomb exploding at the Army Recruitment Center on 125th Street in Harlem. (9) A bomb threat at Stanford University. (10) Two packages with train torpedo explosives mailed from Seattle, Washington. One addressed to the White House, the other to the Washington, DC headquarters of the Selective Services. (11) Twenty-to-thirty sticks of dynamite exploding in the Senate Chamber of the Louisiana State Capitol building. (12) Bail of $180,000 set for an Oakland man accused of possessing grenades identical to those used in an 17 April attack on the Oakland police.

America is bomb central. Zodiac's chasing a fad, what the remnants of the counterculture believe is effective political advocacy. Less than a year ago, he was a monster stalking the imagination, an occult beast beyond understanding, a killer about whom anything could be believed because anything was possible. Now he's just another loser who says that he's got a bomb. What's one more threat when actual bombs go off every day?

At least the bombs are contemporary. The button fad exploded in 1967. It was old hat by late 1968. This isn't to say that people aren't still wearing buttons, but the original idea of the button, of the short meaningless phrase on a piece of tin displayed for the world, of the button as a right-on marriage of consumer choice and political morality, has come and gone. The craze peaks when Horatio Buttons, a New York company, issues tin circles bearing apparently clever phrases. Like: SHAKESPEARE EATS BACON. MARY POPPINS IS A JUNKIE. I LIKE OLDER WOMEN. WHERE'S LEE HARVEY OSWALD WHEN YOU NEED HIM?

One of its buttons says: HERMAN MELVILLE EATS BLUBBER.

Zodiac transforms this button into a joke about Melvin Belli.

MELVIN EATS BLUBBER.

It appears that Horatio Buttons went out of business with the 1968 death of its founder Irwin Weisfeld. Although people in 1970 San Francisco still wear buttons, and while there are surely buttons around town that bear the peace symbol or the phrase BLACK POWER, it's hard to imagine, in this time when the counterculture has gone into revolutionary violence, that there are many people wandering around wearing the 3-year old HERMAN MELVILLE EATS BLUBBER. The wild children are nothing if not brutal in their capacity to abandon fashion. Literary references are counterrevolutionary, a bourgeois scheme to establish class distinction through the production of commodity fetishes. People are being bombed in Cambodia. Right now. Campuses are burning. Right now. No one gives a shit about Herman Melville.

No one but Zodiac.

He suggests that he's been around town and seen these buttons. A more likely scenario is that he saw this button three years ago. Or that he himself purchased HERMAN MELVILLE EATS BLUBBER. And kept it in his piles of junk. The same place as the old greeting cards.

Zodiac is not of the counterculture. He is someone who can't stop looking at the counterculture. This has been obvious since the tradename. "Zodiac" is someone's father's idea of a spooky occult killer. But now we have a letter which proves that he is definitely, absolutely trying to keep up with the kids. And failing. Exactly in the way that someone's father would fail. Like any agéd person who wants to do his thing, he gets the nuances wrong. If it's 1967 and the kids can't stop rapping about *Sgt. Pepper's Lonely Hearts Club Band*, Zodiac's the guy talking about *Rubber Soul*. These are the inevitable tics and accents of someone who isn't a native speaker, whose voice is formed by another tongue. Zodiac is from a different era. One more California person who's been given the keys to the kingdom through the Family Law Act. But doesn't know it. The past is a trap.

Darlene Ferrin and Michael Mageau seem to confirm a pattern that starts with David Faraday and Betty Lou Jensen. Reinforced by Lake Berryessa. Zodiac attacks couples in some state of sexual embrace. Then Paul Stine breaks the pattern.

We can envision Stine's murder as a pre-planned attack. A cab gives Zodiac both a body and the space to steal a bloody relic. What no one asks is this: how many cab rides does Zodiac take on 11 October? Is Stine the first and the last? Or is Stine one of several? What if the determinant factor is not the cab but its driver? Are there other cabbies rejected by Zodiac?

The police theorize that Stine drives Zodiac for roughly twelve minutes. It's enough to get the details of Stine's life, the enforced chit-chat of the cab ride. Young, married, living near Haight-Ashbury, graduate student at San Francisco State University, then a hot-bed of countercultural activism, a perpetual source of student unrest. How do you feel about what's been happening on campus, Mr. Stine? You, who once worked as an intern for the Democratic Party? *I'm sympathetic to the cause and I understand the aims and tactics.*

Each of the victims represents possibility. The children born into a world of birth control and free love. The graduate student from a hotbed of activism, from a place where kids reject privileges that, in the recent past, most people weren't even offered. The victims are faces of a changing society, of a new and unrecognizable America.

If they're poor examples of that change, if one's a divorcée with problems or another's born dirt poor and works his way up or if they're Christians who experiment with each other's bodies before the Sabbath service, well, look at the letters. Look at how Zodiac is aware of the counterculture, tries to use its language, wants to do his thing, but fails at the nuance. Zodiac gazes at the freaks and heads with the eyes of an outsider. Something is happening here. And you don't know what it is. Do you?

Why expect that this killer, the one whose reign of terror derives from the most profound dehumanization, can tell the differences?

†

The 28 April letter makes the papers but barely registers in San Francisco. Zodiac earns Page 10 of *The Chronicle* and Page 50 of *The Examiner.* But the missive gets Zodiac back on Dave Smith's radar. On Friday 8 May, the *Los Angeles Times* gives Smith an extraordinary amount of space. His Zodiac analysis starts on Page 1, runs onto Page 16 and then Page 17. But things have changed. This isn't October 1969. The effect of the article is minimal. No one cares.

More bad timing. Zodiac sends the greeting card on 28 April, makes the news on 1 May. Three days later, a student protest in Ohio on the Kent State campus turns into a massacre. Soldiers from the National Guard open fire on American children. Four people are killed, a teenaged girl weeps over one of the corpses and is photographed as an instant icon of AmeriKKKan chaos. The national wave of student unrest culminates in a Vietnam/Cambodia protest in Washington, DC on 9 May. The nation's capital city is shut down, there are camps everywhere, and in a stunning moment, a drunken Richard Milhous Nixon sneaks into the night and meets protesters at the Jefferson Memorial. Everyone's shocked that he's real, that Nixon isn't just a flickering ghost from Televisionland.

The effect on Nixon's psyche is devastating. This protest and Kent State sends him around the bend, brings out the petty criminal embedded in his character. It ushers in nights of White House boozing and bad judgment that culminate with the Watergate break-in. Prior to this moment, Nixon has been a clear-eyed practitioner of what he saw as a realistic global and domestic politics. Now he's a maniac. He will never recover.

This is the news that competes with Zodiac.

This is what he's fighting against.

And he hasn't killed anyone in over half a year.

chapter twelve

a man in a parked car

AMERICA RIPS APART, bombs itself and Southeast Asia. It's possible that the first half of 1970 is worse than all of 1968. After the President reveals himself at the Jefferson Memorial, there's another student massacre, this one in Jackson, Mississippi. It gets less coverage then Kent State. The dead students are Black men. There's no photo of a crying White girl.

Then there's a quiet period. Not only in San Francisco and the Bay Area, not only in terms of The Zodiac. Throughout the country. Until someone comes up with a new idea, there is nothing left to do. Things happen, things always happen, but the marquee stories are absent.

Someone in Napa County sees a crosshairs scratched into the window of a small private airplane. It sets off a tiny panic. The Sheriffs say that it isn't authentic. It's not Zodiac. It's only The Zodiac.

On 19 June, around five in the morning, in San Francisco, there's three gunshots on the 600 block of Waller Street. This is the same street on which Ann Jiminez is gang banged. The shooting happens eight blocks from the turn-out. At the eastern end of the Haight-Ashbury district, in the spiritual zone of Buena Vista park. It's not exactly Haight-Ashbury, not really, it's the lower Haight, which is predominantly African-American.

The police are called. Two patrolmen arrive on scene and find a SFPD cruiser, its spotlight illuminated. Inside the vehicle, they see one of their brethren. Officer Richard Radetich. Son of a Yugoslavian immigrant, 25-years old.

Shot in the head with a .38 caliber round. His malfunctioning body clutches his police radio. Radetich is alive but won't make it through the next day.

Cops canvas the neighborhood and turn up nothing. Conflicting stories. Some people say that they heard a large heavy car. Some people say they heard a tiny compact one. Some people say they heard multiple shots. Some people say they heard only one. No one saw anything.

Radetich has a wife and an 8-month old daughter. The death poisons his family. His mother dies next year. In 1974, his wife dies of cancer. She is 30-years old. Richard Radetich becomes a symbol, the name brought out whenever there's a discussion of police sacrifice or the bad old days. He makes repeat appearances in every decade after his death.

Four days after the shooting, the SFPD announce that they are seeking a suspect. Wesley Allen Johnson, 26-years old, A/K/A Joe Allen Johnson. The manhunt dominates television and radio and newspapers. Johnson's previous booking photos are broadcast across the region. He's African-American, which in this particular moment and this particular climate, means that he looks as guilty as sin. A witness told SFPD that they saw Johnson fire at Radetich from the driver's seat of a blue 1969 vinyl-topped Camaro. The witness said that Johnson was traveling with another, unidentified individual. Then the story goes dead. Johnson evades police capture. This is neither the first nor the last time that he escapes the law. In 1969, Johnson is arrested after a shootout with the police at a Western Union office. He's wounded in the mêlée, gets brought to San Francisco General Hospital. The staff stitch up his wounds. And then, while no one's looking, Johnson walks away. He disappears. When the cops finger him for Radetich, Johnson has been hiding out for months.

Johnson isn't captured until December 1970. He's picked up in Ohio and extradited back to California. And then, in the blink of an eye, the murder charge is dropped. Although the police have a witness who can place Johnson at the scene, there is no corroborating evidence.

It's useful to think about the death of patrolman Eric A. Zelms. Who saw the face of Zodiac. And was shot three months later.

Vincent Fredericks and Michael Webster. Their trial runs throughout June 1970. It is established that Webster did not touch the gun. Did not shoot Zelms.

Both men are convicted.

Webster, young, Black, gets the same punishment as the man who pulled the trigger. Criminal justice is a story that society tells itself. And if you kill a cop, if you're anywhere near a cop being killed, and if you're African-American, then you are doomed.

And here's Johnson. Charge dropped. The police say there is no corroborating evidence but a witness. In this climate, in this moment, a witness should be enough. Johnson is a Black man facing other charges related to a shoot out with the police. If there is even a scintilla of possibility that he shot Radetich, Johnson would face trial like Michael Webster. A dropped charge can mean one thing. He did not do it. Incontrovertibly. There's other evidence here, an exculpatory thing buried in police files that the public will never see, knowledge that cannot be known.

In 1985, the *Examiner* runs an article stating that the SFPD believe Radetich's murder to be the work of the Black Liberation Army. In 1970, the BLA is where people go when they think the Black Panthers are compromised. They are the main suspects in the Park Police Station attack. But Radetich's murder is an unlikely attribution. If for no other reason than it is never mentioned again.

Two years later, in 1987, there's a new story about Johnson. He lives in Vallejo, and he's in the Solano County Jail awaiting trial on weapons and stolen property charges. And he escapes with five other inmates. Johnson is captured a week later. Final mention of the man comes in 1993, when he's picked up on a murder charge. There appears to be no record of the dispensation.

On 25 June 1970, the *Chronicle* runs a story about Johnson's 1969 escape from the San Francisco General Hospital. Written by Paul Avery. That evening, Thursday night, or Friday morning, an unknown individual goes to an unknown destination and deposits a letter that he's written.

It reads like this:

This is the Zodiac speaking.

I have become very upset with the people of San Fran Bay Area. They have <u>not</u> complied with my wishes for them to wear some nice ✦ buttons. I promiced to punish them if they did not comply, by anilating a full School Buss. But now school is out for the summer, so I punished them in another way.

I shot a man sitting in a parked car with a .38.

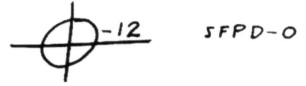

The map coupled with this code will tell you where the bomb is set. You have untill next Fall to dig it up.

A new cipher and the inclusion of a map. Things that no reader can ignore. It's Zodiac's version of a treasure hunt, pulp fiction made real.

Focus on the text. Did Zodiac really think that people would wear Zodiac buttons? And what were these buttons supposed to look like? In this letter he specifies the crosshairs, but in the previous letter he didn't. Assuming that everyone understood that he meant the symbol, how did he verify that Bay Area wore these buttons? Did he wander the Berkeley campus and inspect every bit of tin pinned to a breast? Or is the disappointment that neither the *Chronicle* nor the *Examiner* published follow-up stories about Zodiac buttons? None of it makes much sense, falls apart with any scrutiny. The buttons are gobbledygook. Who is the person that comes up with this scheme? Is this someone that wants friends and has no idea how to make them? Or is this someone, literally, trying to insert themselves into the counterculture?

Barring another miracle, the cipher can't be solved. Zodiac has failed to meet the minimum threshold of characters. Just like last time. And there's fewer repeating characters than the previous unsolvable cipher. It allows for any number of solutions. Without a key or some other apparatus, none can be proved.

Consider the 20 April letter, the one in which Zodiac includes his second bomb diagram. This is a man who knows how to spell photoelectric but misspells "kid" as "cid." Here he writes about Magnetic North, or true north, the magnetic pole to which every compass points. It's different from north on a map. This is navigator knowledge. Zodiac uses it casually, without explication. And yet doesn't know how to spell "kid." This is a character who is smarter than everyone, and wants everyone to know that fact, but pretends to be stupid, someone incapable of the most basic rudiments of writing.

Zodiac says that he can't kill cids because school is out for the summer. Zodiac knows the academic calendar. Does he live near a school? Is he a teacher? A parent? One thing's certain. This is the knowledge that falls away when you become an adult. Unless there is a compelling reason to keep it in mind.

Zodiac claims that he shot a man sitting in a parked car with a .38. It's punishment on the people of the Bay Area. For not wearing Zodiac buttons.

A clear reference to Richard Radetich.

When news of the letter breaks, the SFPD dismisses Zodiac's claim. Their eyes are on Wesley Johnson. In June 1970, no one knows that Johnson won't be held responsible. He's a Black man. A cop is dead. He's guilty as sin.

Zodiac has taken credit for other people's misdeeds, but never before and never again will he claim a crime with an established suspect. He sends letters when a teacher is poisoned in Martinez and when Bobby Salem is killed. SATAN SAVES ZODIAC. When he sends this letter, Johnson is common knowledge. Along with the AM postmark on this letter's envelope, it hints that this letter may be written days before it is sent. Perhaps right after Radetich is discovered but before the cops announce Johnson. By the time Zodiac gets around to mailing the letter, the information is out of date. If this is the case, it's more evidence of his waning interest, of how much air has left the tire, of how the ride is almost over.

There is another possibility. Later reports will suggest that the cops dismiss Zodiac as a suspect because Radetich is killed with a .38 and Zodiac never used a .38. Thin reasoning for a killer who's employed a different weapon at each attack. More likely that once Johnson is established in the cop mind, he excludes other possibilities. But Johnson didn't kill Radetich.

Once Johnson's charges are dismissed, there's no movement in the case. Not an inch of public progress. SFPD has the highest motivation to close this case. And have never come up with a credible suspect. The shooting is exactly what Zodiac promised. What if he really did change his method of collecting slaves?

Could Zodiac have killed Radetich?

He hints at the coming possibility in the 20 April letter. "But there is more glory in killing a cop than a cid because a cop can shoot back."

In 1970, there's a US-101 on-ramp at Oak & Laguna Streets, three blocks north and five blocks east of Waller Street's 600 block. If Paul Stine is murdered in Presidio Heights because the area allows quick egress via the Golden Gate Bridge, then Radetich can be seen as a counterpart. The US-101 funnels into the I-80. Drive from Waller to the on-ramp, take the 101, merge on the I-80, drive unMagnetic North and you're on the Bay Bridge, out of town and on the road to Vallejo. At 5AM in the morning, it won't take more than eight minutes.

Zodiac never again mentions Radetich. It beggars belief that he could shoot a cop and not keep bragging. Or correct the SFPD in their public errors. But, then again, what would happen if Zodiac killed someone, took credit, and no one believed him? If the air is out of the tire, if the ride is almost over, this could only accelerate the end. Zodiac has lost control of his own narrative. The letters have been part of a mutual dialogue between Zodiac and the police and the press. This dialogue has rested on a belief in the killer's statements. What happens when people stop believing?

If Zodiac did kill Radetich, it opens endless speculation. It would mean that a central tenet of Zodiac analysis—that the killings stopped with Stine— is wrong. And that much of the more paranoid speculation is right.

It seems unlikely that Zodiac shot Radetich.

But the possibility must be considered.

†

In the first half of 1970, the San Francisco Police Department experiences the violent murder of three officers. And Zodiac, through his letters or deeds, is connected to each.

The Zodiac lives forever.

chapter thirteen

4-TEEN

THE NEXT FEW MONTHS ARE QUIET. There's an arrangement between SFPD and the *Chronicle*. If a new missive arrives, the response will be silence. Let's see what happens when we aren't taking orders. If the police and the press believe that Zodiac is a compulsion killer, then it's a high risk strategy. It only makes sense if everyone believes that Zodiac's stopped killing.

At the end of July, two letters arrive at the *Chronicle*'s offices. Apparently on the same day. They go unmentioned. Zodiac is speaking and no one hears him.

The first letter is sent 24 July. It reads like this:

This is the Zodiac speaking.

I am rather unhappy because you people will not wear some nice ✛ buttons. So I now have a little list, starting with the woeman & her baby that I gave a rather intersting ride for a couple howers one evening a few months back that ended in my burning her car where I found them.

Taken alone, it makes no sense. What is this Little List that Zodiac mentions? He's still on about the buttons. The third letter in which they're mentioned.

Zodiac references the March 1970 incident. The woman out on Highway 132, the woman who might've been kidnapped. Four months after the fact. If nothing else, the delay should convince the reader that Zodiac had nothing to do with the incident. Why wait? This is someone digging through his own press archives.

Two days later, in the morning hours, another letter is brought to a post office in San Francisco. The second letter reads like this:

This is the Zodiac speaking

Being that you will not wear some nice ⊕ buttons, how about wearing some nasty ⊕ buttons. Or any type of ⊕ buttons that you can think up. If you do not wear any type of ⊕ buttons, I shall (on top of everything else) torture all 13 of my slaves that I have wateing for me in Paradice. Some I shall tie over ant hills and watch them scream & twich and sqwirm. Others shall have pine splinters driven under their nails & then burned. Others shall be placed in cages & fed salt beef untill they are gorged then I shall listen to their pleass for water and I shall laugh at them. Others will hang by their thumbs & burn in the sun then I will rub them down with deep heat to warm them up. Others I shall skin them alive & let them run around screaming. And all billiard players I shall have them play in a darkened dungen cell with crooked cues & Twisted Shoes. Yes I shall have great fun inflicting the most delicious of pain to my slaves

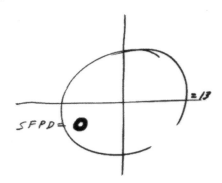

[beginning of new page]

As some day it may hapen that a victom must be found. I've got a little list. I've got a little list, of society offenders who might well be underground who would never be missed who would never be missed. There is the pestulentual nucences who whrite for autographs, all people who have flabby hands and irritating laughs. All children who are up in dates and implore you with im platt. All people who are shakeing hands shake hands like that. And all third persons who with unspoiling take thoes who insist. They'd none of them be missed. They'd none of them be missed. There's the banjo seranader and the others of his race and the piano orginast I got him on the list. All people who eat pepermint and phomphit in your face, they would never be missed They would never be missed And the Idiout who phraises with inthusastic tone of centuries but this and every country but his own. And the lady from the provences who dress like a guy who doesn't cry and the singurly abnormily the girl who never kissed. I don't think she would be missed Im shure she wouldn't be missed. And that nice impriest that is rather rife the judicial hummerest I've got him on the list All funny fellows, commic men and clowns of private life. They'd none of them be missed. They'd none of them be missed. And uncompromiseing kind such as wachmacallit, thingmebob, and like wise, well-nevermind, and tut tut tut tut, and whatshisname, and you know who, but the task of filling up the blanks I rather leave up to you. But it really doesn't matter whom you place upon the list, for none of them be missed, none of them be missed.

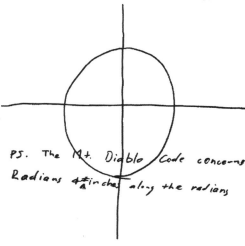

PS. The Mt. Diablo Code concerns Radians 4 inches along the radians

Here's the Little List promised in the previous letter. The sole instance where one letter directly prefigures the content of another. John the Baptist arrives before Jesus. The second letter predates the first, in concept if not execution.

The final method of torture, the one about billiard cues and twisted shoes, is lifted from a stanza in "A More Humane Mikado," a song in Act II of Gilbert and Sullivan's *The Mikado*.

> *The billiard sharp who any one catches,*
> *His doom's extremely hard —*
> *He's made to dwell —*
> *In a dungeon cell*
> *On a spot that's always barred.*
> *And there he plays extravagant matches*
> *In fitless finger-stalls*
> *On a cloth untrue*
> *With a twisted cue*
> *And elliptical billiard balls!*

Which gets us to the Little List.

It's a transcription of the song "As Some Day It May Happen," from Act I of *The Mikado*. Sung by the character Ko-Ko, the Lord High Executioner. *The Mikado* is a Nineteenth Century light opera, entertainment for mon-eyed English audiences that features monstrous word play and unfortunate singing. The genre's gone out of style but once was the finest in middle brow entertainment.

On 3 April 2013, a user on zodiackillersite.com posts a discovery. The user calls themselves Tahoe27. They prove that Zodiac works off a slight vari-ant, with modified lyrics, of "And Some Day It May Happen." This version appeared in a 1960 Televisionland adaptation of *The Mikado*. Groucho Marx played Ko-Ko. Marx is a vaudevillian comedian who starred in a series of groundbreaking films in the 1930s and 1940s before transitioning into the cantankerous, wise-cracking uncle of Televisionland. The soundtrack was released on vinyl LP.

This is an era before Betamax, before VCRs, before DVDs and BluRay collected season sets, before Internet piracy, before TiVo, before streaming. Once a television show is gone, it's gone. Zodiac must work off the record.

He can't follow, not exactly, every word sung by Groucho. Certain phrases are obscure. Zodiac renders his best phonetic spelling.

Groucho sings: "And all children who are up in dates and floor you with 'em flat." Zodiac writes: "All children who are up in dates and implore you with im platt."

Groucho sings: "And the people who eat peppermint and puff it in your face." Zodiac writes: "All people who eat pepermint and phomphit in your face."

The killer's motivations were never clear. Now they are obscure in the extreme. This letter, a transcription of Groucho Marx singing light opera, is important enough to be heralded in an earlier letter?

Perhaps the source material opens up a metaphor. Back when there was a functioning recording industry, there was a predictable pattern for almost every artist who experienced mass market success. Years of struggle followed by a commercial breakthrough followed by the disorienting mechanisms of fame. A changed life followed by a period of introspection and confusion and wrestling with one's own fortune. Followed by the inevitable conclusion that the success was the not the result of luck and timing, but rather derived from the artist's individual character and omnipresent talent. Followed by the recording of tedious music displaying none of the bravado or verve of the original success. There's a spirit of innocence that comes with being ignored. Once the world pays attention, it's impossible to maintain what brought that attention.

A classical period is always followed by decadence.

1970 always comes after 1969.

Zodiac can't do what made him famous, feels attention drifting, devises new schemes to improve on the original. But the original is perfect. Everything is flawed in comparison. Some people only have one good idea.

It must make an absolute hell of the *Chronicle*'s silence.

In the past, he's received front page treatment and foreign correspondents. Now he's sent an important letter and gotten nothing. There's waiting followed by confusion and doubt. Did the paper not publish? Or was it lost in the mail? What's gone wrong? Zodiac had it, he held it in his hands, thought it was his forever, and now it's gone so fast.

There's the PS. Placed over the symbol and containing a note about the treasure hunt. He uses another technical term. Radian. A unit of measurement related to angles. More navigation, more knowledge, mountaineering. No explication. This is the deep territory.

†

There are months of silence.

†

On 12 October, a year and a day after the death of Paul Stine, the *Chronicle* publishes an article by Paul Avery. Page 5.

GILBERT AND SULLIVAN CLUE TO ZODIAC. The article reports on the July letters. The police caught *The Mikado* reference. They attribute the change in lyrics and the phonetic nonsense to a flawed memory. They've been conducting a wide search for individuals who once performed the role of Ko-Ko. None of these leads has turned up anything.

Avery also writes of a card that arrived at the *Chronicle* on 7 October. The card looks like this:

(front)

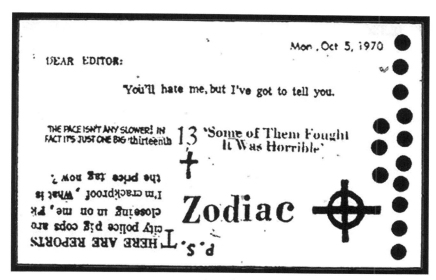

(rear)

There's no original writing. The text is cut-and-pasted from area news-papers. Thirteen holes are punched along one of its vertical sides, presumed representations of collected slaves. There's a cross at the center, a Zodiac crosshairs at the bottom right. The stamp commemorates the Apollo 8 mission of 1968, the first manned spaceflight to reach lunar orbit.

All previous mailings have been sent in envelopes bearings stamps from the Prominent American series. The series is illustrated with the likenesses of Americans who achieved in public life. In the 1969 mailings, the envelopes were over stamped. Usually two, sometimes four. One time six. Other than the 20 December 1969 Belli envelope, no image of these envelopes have appeared in the press. The Belli envelope is an anomaly. It doesn't bear the usual 6¢ stamp, doubled or otherwise. It's got six 1¢ Thomas Jefferson stamps.

The Apollo 8 stamp looks like this:

During the flight, as the astronauts are broadcast across Televisionland, they read from the Biblical creation story in *Genesis*.

IN THE BEGINNING, GOD...

Apollo 8 launches on 21 December 1968. 5:51AM California time. About six hours after David Faraday and Betty Lou Jensen are found on

Lake Herman Road. It's not exactly the same day. But it's close. This feels like a Zodiac joke.

The source materials suggests someone with broad reading habits. DEAR EDITOR: looks to be clipped from the "Our Readers' Rights" letter column that appears in *The Press Tribune* of Roseville, California. Right outside of the state capital of Sacramento. This phrase can be found in other newspapers, but only the *Press Tribune* uses all caps followed by a colon. THE PACE ISN'T GETTING ANY SLOWER is from the 25 September installment of a comic strip called *Smidgens*. It appears in that day's *Oakland Tribune*. SOME OF THEM FOUGHT / IT WAS HORRIBLE are both subheaders on Page 5 of the 25 September *Examiner*. THERE ARE REPORTS is on Page 54 of the 23 September *Chronicle*. This page is also the origin of CITY POLICE and the CLOSE in CLOSEING. MON, OCT. 5 1970 is from the *Oakland Tribune*.

Two publications in San Francisco, one in Oakland, one outside of Sacramento. If one imagines a geographical center, it's the rough Vallejo area.

There is an unknowability in Zodiac correspondences.

There are the three letters sent on 31 July 1969, the 4 August letter apparently hand delivered to the *Examiner*, the dripping pen card authenticated by the inclusion of a cipher, and then three more letters authenticated with Paul Stine's bloody shirt. These are the correspondences from 1969. All of them are from the genuine issue original.

But the letters of 1970?

They're authenticated on hope and prayer and belief in the consistency of handwriting and a tone of voice. It's possible that all of the 1970 letters are hoaxes, that none come from Zodiac. That they come from The Zodiac. It's possible that some are from the genuine issue original and others are the work of hoaxers. Barring a major breakthrough, one that proves what Zodiac wrote and what he didn't, we take it on faith that authorship of these mailings can be deduced from context.

But.

On 4 or 5 October 1970, the international newswire Reuters sends out a story. Reuters has clients that are newspapers but it also services radio and television stations. It's a small story, doesn't get picked up in many places, the only extant evidence is two papers that published in Florida. *The Miami News* and *The Orlando Sentinel.* But this story must pop up elsewhere, must appear on a radio station or a Bay Area newspaper yet to be discovered.

In the *Miami News,* the story runs with the headline SEARCH FOR ZODIAC KILLER STILL ON—A YEAR LATER. Most of the article is standard Zodiac rehash. Reign of terror, disappearance, victims.

But there's new information: "The mystery killer now claims 13 victims, though only the police and the San Francisco Chronicle know about his supposedly ever-rising tally. The newspaper has decided not to cater to his boastfulness any more. It wrote nothing on his last two communications, received in July."

SFPD's Dave Toschi tells Reuters a letter is overdue, that they're waiting for the next one. Towards the end, there's an operative sentence: "Toschi claims he is closer to identifying the Zodiac than a year ago."

This Reuters story appears in the Florida newspapers on 5 October 1970. The same day as the card is postmarked. The card says the following: "There are reports that city police cops are closeing in on me..."

Other than this Reuters report, there's been total silence.

From 8 November 1969, almost all of his communications are responses to news of The Zodiac. This is the first time that he says it. There are reports. I've been reading your papers, I've been listening to your radio. This is the method of authentication. Do the letters come in response to some recent news? Do they display that creepy attention to detail?

Zodiac hears or reads the Reuters report. He learns that his July letters did not go astray. He must encounter the story in the morning and spend the day putting together the index card. He mails it in the afternoon.

THERE ARE REPORTS comes from Page 54 of the 23 September *Chronicle.* But Zodiac couldn't have cut-and-pasted before the Reuters story. There were no reports prior to 4 or 5 October. The card is an idea, a thought, a response to new stimuli. Zodiac didn't buy these newspapers for the purpose of a mixed-media mailing. They're what he reads in his normal daily life. He keeps them for weeks. Zodiac owns a 3-year old button. Zodiac has a back catalog of greeting cards.

Zodiac is a collector.

From the first cipher, the knowledge was there.

Slaves in the afterlife.

†

Avery publishes his Gilbert and Sullivan article. The two letters and the index card don't make much noise. Page 5 in the *Chronicle*. Page 24 in the *Examiner*. Down in Los Angeles, it's a different story. Dave Smith gets a front page screaming headline in *The Los Angeles Times*. NEW ZODIAC BOAST. CLAIMS 13 VICTIMS IN TWO NOTES.

But nothing happens.

It's quiet until 27 October, when Paul Avery publishes a new article. Page 4. A 'JACK THE RIPPER' THEORY ON SLAYINGS. Over the last few months, the mutilated bodies of African-American women have been found around San Francisco. On 4 August, the corpse of Brenda Joyce Vance is discovered on the 1200 block of Golden Gate Avenue. Broken neck, burned body. On 30 August, 22-year old Janice Smith is found in an abandoned building at 959 Webster Street. Stabbed 15 times, bludgeoned, sexually mutilated. On Saturday 24 October, the body of 16-year old Jackie Truss is found on Laurel Street between Jackson & Pacific Avenue. One block north and four blocks east of Paul Stine. Truss is naked, burned, rope marks on her wrists, disemboweled, throat and eyelids slashed, skull smashed after death. The three women worked as prostitutes. Avery ties these deaths to a dim memory of Jack the Ripper. London 1888. Who was down on whores and liked ripping them up.

The transhistorical identification attempts to solve a problem. No one has a clinical name for serial killers. Historical antecedent is the only recourse. It happens in December 1969, when North Hollywood's *Valley Times* asks: ANOTHER ZODIAC?

The murders go unsolved until May 1973.

The SFPD arrest Stanley Nelson, 38. His wife tells the police that Nelson enlisted her help in disposing two bodies. When the SFPD arrest Nelson, he's in prison for another crime. He attacked a prostitute in November 1970. She survived. When he goes inside, the killings stopped. Other prostitutes identify Nelson as a man with whom they've had bad experiences. In 1958, Nelson slashed a woman in Salinas. He served ten years on that one. Nelson is African-American. This is not like the prosecution of Michael Webster or SFPD putting the Radetich rap on Wesley Johnson. This is a dude who did that shit.

America's serial killer moment has been mined for ore, turned into relentless media, analyzed, obsessed over, given birth to countless podcasts, the sound of droning voices with blood in their throats.

But no one, not once, has gone back to Stanley Nelson.

Because he killed poor Black women.

Jackie Truss is not anointed with the sparkle of the White world. There's no romance here, no Jeffrey Dahmer mugshot.

There's only squalor and malice.

The True Crime genre has forgotten that these women ever died. Let alone lived. As of this writing, 15 April 2021, when one uses Google to search for Stanley Nelson and Jackie Truss, there is not a single result.

Avery's article ends with the following paragraph:

> During the year he prowled Whitechapel, the Ripper would stalk his victim, kill and disappear into the fog. He then would post letters to police and newspapers boasting of his latest slaying. After the seventh murder he was never heard from again.

Can Avery write these words about a Presidio Heights murder and not think ZODIAC?

Someone believes that's what he's doing.

On the same day as Avery's Jack the Ripper article appears, an unknown individual goes to an unknown destination and deposits an envelope in a San Francisco mail box. Another greeting card.

It looks like this:

(rear of exterior)   (front of exterior)

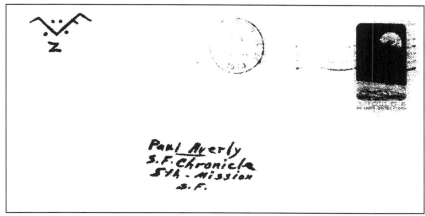

(envelope)

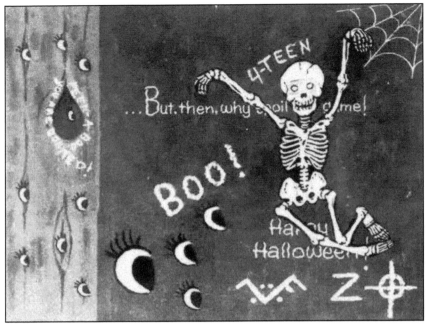

(interior)

On the inside of the envelope, Zodiac writes the following:

The front skeleton and Secret Pal text are part of the card's original design. Zodiac writes "14" on the skeleton's hand and glues a pumpkin over the figure's pelvis. On the card's rear exterior, Zodiac creates a cross from the words PARADiCE and SLAVES. In the resulting quadrisections, he writes: BY FIRE, BY GUN, BY KNiFE and BY ROPE. On the interior, Zodiac glues another Halloween skeleton, puts an orange mask across its eyes, and uses white ink to write PEEK-A-BOO YOU ARE DOOMED!, the word BOO!, 4-TEEN, a Zodiac logo, and a symbol that looks like a flying V. Surrounded by four dots. This symbol also appears on the envelope, where Zodiac has misspelled Avery's last name. AVERLY.

The card is postmarked 27 October 1970. In the evening. On the same day as the Jack the Ripper article. Like the 5 October card, none of this was planned. It's all produced with material that's hanging around the home. The Halloween decorations, the white ink, the greeting card.

The message on front—FROM YOUR SECRET PAL—seems sinister. But is not. Secret Pal clubs are groups of women who exchange cards after pulling the name of another member of their club, and then, after about a month, exchange another card that reveals their identity. Almost every card has the same phrase. FROM YOUR SECRET PAL. Perhaps Zodiac bought this card. But maybe Zodiac lives with a woman who has an active circle of friends.

There's no copyright, no visible manufacturers mark, presumably covered with white correction fluid. In 1971, Avery prepares a document given the ad hoc title *The Avery Report.* It's an overview of The Zodiac. It circulates amongst law enforcement. In the *Report,* Avery writes that this card was manufactured by the Gibson Greeting Card company. The artwork and the color choices do not look current. By 1970, the Summer of Love's freaked out graphic design, the concert poster acid visions, have infected American commercial illustration. Motor spirit dominates advertisements for vacuum cleaners and new cars. The card has none of this. The artwork and color choices look as if they're from an earlier era. The late 1950s through, maybe, 1966. More old junk.

When it's received at the *Chronicle,* the card is interpreted as a threat against Avery. He's destined to be Zodiac's fourteenth slave. In his *Report,* Avery writes: "The number 14 (4-TEEN) was present, but could not be precisely figured if either [Zodiac] had taken 'slave' number 14, or if I was to be victim 14."

The card is provoked by an article. An article about a teenager killed in Presidio Heights. An article that links the murder to a killer who mailed anonymous taunts. It's only been two days since publication. And even the article's author has forgotten Jackie Truss.

A dead teenager found in Presidio Heights. 4-TEEN. First notice of Jackie Truss runs in the Sunday 25 October *Chronicle-Examiner*. When she's found, her body is disemboweled. Where is the pumpkin placed? Over the skeleton's lower torso. Her skull was crushed in death. The card's interior skeleton has a broken skull. It can't be determined if the cracks are original or added by the artist.

On 30 December 2013, Tahoe27 again proves their salt.

They discover the source material for BY FIRE, BY GUN, BY KNiFE, BY ROPE. It comes from a 1952 comic book, from the cover of *Tim Holt #30*:

(cover detail)

There are potential Zodiac inspirations that are disputable. And then there are the ones that are not. There's a reason why this cover appeals to Zodiac. On 27 September 1969, after he stabs Bryan Hartnell and Cecelia Shepard, the killer writes on Hartnell's car door:

Vallejo
12-20-68
7-4-69
Sept 27-69-6:30
by knife

Parts of this message—in particular "by knife"—were kept secret from the press. When the door was photographed, the Napa Sheriffs physically blocked its bottom. The detail somehow made it into papers from New York and Ohio, but until Graysmith's *Zodiac*, the full message never appeared in California. Unless someone is receiving newspapers from distant locales and picking up on one additional detail, this mailing must be Zodiac.

.

†

If you want the front page, threaten a journalist.

The press is nothing if not self-obsessed with its own place in the social hierarchy. On Halloween Day, Zodiac makes the *Chronicle*'s front page. ZODIAC HALLOWEEN THREAT. Paul Avery doesn't have the byline. Paul Avery is the headline. Zodiac makes the newswires. Zodiac makes the front page of *The Los Angeles Times*.

A man named Phil Sins—actual name, no pseudonym—sees the story and writes to Avery. He tells Avery about a girl in Riverside, California. She was killed. Her murderer sent in letters. Boasting about killing her. Riverside County is down near Los Angeles. It's where Cecelia Shepard lived.

Phil Sins thinks that The Zodiac killed a girl in Riverside.

chapter fourteen

it's not the way you kiss
that tears me apart

THIS IS REALITY LAYERED UPON ITSELF, as if Charlie is right, and there is no time and thus no morality. Phil Sins writes Avery. Avery phones the Riverside Police Department. The Captain sends Avery material. Avery receives the material in early November. A few hours later, the reporter is so energized that he flies to Riverside and conducts his own investigation. The result is Page 1 of the 16 November *Chronicle*. NEW EVIDENCE IN ZODIAC KILLINGS. The article isn't only about Riverside. Avery also interviews the woman from March 1970 out on Highway 132.

This is a new Avery. If his Zodiac reporting has never been perfect in its accuracy, past distortions are first draft journalism. Now things have changed. Zodiac sends the Halloween card, puts Avery into the story, makes the reporter part of the text. Avery runs with the new role. He's breaking his own leads, has lost all objectivity. Get that in the mail, interpret it as a death threat, and you'll believe everything.

This first layer is Avery time. November 1970. The second layer is 30 October 1966. The night before Halloween. There's an 18-year old girl named Cheri Jo Bates. She's a student at Riverside City College. Sixty miles outside of Los Angeles. Small town life in shadow of the myth machine.

Newspapers take pleasure in bestowing pulchritude on female crime victims. Everyone's a luminous angel when they're dead and gone. Whenever someone writes about Cheri Jo, it can't be avoided. She is always described as beautiful. In her case, this isn't a rewrite of journalistic bloodlust. Cheri Jo looks like the living embodiment of what people call the California Girl, what happens when Oakies escape to the West Coast and bake beneath the sun. The promise of tomorrow in the vibrant flesh of the now.

30 October 1966. Cheri Jo lives with her father in a 3 bedroom house at 4195 Via San Jose. At the intersection with California Avenue. Her mother moved out in 1965. Her brother's away in the Navy. Cheri Jo's got a boyfriend named Dennis Highland. They've been dating for two years. Dennis is up north attending San Francisco State. Just like Paul Stine. On the morning of 30 October, Cheri Jo eats breakfast with her father and the two attend church services. They're Catholic. They come home. Cheri Jo's father goes to the beach. Cheri Jo doesn't go with her father because she studies on the weekends. Her weekdays are packed. In the morning, she attends classes. In the afternoon, she works at a local bank. Cheri Jo's got a plan. She wants to be a stewardess. The airlines require a minimum age of 20 and two years of college. Cheri Jo's biding her time, attending Riverside City College. Around 3PM, Cheri Jo's father calls home. He's gonna invite his daughter to dinner at a friend's house. The line's busy. Her father calls again. 5:15PM. The line is still busy. The father heads home. Cheri Jo's gone. But she's left a note. DAD—WENT TO RCC <u>LIBRARY.</u> Depending on the source, the note is on the kitchen table or taped to the refrigerator. Cheri Jo's father takes a shower and goes to his friend's for dinner. Before he leaves, he gets a call from Cheri Jo's friend Stephanie. She leaves a message, wants Cheri Jo to call back. Earlier in the day, Cheri Jo calls Stephanie, asks if Stephanie can go to the library. Stephanie says that she can't. Cheri Jo's father comes home around midnight. Cheri Jo's not there. He's worried but Cheri Jo's a popular girl, she's got a lot of friends, she's a legal adult, she's probably out having fun.

Around 6AM, a Riverside Community College groundskeeper finds Cheri Jo's body near campus. On a present day map, it's impossible to find this location. The college has conquered the surrounding territory.

The center of Riverside City College is the Quad, a series of buildings forming an irregular rectangle and enclosing an expanse of green. In 1966, the campus library is in the north side of the Quad. The library is too small for its holdings and an ever-expanding student body. The library had to take over other buildings that belong to the school, including one right next door to the Quad. It's an old house. The librarians have named the annex buildings after Ivy League colleges. The old house next door is called Harvard. The Quad and Harvard are located on the south side of Terracina Drive. On the north side of Terracina, there's a ravine that leads down to RCC's athletic fields.

Harvard is in the neighborhood that abuts the RCC campus. Recognizing California's massive demographic boom, the college bought the nearby buildings. Land for future expansion. Harvard's unique. It's in use. The other structures are either storage or derelict and empty, and the neighborhood sits dark and unlit. It is crisscrossed by dirt pathways and driveway. Cheri Jo is found in a driveway off Terracina Drive between Harvard and an empty house. Her Volkswagen Bug is in front of the Quad.

The scene looks like this:

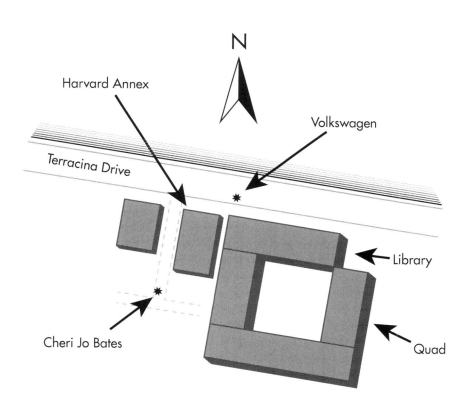

The cops come up with a timeline. Only a few junior colleges in California have Sunday library hours. RCC is one. The library opens at 6PM. Closes at 9PM. Around opening, Cheri Jo parks her Volkswagen Bug on Terracina Drive, goes into the library and checks out three books on the Electoral College. The books are found in her car. They're stamped with the date and time. Witnesses place her outside of the library. These witnesses are not close friends. They're people who see a blonde and a Volkswagen. The cops theorize that Cheri Jo hangs around the library for several hours, possibly until closing. She comes outside and tries to start her car. But her car won't start. Something's wrong. A wire has been torn from the ignition coil. As Cheri Jo's struggling, someone comes up and offers help. This person says that their car is parked down the street. The two walk past Harvard, this person grabs Cheri Jo, drags her down the driveway. And stabs her until she is dead, until she is lying face down in gravel waiting to be discovered by a groundskeeper.

Everything about this scene is small. The scale isn't apparent from photos or Google Maps. Look at mediated depictions and you miss the most important fact. Every story told about the death of Cheri Jo happens in an area no bigger than an East Coast suburban backyard. The library is cramped, inadequate to the student body who study cheek-to-jowl. The library is full of people who know Cheri Jo. They're different than the witnesses who put Cheri Jo outside around 6PM. These library people are friends with Cheri Jo. None remember seeing her. Cheri Jo is someone who you remember. She's beautiful.

At autopsy, her stomach contents indicate that she had eaten two-to-four hours before death. If news reports are accurate, Cheri Jo ate roast beef before she left home. Somewhere before 5:15PM. Her body temperature indicates a time of death between 7:30PM to 9:30PM. Just like the stomach contents. There are witnesses who say they hear screaming around 10:15PM to 10:30PM. If these recollections are accurate, the screaming can't be Cheri Jo. But 30 October is the day that the clocks change. Daylight saving time. This is an era before digital time-keeping. Maybe everyone forgets. Maybe these screams happen at 9:15PM to 9:30PM. It still leaves Cheri Jo in a tiny library for three hours. Where no one sees her. And everyone always sees Cheri Jo. You can't miss her. Unless she's not there.

The library, right now, is packed with students. There's about fifty people inside. Some stay until closing. To account for no one seeing Cheri Jo in the library, the cops theorize that maybe she didn't stay until closing. Maybe she left earlier. But this makes no sense. The distance to her car from the northern entrance of the Quad is no more than thirty seconds. If Cheri Jo leaves before closing time, say around 8PM, she's still got to hang around for more than an hour. Doing what?

Maybe it's all true. Maybe Cheri Jo does go into the cramped library and maybe somehow goes unrecognized. Maybe she comes out at 9PM and can't get her car started and someone says, hey, Cheri Jo, my car's just over on Fairfax. They walk together alongside the library. They reach a dirt path to their right, her assailant drags her into an abandoned neighborhood. She's stabbed to death. Maybe no one notices the body, no one walks down the driveway for the entire evening.

Or maybe it starts earlier.

When Cheri Jo's dad tries to call home, the line's busy. Both times. There's a note left about the library, but it's odd and formal. DAD—WENT TO RCC <u>LIBRARY</u>. If you're abducting someone and know where you're leaving the body, isn't this exactly the note that you'd make them write?

But why would anyone do this?

At the crime scene, there's a military boot heel print, size 8 to 10, and a torn-off men's Timex watch. Cheri Jo fought like hell. She's got her attacker's skin and hair under her fingernails and there's blood at the scene that does not belong to Cheri Jo. She kicked so much that one cop says the dirt looks as if it were worked over by a tractor. She fought like hell. That much is apparent. She did not go quietly.

No one will ever know what happened. Even when the inevitable occurs, even when DNA from recovered genetic matter is matched in a vast database of state surveillance, the details will remain lost. It's a mystery, an ambiguity, and this silence is like any other. It demands to be filled by noise.

Cheri Jo isn't much older than David Faraday or Betty Lou Jensen, she's just out of high school, only enrolled in September. She's a lower middle class kid killed before she really does anything. Had Zodiac not sent the Halloween Card which gets Avery on Sins's radar, it is entirely possible that Cheri Jo would be a very sad forgotten story.

Four years after she's killed, she stops being Cheri Jo Bates.

She becomes Zodiac Victim Cheri Jo Bates.

We know nothing of her thoughts or her personality. We have no idea if she was nice or cruel or waspish or how she sounded when she laughed. We have no idea if she had a single original thought. None of this is important to the world.

Only her death matters.

And what happens after.

The Zodiac lives.

†

Cheri Jo's murder makes a small splash. Hits the newswire, transmitted around America. 1966 is pre-Summer of Love, pre-Revolutionary politics. California can be surprised by the death of a young person. Especially if she's beautiful. Especially if the killing has the symbolic resonance of a student in a college driveway. Give it three years and this story might be local only.

The 1966 coverage tells the same tale as above, allowing for minor variations. These are the elements: dead blonde former high school cheerleader, disabled car, small blade, wound to the throat and other parts of the body, found at college. It's enough information to make a semi-accurate recreation of the crime scene.

Which is exactly what someone does.

On 29 November 1966, someone mails a letter to the Riverside PD and *The Press-Enterprise,* a local newspaper. The letter is composed on a typewriter. The mailed copies are produced through several sheets of carbon.

Carbon sheets are crude duplication technology. They're placed between pieces of paper. Pressure from the writing implement causes the carbon to deposit an inky impression on the bottom piece of paper. It's an inexact duplicate, legible, but it obscures the source of origin. There's enough distortion that the cops can't trace the typewriter.

The letter reads like this:

THE CONFESSION

BY_____

SHE WAS YOUNG AND BEAUTIFUL. BUT NOW SHE IS BATTERED AND DEAD. SHE IS NOT THE FIRST AND SHE WILL NOT BE THE LAST. I LAY AWAKE NIGHTS THINKING ABOUT MY NEXT VICTOM. MAYBE SHE WILL BE THE BEAUTIFUL BLOND THAT BABYSITS NEAR THE LITTLE STORE AND WALKS DOWN THE DARK ALLEY EACH EVENING ABOUT SEVEN. OR MAYBE SHE WILL BE THE SHAPELY BLUE EYED BRUNETT THAT SAID XXX NO WHEN I ASKED HER FOR A DATE IN HIGH SCHOOL. BUT MAYBE IT WILL NOT BE EITHER. BUT I SHALL CUT OFF HER FEMALE PARTS AND DEPOSIT THEM FOR THE WHOLE CITY TO SEE. SO DON'T MAKE IT TO EASY FOR ME. KEEP YOUR SISTERS, DAUGHTERS, AND WIVES OFF THE STREETS AND ALLEYS. MISS BATES WAS STUPID. SHE WENT TO THE SLAUGHTER LIKE A LAMB. SHE DID NOT PUT UP A STRUGGLE. BUT I DID. IT WAS A BALL. I FIRST PULLED THE MIDDLE WIRE FROM THE DISTRIBUTOR. THEN I WAITED FOR HER IN THE LIBRARY AND FOLLOWED HER OUT AFTER ABOUT TWO MINUTS. THE BATTERY MUST HAVE BEEN ABOUT DEAD BY THEN. I THEN OFFERED TO HELP. SHE WAS THEN VERY WILLING TO TALK TO ME. I TOLD HER THAT MY CAR WAS DOWN THE STREET AND THAT I WOULD GIVE HER A LIFT HOME. WHEN WE WERE AWAY FROM THE LIBRARY WALKING, I SAID IT WAS ABOUT TIME. SHE ASKED ME "ABOUT TIME FOR WHAT". I SAID IT WAS ABOUT TIME FOR HER TO DIE. I GRABBED HER AROUND THE NECK WITH MY HAND OVER HER MOUTH AND MY OTHER HAND WITH A SMALL KNIFE AT HER THROAT. SHE WENT VERY WILLINGLY. HER BREAST FELT VERY WARM AND FIRM UNDER MY HANDS. BUT ONLY ONE THING WAS ON MY MIND. MAKING HER PAY FOR THE BRUSH OFFS THAT SHE HAD GIVEN ME DURING THE YEARS PRIOR. SHE DIED HARD. SHE SQUIRMED AND SHOOK AS I CHOAKED HER, AND HER LIPS TWICHED. SHE LET OUT A SCREAM ONCE AND I KICKED HER HEAD

TO SHUT HER UP. I PLUNGED THE KNIFE INTO HER AND IT BROKE. I THEN FINISHED THE JOB BY CUTTING HER THROAT. I AM NOT SICK. I AM INSANE. BUT THAT WILL NOT STOP THE GAME. THIS LETTER SHOULD BE PUBLISHED FOR ALL TO READ IT. IT JUST MIGHT SAVE THAT GIRL IN THE ALLEY. BUT THAT'S UP TO YOU. IT WILL BE ON YOUR CONSCIENCE. NOT MINE. YES, I DID MAKE THAT CALL TO YOU ALSO. IT WAS JUST A WARNING. BEWARE...I AM STALKING YOUR GIRLS NOW.

CC. CHIEF OF POLICE
    ENTERPRISE

The Confession is covered. The papers don't give every detail. Enough to get the general sense. A killer takes credit for murdering a teenager and writes in with details of the killing and threatens more murders.

Months later, in April 1967, three more letters are sent. One is mailed to Cheri Jo's father at the haunted house on Via San Jose. It looks like this:

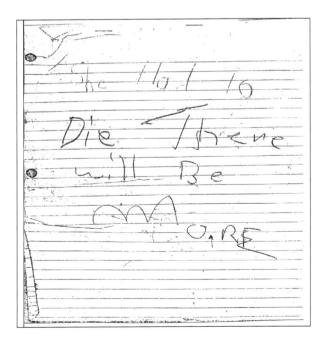

The other two letters feature slightly different text, employ capital letters. They look like this:

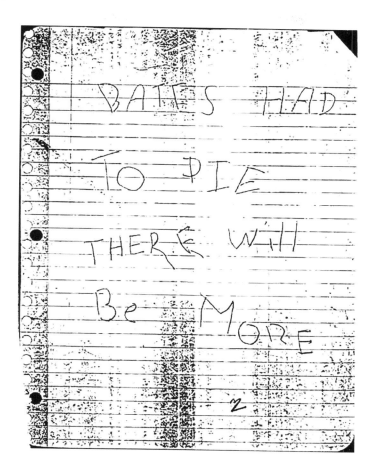

Each letter's respective envelope bears two Abraham Lincoln 4¢ stamps. The latter two letters conclude with a symbol. The symbols look like this:

When these letters arrive, no one's thinking Zodiac. Zodiac doesn't exist. This is cruelty from a crank writer. It's an intimation of the coming violence, a sick joke, an affront to the dignity of Cheri Jo and her father. A sign of the times.

Two years later, Zodiac starts the campaign with a triple mailing. A letter to the *San Francisco Chronicle,* a letter to the *San Francisco Examiner,* and a letter to the *Vallejo Times-Herald.* The first two are double stamped. The *Herald* letter is quadruple stamped. All stamps from the Prominent American series. Each decorated with a portrait of Franklin Delano Roosevelt. When word of Zodiac's letters hits the news, cops in Riverside start thinking about The Confession. People start thinking Cheri Jo and then they start thinking ZODIAC.

Riverside contacts Napa, where Zodiac killed BY KNiFE. This happens in late October 1969, after Dave Smith's article that creates The Zodiac. A memo is sent by Sergeant H.L. Homsher of Riverside. Homsher includes the confession letter but makes no mention of the three subsequent letters. At this time, anyway, Riverside doesn't think that the confession letter was sent by the same person who the subsequent mailings.

†

At the tail end of the Twentieth Century, the Riverside autopsy report leaks. The intimate details of Cheri Jo's murder flows into a stream, becomes part of the Internet's progression of brutal death and merciless pornography. Without going too much into the details, without dragging Cheri Jo back through the driveway's dirt, the report offers clarity.

Whoever authored the Confession letter was not the murderer. Many of the letter's details are flat out wrong. Cheri Jo did not suffer the wounds described by the writer. There is zero evidence that she was kicked in the head. And she did not, definitely did not, go like a lamb to the slaughter. Cheri Jo fought like hell. She fucked up the assailant. She did the best that she could. But there's a disparity between fingernails and a knife. The knife always wins. Cheri Jo dies. One detail in the Confession convinces the cops that the writer is the killer: the disabled car. The cops don't remember that this information appeared in the press.

Read the letter and another thing makes itself apparent. The writer has no idea where Cheri Jo Bates was killed. The operative sentences are: "I TOLD HER THAT MY CAR WAS DOWN THE STREET AND THAT I WOULD GIVE HER A LIFT HOME. WHEN WE WERE AWAY FROM THE LIBRARY WALKING, I SAID IT WAS ABOUT TIME."

The October 1966 coverage is vague about where the body is discovered. It sounds as if Cheri Jo is found almost anywhere. But she was left in a specific place, one requiring some familiarity with the campus. It's not down the street and it's not away from the library. It's right next door and in a driveway. From the library, it's the length of a baseball's flight across a suburban backyard.

The Confession is a hoax. The writer did not kill Cheri Jo.

But could this not have been the beginning of an era?

Zodiac takes credit for crimes that he did not commit.

A few things support the possibility. There's the spelling errors. In the Confession, the writer spells victim as "victom." The same error appears in the 20 December 1969 Zodiac letter to Melvin Belli. In the Little List letter, Zodiac offers the following torture method: "Some I shall tie over ant hills and watch them scream & twich and sqwirm." In the Confession, we find: "SHE SQUIRMED AND SHOOK AS I CHOAKED HER, AND HER LIPS TWICHED." Same spelling error. The beginning and the end of the Confession sound like the Little List. A fantasy vision of future victoms, the ones who'll get it next.

Zodiac writes by hand, so victom is an intentional misspelling. The Confession is composed on a QWERTY typewriter: "I" is next to "O." Zodiac's Little List is a weird joke, a transcription of Groucho Marx singing *The Mikado*. The Confession's future victims are part of a scheme to bring fear to Riverside's women.

The commonalities are genre convention. It's like writing Science Fiction space opera. If the meat of your text is intergalactic travel, it'll be strange if there aren't extraterrestrials or spaceships. If you're the big bad killer writing to the cops and the press, you're working in a genre established by the spurious London 1888 correspondences. Jack the Ripper theory. It'll be strange if you don't write about murder and victims and potential future victims and ask to be published. And while Zodiac is an innovator of the form, there are some notes that one must play.

The differences are more illustrative than the similarities. In 1969 and 1970, Zodiac mails fifteen correspondences and never personalizes. Zodiac might write of killing but never names the victims. The one time that he describes a victim's pain is in the 4 August letter: "He ended up on the back seat then the floor in back thrashing out very violently with his legs; that's how I shot him in the knee." But this is neither gloating nor delight. It's clinical detail offered as corroborating evidence. The Zodiac dead are abstract concepts, pawns on a chessboard. The Confession is ultra-personalization. It's about humiliating Bates. This is what I did to her. When Zodiac personalizes, he talks shit about cops, he says they fucked up. He sends a card to Paul Avery. He writes to the most famous lawyer in San Francisco. Zodiac is a man in a man's world. Reaching out to his peers.

Could Zodiac have been inspired by the Confession and sent in the next three letters? After all, there's that symbol. Very serious people believe that it looks like a "Z." But this is either pareidolia or apophenia, the seeing of things that aren't present because the human brain takes in new data and matches it to pre-existing patterns. Look again at the symbol:

It's as easily a 2 as a Z. Or a sideways 3 atop a 2. Or a conjunction of the letters M and L. In the first four letters sent by Zodiac, one can witness an evolution. In the initial three letters, sent 31 July, there is no mention of the tradename. Zodiac doesn't know what to call himself. Is he the murderer or the killer of the two teenagers last Christmass? If the tradename exists on 31 July, it'll be in the cipher. But it's not there, despite Zodiac promising that the cipher contains his identity. In the three days between the first letters and the 4 August correspondence, the killer comes up with the tradename.

Is it a dimly remembered echo of *Charlie Chaplin at Treasure Island*? Maybe. Anything's possible. Maybe it's something else. Maybe it's just dad trying to sound spooky.

In 1970, the cops and Paul Avery are people who believe everything. They think that Zodiac has a plan, that they're fighting an evil mastermind out of pulp fiction, that everything makes cohesive internal sense and is planned from the beginning. Exactly what Zodiac wants them to believe.

It's the easier idea.

The BATES HAD TO DIE notes have a progression resembling the first three Zodiac letters. The letter to Bates's father is probably the first composed. Unlike the other two, it's not written in all caps and bears no symbol. Which is similar to Zodiac's first three letters. He goes from being the killer to the murderer, adapts as he writes.

But, again, the Bates letters are so personalized. The writer is networked into Riverside, has a grudge against Bates or her father. And unless Zodiac calls the relatives of Darlene Ferrin on the night of her murder, at best a tentative speculation, he never demonstrates interest in the victims. Their deaths aren't the point. Their bodies are props, fuel for the fire. The victims aren't individuals. He never use their names, even after they've appeared in print. "The girl." "The boy." "The cab driver." "The woeman and her baby." "A man in a parked car."

And the Bates letters are *mean*. This is one emotion that never registers in the Zodiac correspondences. Zodiac is a brutal killer, Zodiac is a beast. But Zodiac takes no pleasure in cruelty for its own sake. There's no delight in humiliation. He's got a god's eye view of the matter. The Bates letters are sent from the gutter.

What about the stamps?

On the surface, the double stamping of BATES MUST DIE looks like Zodiac. But there's a subtle difference. On 7 January 1963, the United States Postal Service establishes a fixed-rate on the first ounce of any letter. 5¢. Each additional ounce requires another 5¢. On 7 January 1968, this is changed to 6¢ for the first ounce and 6¢ for each additional. The Bates letters are sent under the 1965 rates. Each use two 4¢ Abraham Lincoln stamps. Once those letters hit the 5¢ threshold, the additional three cents add nothing.

Zodiac always stamps to exact postage. If he exceeds what's required, the extra stamp is there to ensure delivery. But he never wastes a cent. Zodiac uses six 1¢ Thomas Jefferson stamps on the 20 December 1969 letter to Melvin Belli. Exact first ounce postage. On the 31 July letter to the *Vallejo Times-Herald,* Zodiac uses four 6¢ stamps. It's over kill, but it's to-the-cent postage for four ounces. Subsequent commentators have speculated that Zodiac believed that the extra postage would speed the letter's delivery to Vallejo. This is possible, but it's an assumption based on seeing a reproduction of a thing rather than the thing itself. How does anyone know how much that first letter weighs? And how much does anyone know what Zodiac thinks that it weighs? Given that it's the first letter, it's as likely that he quadrupled stamped it and then realized that the extra postage was unnecessary. Which would suggest someone with a great deal of postal knowledge. And a letter scale.

The Bates letters aren't like this. They're sent by someone who might not know the correct postage.

Zodiac is a stickler for detail, Zodiac knows enough about the postal system to get Sunday postmarks, Zodiac puts in the work. Everyone else scrawls bullshit on a piece of paper. Zodiac might fuck up when he's killing, leaves fingerprints on the scene. But Zodiac never fucks up delivery.

†

Avery gets two more days out of Cheri Jo Bates. 17 and 19 November. More details emerge, Avery writes himself into the story. Avery has become the story. Before he goes to Southern California, the Riverside PD do not see BATES HAD TO DIE as related to the case. Dozens of crank letters have arrived. Riverside believes the trio are examples of the genre.

Paul Avery looks at the file. Paul Avery sees the symbol. Paul Avery sees Z. Paul Avery sees ZODIAC. There's an informal comparison of handwriting against that of Zodiac. It turns out that Zodiac fever is contagious. Now the cops think that the letters say ZODIAC.

As Avery and the cops talk, new evidence comes to light. Roughly a month after 30 October 1966, a college janitor discovers a poem written on a desk. Somehow it ends up in the police archives. No one pays any attention. But Paul Avery is infected with Zodiac fever and the disease is contagious. Everyone looks at this poem and everyone thinks ZODIAC.

The poem reads like this:

Sick of living/unwilling to die

cut.
clean.
if red /
clean.
blood spurting,
   dripping,
    spilling;
all over her new
dress.
oh well,
it was red
anyway.
life draining into an
uncertain death.
she won't
die.
this time
someone ll find her.
just wait till
next time.

      rh

There are undeniable ambiguities in Cheri Jo Bates's death. But this is idiotic. This is Zodiac fever. The heat in the body goes to the brain and produces hallucinations. Assume that somehow the poem describes an attack on a woman. None of the details match Cheri Jo. She wasn't wearing a dress. She died. There isn't going to be a next time.

Think about the poem for more than a millisecond, let it pass through a brain uncooked by Zodiac fever, and the words make sense. This is moody teenager suicide poetry. It's titled "Sick of living." It uses a slightly complex perspective—someone writing about themselves in the third person—but otherwise is very simple. A girl tries to kill herself. No one notices until the last minute when she's saved from the attempt. But she's going to try again.

Writing like this has been a staple of college campuses for as long as there have been college campuses. If you're a young adult, you're moody. Some kids self-harm. Some kids booze and dope. Some kids write awful poetry. This has nothing to do with Bates.

But Paul Avery gets that Halloween Card, Paul Avery becomes part of the text. Paul Avery gets energized. Paul Avery gets Zodiac fever. He's breaking stories. He's the new Sheriff in town. Which must embarrass the actual cops. A bohemian from the *Chronicle* is doing their job. Either they discredit Avery. Or they catch Zodiac fever and get on board. The cops chose the latter. They incorporate new data.

Sherwood Morrill is the California State Bureau of Criminal Investigation's handwriting expert. Avery gets the poem to Morrill—either through his own initiative or via Riverside PD—and Morrill authenticates the text. It's written by Zodiac. It tells us everything that we need to know about this expert, his field, and his body of expertise. A poem etched into a desk with a ball-point pen cannot be compared against samples of someone using felt-tip pen on paper. It's impossible. But it happens anyway. And comes up ZODIAC.

Whenever a new Zodiac letter arrives, the SFPD uses Morrill. Whenever there's a new suspect name, a handwriting sample is acquired. It's sent to Sherwood Morrill. Who compares it against the Zodiac letters. If the sample doesn't match, he discredits the suspect. But this man just said that a suicide poem from 1966 is a Zodiac death-note. What does that say about the process? What does that say about the people who've been excluded?

Later, in 1972, Morrill tells a reporter that he's excluded 8,000 Zodiac candidates. It might not be true, could be an old man who likes attention. But it also might be accurate. 8,000 names. Excluded by this man.

Zodiac did not write this poem. It doesn't matter. Everyone's caught Zodiac fever. Cheri Jo Bates becomes a prop, an expanding story, something that tells the cops new things about an old mystery. All future Zodiac candidates will be evaluated by two new questions.

Were they in Riverside in October 1966?

Do they have some connection to the initials RH?

On 18 November 1970, Ken Narlow of the Napa Sheriff's Department and Dave Toschi and Mel Nichol of the State Crime Bureau go to Riverside. They confer with the police chief. The meeting is nine hours long.

The meeting ends with a conclusion. Everyone's caught Zodiac fever. There's a definitive link between the murder of Cheri Jo Bates and the Zodiac. These men are convinced that Zodiac killed Bates. Documented by Avery, who writes: "[Law enforcement] also think that for some reason, Zodiac has attempted to hide his connection with Miss Bates' murder—a distinct contradiction for his style now in which he brags about his killings in letters sent to the *Chronicle.*"

These men worked when criminal justice was a story told to maintain social cohesion. There's no DNA. Police work is barely professionalized.

But this too is idiotic.

The cops have taken the presumed evidence and fashioned a narrative by working backwards. If you invent convolutions to explain a phenomenon, then your story is false. *Zodiac is hiding his connection. For some reason.* Five days earlier, no one knew about Cheri Jo Bates. Now the narrative has shifted. Rather than put these details in the order which they arrived, after everything else, they're put first and everything that came before is informed by the new information. The Bay Area killings and the letters are seen as a sequel. If Zodiac has the good luck to murder in San Francisco, and if this luck brings in a police department that can believe anything, and if their credulity allows Zodiac to escape detection, then this is the acme of that process. This is when it becomes definitive. Zodiac will never be found.

Avery writes something else: "While it cannot yet be said with certainty, it is considered 'quite possible' the library poet—known to be Zodiac—also authored the confession letters. These are considered authentic because they revealed facts about the slaying that only the killer could have known."

Zodiac wrote the poem. That's what Morrill says. That's what Avery says. That's what the cops say. But maybe Zodiac didn't write the letters.

But without the letters, the poem can't be linked to Zodiac.

Initial evidence displaced for subsequent developments. This is not an investigation. This is fan fiction.

In the 16 November article, Avery writes about the woman from Highway 132. He tracks her down, interviews her, relays more and shifting detail about her encounter. The operative sentences are: "Police, however, feel she did meet with and escaped from Zodiac. They base this on a thorough examination of details of her story. And also because of a Zodiac letter received by the Chronicle: in which he bragged about his near miss..."

Here we see the process. The story is true because Zodiac wrote about it and because it reinforces what we know about Zodiac. But everything that we know about Zodiac comes from what Zodiac has told us. Back in November 1969, Zodiac writes a letter that ends with the following sentence: "To prove that I am the Zodiac, Ask the Vallejo cop about my electric gun sight which I used to start my collecting of slaves." It's a call-back to Zodiac's *Popular Science* quote on 4 August 1969: "What I did was tape a small pencel flash light to the barrel of my gun. If you notice, in the center of the beam of light if you aim it at a wall or celling you will see a black or darck spot in the center of the circle of light about 3 to 6 inches across. When taped to a gun barrel, the bullet will strike exactly in the center of the black dot in the light. All I had to do was spray them as if it was a water hose; there was no need to use the gun sights."

The operative phrase in the November letter is this: "... which I used to start my collecting of slaves." Written long before anyone has discovered the Bates connection. His first kills occurred in December 1968 out on Lake Herman Road. He could be lying. Zodiac lies. He did not scope a .22 pistol with a pencil light. He copied nonsense out of *Popular Science*. But if the police believe the accuracy of his claim about Highway 132, then why don't they believe this statement? How can they discern the truth from a lie? Or do they believe that everything Zodiac writes is true? But if everything that Zodiac writes is true, the earlier letter means that he didn't kill Bates. They didn't believe Zodiac when he wrote about Richard Radetich. But now they believe that he abducted a woeman on the highway?

Zodiac lists his kills on Bryan Hartnell's car door. He writes them with a black felt-tip pen. They start with Lake Herman Road. But Zodiac is hiding his connection to Bates. For some reason. Which means Zodiac lies. But they've just used his writing to verify Highway 132.

The contradiction is ignored.

That's Zodiac fever.

†

On 25 November 1970, the *Chronicle*'s world famous gossip Herb Caen writes a column. One paragraph is about Paul Avery.

Colleagues at the *Chronicle* are worried. What if The Zodiac mistakes them for Avery? What if The Zodiac assassinates them instead of Avery? Caen writes that Avery's colleagues have come up with a solution.

They've started wearing lapel pins that say: I AM NOT PAUL AVERY.

Gallows humor from the international brotherhood of degenerate newspapermen. At long last, Zodiac gets his buttons.

Caen also writes that Avery has asked the Department of Motor Vehicles for personalized license plates. These plates are a new thing, only just signed into law by Governor Reagan. Avery asks for one word.

ZODIAC.

ADDENDUM

The preceding chapter was written in April 2021. On 2 August 2021, the Riverside Police Department announced that it had verified the authorship of the three BATES HAD TO DIE letters. Investigation of Bates's murder is now, formally, severed from any attempt to find Zodiac.

In 2016, the RPD received an anonymous letter. Its author stated that, in their turbulent youth, they composed the BATES HAD TO DIE letters. DNA was extracted from a stamp on the 2016 envelope. Through genetic genealogy, it was tracked to its sender.

He was not Zodiac.

The preceding chapter has been left unmodified, as it now proves an underlying thesis of this book: that the authenticity of Zodiac correspondences can be determined through analysis of the greater context and each letter's contents.

The importance of the RPD statement can not be overstated. From Paul Avery's original reporting, it's clear that Cheri Jo Bates was moved into the category of Zodiac victim on the basis of BATES HAD TO DIE.

The article in question, dated 16 November 1970, contains the following:

> The three "BATES HAD TO DIE" notes and the desk poem were not connected to each other at the time, or to the confession letters received a few months earlier. They were decided to be the works of a sick-minded hoaxer... The notes were routinely tucked away and the desk

stored in the evidence vault... They remained there until last week when The Chronicle learned of their existence, examined them, and pointed out to Riverside Police:

> • That the penciled printing bears eerie and strong resemblance to that of Zodiac's felt-tip pen lettering in the numerous communications he has sent to this paper.

> • That the printing on "BATES HAD TO DIE" envelopes seemed to match exactly the desktop writing.

> • And perhaps the most meaningful discovery was that two of the three notes had been signed with a "z."

> ...At the conclusion [of a conference between RPD and Paul Avery], Captain Cross immediately forwarded the three notes and a photograph of the strange desk poem to Sacramento for examination by specialists of the State Bureau of Criminal Investigation and Identification.

...If the man who signed the notes "z" is, as police here now tend to believe, Zodiac, they consider it likely that he is also the killer who sabotaged Miss Bates' car and then lured her to her death.

None of these observations were accurate. For fifty-one years, they have clouded and poisoned the memory and name of Cheri Jo Bates.
   Zodiac fever.

chapter fifteen

one more sad
pathetic bastard

IT'S 1971. NO ONE'S HEARD A PEEP SINCE OCTOBER 1970, there's no developments. A template is set with Avery's scoop, a shifting of possibility. When February rolls around and two young women go missing, the press and law enforcement speculate as to Zodiac's involvement. The first woman is a co-ed from Humboldt State College. Her name is Sharon Wilson, she's 20-years old. She disappears. At roughly the same time, Lynda Kanes also goes missing. She attends Pacific Union College, the Seventh Day Adventist school where Bryan Hartnell and Cecelia Shepard were students. The magic word appears in the press, heavy speculation. Zodiac fever. Both women are found dead, both cases are solved by the end of the year, suspects are convicted in each killing. Neither is Zodiac. They're not even The Zodiac. But this spurt of news is enough. It shakes loose the genuine original.

On 13 March 1971, an unknown man goes to an unknown location in Pleasanton, southeast of Martinez and Benicia on the I-680, and deposits a letter in a mail box. It's addressed to *The Los Angeles Times.* It reads:

This is the Zodiac speaking

Like I have allways said, I am crack proof. If the Blue Meannies are evere going to catch me, they had best get off their fat asses & do something. Because the longer they fiddle & fart around, the more slaves I will collect for my after life. I do have to give them credit for stumbling across my riverside activity, but they are only finding the easy ones, there are a hell of a lot more down there. The reason I'm writing to the Times is this, They don't bury me on the back pages like some of the others.

It's Zodiac. He's happy to claim Cheri Jo Bates. Someone else did the heavy lifting. Now the police and Paul Avery are in the driver's seat. Zodiac writes that there's more activity. "Down there." Southern California. And he's abandoned the *Chronicle* because the *Chronicle* and *Examiner* bury him. The *Times* always affords Zodiac front page real estate. He's good for circulation, sales, brings in the punters.

News breaks on 16 March. Paul Avery writes a story that gets a biopsy on Page 1 of the *Chronicle*, two paragraphs that run on to Page 16. Avery makes fun of Zodiac's claim of 17+. The article ends like this: "... Zodiac has written to the Chronicle often, although with no pattern of regularity."

No one, not Avery, not his colleagues, not SFPD, has noticed that there is a pattern. Zodiac writes after media mention of The Zodiac. Not every time. Enough to make it definitive. And no one's noticed.

The *Times* is caught with its hands in the cookie jar. For the first time in a very long while, a Zodiac letter doesn't make Page 1. The *Times* puts it on Page 3. Observation changes the nature of the observed.

It's quiet for ten days and then on 26 March, the *Chronicle* gives Avery the front page. ZODIAC HINTS OF A BODY NEAR TAHOE. A new mailing has arrived, another cut-and-paste postcard like 5 October 1970. Zodiac takes credit for the disappearance of a woman named Donna Lass, 25, last seen September 1970 in South Lake Tahoe.

The card looks like this:

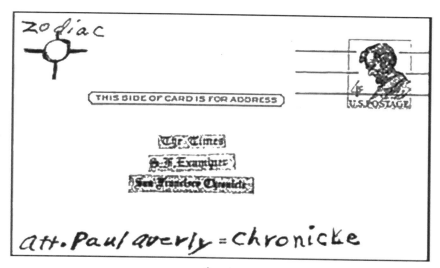

(front)

(rear)

It's the cut-and-paste method of the 5 October 1970 card, uses multiple sources for material. SOUGHT is on Page 54 of the 15 March *Examiner*. AROUND IN THE SNOW comes from Page 14 of the 16 March *Chronicle*. SIERRA CLUB is from either Page 9 of the 19 March *Examiner* or Page 6 of the 20 March *Examiner*. PEEK THROUGH THE PINES and the illustration come from a condominium advertisement that runs on Page 37 of the 19 March *Chronicle* and Page 15 of the 19 March *Examiner*. THE TIMES, one of the addressees, is taken from almost any page of any edition of the *San Mateo Times*.

The method of composition can't be ignored, but everything here looks like an imitation. There's no innovation. The author gets the victim number wrong. By the time that Donna Lass goes missing in September 1970, Zodiac's sent in two correspondences claiming thirteen victims.

This mailing is cut-and-pasted onto a pre-paid post card issued some time after 7 January 1963, when the rate for a postcard is established at 4¢, and before a 1968 hike makes the cost 5¢.

In 1971, this card lacks proper postage.

There's neither cancellation nor postmark. When it enters the postal system, it's flagged for lacking postage. Someone realizes the nature of the thing before them and forwards the card to the *Chronicle*.

Without a postmark, we have no idea from where it was sent. Or when it was mailed.

It's addressed to three different newspapers. This, along with the improper postage, violates everything in the previous mailings. Zodiac is a stickler for delivery. Zodiac wants these mailings read, printed. He never fucks up a letter.

It's probable that the card is from a copycat.

Which makes the *Los Angeles Times* letter something special. No one knows it yet. The correspondence of 13 March 1971 is the last indisputable Zodiac mailing. Possible letters will not arrive again until 1974. An era has ended. The game is over, the air's out of the tire, the ride is over.

Zodiac is gone.

For good.

†

People search for Donna Lass and come up with nothing. She's never found. A few more 1971 murders earn press mentions for The Zodiac. These come to nothing. Zodiac is gone, the cops failed to catch him, the letters have ceased.

The story never ends. It continues in April 1971 with the cinematic premiere of *Zodiac*, later retitled *The Zodiac Killer*. The film is schlock. The screenplay takes a day-and-a-half to write, the shooting schedule is a few weeks, the footage is edited in less than a month. The director is Tom Hanson, a former restaurateur. He doesn't want to make a film. He wants to create an event. He wants to trap The Zodiac. Hanson spends $13,000 on the film. It premieres at San Francisco's Golden Gate 2 Cinema, smack dab at the intersection of Taylor & Market Streets. The Zodiac is such an egomaniac, thinks Hanson, that the killer will come see himself on the screen. There's no way he won't show up. When attendees buy their ticket, they're given a small card that reads: I THINK THE ZODIAC KILLS BECAUSE....

Followed by a space for attendees to write in assumed motivations. When they drop it off, they'll be entered into a contest. They can win a motorcycle. Hanson stacks the cinema with cronies. The cards are analyzed in real time. If anyone's handwriting matches Zodiac, Hanson and cronies will apprehend the killer. Despite stories from later decades, the scheme comes to nothing. Hardly anyone attends. The film closes before the scheduled end of its run.

The Zodiac Killer opens with the following title:

> The motion picture you are about to see was conceived in June 1970. Its goal is not to win commercial awards but to create an "awareness of present danger". Zodiac is based on known facts. If some of the scenes, dialogue and letters seem strange and unreal, remember - they happened. My life was threatened on Oct. 28, 1970 by Zodiac. His victims have received no warnings. They were unsuspecting people like you---
>
> *Paul Avery, Reporter*
> *San Francisco Chronicle*

Avery is credited as a consultant. Throughout the film, there're resonances from someone who remembers. Recreations of the attacks are surprisingly accurate, two letters are quoted almost verbatim. There's a crazy version of Highway 132. There's an echo of SATAN SAVES ZODIAC. One scene recreates the 20 November 1969 spectacle of David Martin, a man with so much motor spirit that he held his daughter hostage, saw pressed tight against her throat. Hanson says that he only met Avery a few times. But the microdetails argue for deeper involvement. One scene recreates Zodiac's SFPD encounter. The cops let him go. If this is from Avery, it's confirmation that press and law enforcement believe Zodiac over the official story.

On 13 April, Avery gets Page 1. KNIFE MURDER OF GIRL 18— FEARS OF ZODIAC. Kathy Bilek is found on Easter Sunday, knifed to death, close to where Deborah Gay Furlong and Kathy Snoozy were killed. The two girls murdered 3 August 1969. Their deaths invited Zodiac speculation. He took credit for the killings in November 1969. Bilek isn't killed by Zodiac. She's killed by Karl Werner, who's arrested and convicted for the murders of Bilek, Furlong and Snoozy.

On 31 July 1971, someone mails another card to the *Chronicle*. No image has ever circulated. We know what it says: "NEAR MONTICELLO SOUGHT VICTIMS 21 ...... IN THE WOODS DIES APRIL."

Another letter is sent to the *Chronicle*. It looks like this:

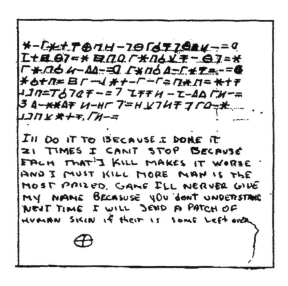

The cipher decodes to:

TIS THE ZODIAC SPEACKING
WHY CANT YOU STOP ME I CANT
STOP KILLING STOP LISTENING
T PHONYS IF THIS IS NOT ON THE
FRONT PAGE IN A WEEK I WILL SKIN
3 LITTLE KIDS AND MAKE A SUIT
FROM THE SKIN

Each correspondence claims 21 victims. The cipher arrives after the card, which did not appear in the press. It's probable that they have the same author. Neither mailing is from Zodiac. They're from The Zodiac.

†

Just before Christmass, Hollywood releases Don Siegel's *Dirty Harry*.

The film is a masterpiece, expression of a violent libertarian ethos that freaks out a liberal elite who reject state-sponsored violence but embrace radical bombings. It captures San Francisco unlike any other film, the San Francisco far from tourist landmarks. One scene is set by a Hunter's Point oil tank. Another is on Mount Davidson.

Siegel is a journeyman director. He's honed his craft for decades, works at perfection. Near *Dirty Harry*'s very beginning, there's a bird's eye shot from the top of a skyscraper, a circular pan establishing almost every location that appears in the subsequent 100 minutes. It's how cinema is supposed to work.

The film stars Clint Eastwood as Harry Callahan. A tough cop with a short fuse. He's up against a killer who calls himself Scorpio. Scorpio likes writing letters. Scorpio's letters are exact visual duplicates of Zodiac's letters. The film's climax involves a school bus full of kiddies.

The filmmakers admit the similarity but deny that the film is about The Zodiac. Public relations bullshit. The Zodiac is the unmoved mover of

Dirty Harry, the secret star, the invisible ghost in every millimeter of celluloid. It's there in the first shot, double exposure montage of a memorial in the Hall of Justice. The memorial commemorates fallen police officers. The montage starts with the first dead. 1878. Ends with the most recent. And there are the names. Eric A. Zelms. Richard P. Radetich.

If Dave Toschi and Bill Armstrong can't close the case, Hollywood's sending Clint Eastwood. He'll finish things in a way that doesn't give two shakes of a stick about the liberals or the Blacks and all that whinging about civil rights and the Constitution and Supreme Court rulings and due process. Clint Eastwood closes cases like a White man. With a sneer, a wisecrack, and a bullet.

The Zodiac becomes a screen god. Instant apotheosis.

In later years, a rumor arises that Harry Callahan is based on Dave Toschi. Just like how Steve McQueen's character in *Bullit* was based on Toschi.

Assume that the person who starts this rumor is Toschi.

†

Before the release of *Dirty Harry*, a long and pathetic saga begins. It's August 1971. A man named Don Cheney speaks with Dave Toschi and Bill Armstrong. He tells them about a conversation with a friend named Arthur Leigh Allen. This happened back in December 1967 or January 1968. Allen lives in his parents' basement in Vallejo. 32 Fresno Street. Allen tells Cheney that he's thinking about going on a kill spree. Allen mentions "The Most Dangerous Game." Allen thinks that he could get away with it. When he embarks upon his reign of terror, Allen's going to call himself Zodiac. And shoot people with a pencil light taped to the barrel of his gun.

Toschi and Armstrong hear Cheney. Their eyes go wide. This is it. They call Sergeant Jack Mulanax of the Vallejo PD and give him the dirt. Vallejo PD conducts a low-level investigation, talks to people on Fresno Street. The neighbors all like Allen. Talks to former employers. They're more ambivalent. Allen worked as a school teacher but something happened and now he works as a junior chemist at the Union Oil refinery across the Carquinez Straight. The three investigators arrange to meet with Allen at his place of employment.

Allen walks into the room and Toschi *knows*. This dude smells all wrong. This guy is as wrong as wrong can get. This guy is the definition of wrong. Brother, this dude is *Zodiac*.

They ask Allen if he remembers any conversation about a kill spree. Allen says he can't recall something like that. They ask if he's read about The Zodiac. Allen says that he skimmed the initial articles but stopped after a while. He found the whole thing too morbid. Allen says that he was questioned by Vallejo PD after the Lake Berryessa attacks. Which is true. It's there in the files, 10-6-19, 4:05PM: "Went to Elmer Cave School and contacted Arthur Lee ALLEN. WMA, 35 years dob 12-18-33. Resides 32 Fresno St, is single lives with his parents. Arthur 6'1", 241, heavy build and is bald. On 9-26-69 Arthur went skin diving on salt point ranch, stayed overnight and returned to Vallejo 9-27-69. This is at approximately 2 to 4:30PM. Is a student at Vallejo Jr College and works park time as a custodian at Elmer Cave School."

Speaking in August 1971, Allen elucidates his 9-26-69 movements. He went to Salt Point Ranch in Sonoma County near Fort Ross. He was skin diving. He went alone but became acquainted with a serviceman stationed on Treasure Island and the serviceman's wife. He doesn't remember the man's name but has it written down somewhere. When he returned on 9-27-69, he talked to his neighbor. Unfortunately, this neighbor died a week later. With no prompt, Allen says: "The two knives that I had in my car with blood on them, the blood came from a chicken that I had killed."

Mulanax will look into the files and find no record of the previous conversation. The detective who interviewed Allen, Sergeant John Lynch, has no memory of the encounter. But it happened, it's there in the files, it's as plain as day. What's missing is any hint of how Allen got on Lynch's radar. Someone had to tell Vallejo PD. We have no evidence of whom.

Allen tells the cops that he was in Riverside when Cheri Jo Bates was killed. This contradicts his earlier statement of not following news reports. He has an interest in guns but only owns .22 caliber firearms. The cops notice that Allen is wearing a watch. It's made in Switzerland by a company called Zodiac. The company's logo is a circle quadrisected by a cross. But the early Zodiac letters establish that the logo predates the tradename. Not that the cops care. Not in this moment. Not when Allen smells so wrong. Not when The Zodiac sits before them. Not when he stinks to high heaven.

Allen says that he wants to help in whatever fashion he can. He says that he looks forward to the day when people stop referring to police as pigs. Allen can't remember any other conversations he might have had about The Zodiac but thinks that maybe he did talk about the case with old co-workers. But he can't remember. Allen says "The Most Dangerous Game" was the best thing that he read in high school.

Thus ends the dialogue.

Mulanax completes his report with an understatement of the century: "After interview with Allen, it was opinion of all three investigators that further investigation was warranted."

†

For the next year, Allen will be on the cop radar.

It'll culminate in September 1972. A raid on a trailer in Santa Rosa. But most investigation occurs in the weeks following the interview.

Arthur Leigh Allen is ghastly. He's a pedophile. He will spend much of the 1970s in trouble with the law. When Allen realizes the cops think that he's The Zodiac, he goes out of his way to make people believe that maybe he is the killer. Until he dies in the early 1990s, he'll never stop flashing the watch. He's one of those sorry people who believe that they're the center of the universe despite everyone else thinking that they're a microscopic speck of dust embedded in another microscopic speck of dust that's trapped beneath an important person's toe-nail. Now the cops confirm what he's known for his whole life. Allen matters. He will do anything to keep the focus. In later years, he'll give interviews, he'll write letters, he'll keep track of The Zodiac, and all the while he'll protest his innocence. Everyone will find this very hard to believe. Despite there being zero evidence that he is Zodiac. Allen has pedophile stink upon him, there's something desperately wrong, he's unsavory, and even when he's tells the truth, he visibly attempts to emote what he's identified as sincerity in others.

We don't know how the Vallejo cops hear about Allen in 1969.

But we know how SFPD hears in 1971.

Don Cheney and his business partner, Santo Paul Panzarella, contact the Manhattan Beach Police Department. Down near Los Angeles. They tell MBPD a story. Allen planned it all out. Back in late 1967 or early 1968. The entire spree in advance. Including the tradename. But it's the same as the symbol on BATES HAD TO DIE. Arthur Leigh Allen couldn't have invented the tradename in 1967 or 1968 because it didn't exist until 4 August 1969. The killer invents as the situation shifts. Cheney presents a narrative of it being there from the beginning.

MBPD contacts SFPD. Toschi gets in touch with Cheney.

On 19 July 1971, MBPD sends a memo to SFPD. Its most important sentence is this: "The recent killings in the Grass Valley Area by an unknown subject, middleaged [sic], brought the suspicion into focus."

1971 is a bad year for Clarence Otis Smith. He's a six-foot-five garbage collector. In January 1971, a 19-year old preacher named Everett Richardson moves into the house Smith that shares with his wife and children. It's probable that Richardson, who says that he's 19 but looks 35, is having an affair with Smith's wife. Richardson was ordained through the mail. Smith tells Richardson that the house is filled with demons. Richardson sees the demons on thirty-four occasions. Richardson and Smith cover the windows with aluminum foil. Everyone prays to get rid of the demons. Smith's 15-year old stepdaughter gets possessed. Richardson performs an exorcism. The demons leave the stepdaughter. The preacher asks the girl to marry him. The girl runs away from home. Richardson gets Smith's wife pregnant. Richardson tells Smith that the father is Jesus Christ. Jesus Christ speaks to Smith. Jesus Christ uses the vocal chords of Richardson. Jesus Christ speaks in old English type of language. Smith and Richardson visit a physician in Colusa. The physician circumcises Smith and Richard. It's an act of purification. 25 June 1971. Smith is driving a garbage truck. His son is in the passenger seat. Smith's sleepy. He crashes the truck down a ravine. His 8-year old son dies. Smith is ejected but survives. On 2 July 1971, Smith tells Richardson that he's going to kill the preacher unless the preacher and Smith's family get out of the house. Now. Everyone goes to a Sacramento hotel. Smith is alone in the house. On 10 July and 11 July and 12 July, Smith is drinking and telling people how much he hates hippies and that the longhairs have stolen his power tools and how's going to get even. He shows his friends a big knife. One says, "God damn, that's a beautiful knife." Smith threatens to kill the friend if he ever again takes the Lord's name in vain. Later, while confessing his culpability, Smith says that Richardson told him that hippies stole the power tools and Richardson tells Smith that he has to get even. In truth, the power tools are stolen to pay for the hotel in Sacramento. On the morning of 12 July, Smith's family and Richardson come back to the house. Smith is in a good mood. He and Richardson drink. Smith is wearing unbroken eyeglasses. That night, about three miles from the Smith house, people are at the Dog Bar campground on the Bear River. They're in tents. They're enjoying natural beauty. Smith comes to the campground. And it's absolute chaos. His knife is huge, it's a rounded blade that he made himself, people think it's a sickle, he's attacking people, he's drunk, he's laughing, he's a big balding giant, he's killing two, he's wounding another three, people have guns that they're trying to fire at Smith. Smith is getting injured, he's bleeding, he's taking guns away from people, he's leaving his broken eyeglasses at the scene, he's disappearing in the darkness. Richardson and Smith's wife help Smith flee to Mexico. He's arrested and extradited to Texas before being brought back to California.

News of the massacre breaks. Hits the *Los Angeles Times*. Don Cheney and his business partner see the article. They think Arthur Leigh Allen.

They think ZODIAC.

Cheney's story, told to MBPD before Smith is apprehended, doesn't contain a scrap of evidence linking Allen to the campground. By the time that SFPD and Vallejo interview Allen, Smith has been named in public.

The massacre is deleted from their story.

†

After the interview with Allen, SFPD and Vallejo get in touch with Allen's brother. He's not hostile to the idea that Allen might be The Zodiac. But he doesn't think it's true. He knows that something is wrong with his brother. He says that Allen made advances at Cheney's child. The brother doesn't suggest that this is why Cheney told the story to the SFPD. But Mulanax thinks this might be the case. It's a rare moment, a disconnect between SFPD and Vallejo. Armstrong and Toschi believe everything. Mulanax is more skeptical.

Allen's presumed guilt is based on Cheney. And Cheney doesn't, not once, offer a single piece of evidence that wasn't in the media. He reveals nothing new. Only what the world knows. This is the disqualifier. Even when the cops raid Allen, even with decades of investigation, they uncover zero pieces of information resolving Zodiac mysteries. Anyone can fudge the details. Almost any White male in the Bay Area can become The Zodiac. But how to know when the genuine issue is found? Details of the suspect must enhance knowledge of the case. Without contortion, without bending facts. Mysteries must be solved.

In April 2018, the Sacramento Sheriffs arrest Joseph James DeAngelo on suspicion of being The East Area Rapist/Original Night Stalker. These seemingly disconnected crime waves—a 1970s Sacramento/Bay Area serial rapist and a 1980s Southern California serial killer—are linked by DNA evidence that is then linked to DeAngelo. When his name is announced, people research DeAngelo's life. He was law enforcement, he was arrested for petty theft in July 1979. These details lend themselves to knowledge of the crimes, enhance and explain things that have been unresolved. Like: why the East Area Rapist was good at evading the police. Like: why, in 1979, the East Area Rapist abandons Sacramento and goes to Southern California. During one attack, a victim hears the East Area Rapist sobbing about a woman named Bonnie. In 1970, DeAngelo gets engaged to a woman named Bonnie, who soon breaks the betrothal.

There is none of this with Arthur Leigh Allen. There is not a single piece of information about Allen that makes sense of unknown Zodiac.

It's possible that Cheney and Allen did have a disquieting conversation about "The Most Dangerous Game." The rest didn't happen. Allen couldn't have told Cheney about Zodiac because Zodiac did not exist.

Allen looks nothing like any description of Zodiac. He's bald by 1969, heavier than any victim statement. And he's too tall. He's 6'1". When Zodiac wears military boots at Lake Berryessa, these add about an inch and a half of height. If Allen is Zodiac at Lake Berryessa, and wears these boots, he'll be over 6'2". Bryan Hartnell says he can't judge Zodiac's height because everyone looks short. Bryan Hartnell is 6'7". He can't judge height on average people.

But 6'2" is not average. 6'2" is six inches above average.

Allen isn't Zodiac. But SFPD has Zodiac fever. They look at a desktop poem and see ZODIAC while being unsure about letters that brought them to the desktop poem. They can believe anything. And Allen smells wrong. He smells so wrong.

Armstrong and Toschi and Mulanax spend August 1971 interviewing people who know Allen. It becomes apparent that Allen is an inveterate pedophile. He was working as a teacher and got fired after complaints from parents. He got fired from a gas station because he was too interested in children. He made advances at Don Cheney's kid. Allen's brother admits that this is a serious issue.

The pedophilia is the best argument against Allen as Zodiac. Ignore the perversion itself. Think about its effects. It's gotten Allen fired from every job that he ever had, ruined any hopes of his envisioned life. It'll put him in a state mental hospital. It's kept him in his parents' basement, alienated him from friends and family. Along with the Zodiac accusation, it's the defining aspect of his life. Allen's no genius but he's not an idiot. He knows that pedophilia is a terrible life choice. And he keeps doing it. Long after it's become clear that it's destroyed everything. He can't stop.

What's the one definitive fact that we can state about Zodiac?

Zodiac stops.

He stops killing. He stops writing.

In 1971, everyone knows that pedophiles exist. But the word isn't in common circulation, isn't the default Internet taunt. And no one knows what to do about pedophiles, not yet. They tend to get fired and shunted along. An unfathomable number slip through the cracks. Criminal justice hasn't caught up. In 1974, Allen is arrested. He molests a boy in his trailer. He spends years at the Atascadero State Hospital for the Criminally Insane. While there, he writes letters that mention Zodiac. He knows his mail is monitored. He knows that these letters are sent to SFPD. He knows these letters are going to Toschi. But Allen needs the attention. No one has ever paid him any mind.

Allen is ghastly. He creeps everyone out. Allen is hurting kids. But he's also a man for whom, in the late 1960s and early 1970s, there is no social remedy. What do you when someone smells this wrong and there's no obvious redress?

You read the newspapers.

You see the magic word.

You call the police.

You say the magic word.

ZODIAC.

On 6 October 1969, this is not enough. John Lynch of Vallejo PD hasn't lived through the murder of Paul Stine or the Zodiac era.

But in August 1971?

Everyone knows about Cheri Jo Bates. And there's been articles about the forthcoming *Dirty Harry.* There's a humiliation on the horizon. Hollywood is cracking the case that the cops can't.

Zodiac fever.

†

On 26 March 1972, the *Examiner* asks: WHERE HAS ZODIAC GONE? On 28 June, the paper runs: 'ZODIAC' PET KILLER AT LARGE. It's a story about thirty murdered animals. More grasping for historical antecedent. Society doesn't have a name for serial killers, but the Bay Area has ZODIAC.

In April, a woman is attacked in Marin County's Tamalpais Valley, just over the Golden Gate Bridge from San Francisco. Most people don't think it's The Zodiac. Ken Narlow of the Napa Sheriff's Department disagrees. There's nothing until November, when a sheriff in Santa Barbara attempt to link The Zodiac with the 1963 killings of two high school students. Shot with a .22 rifle. Cheri Jo Bates redux. There are a hell of a lot more down there.

On 17 November, Darlene Ferrin's sister, Pamela Hyman, makes a phone call about another sister. This other sister has been missing for five months. Pamela thinks The Zodiac got this sister too. It's not the first time that Darlene's relatives act out of grief.

That's it. A year goes by and there's no Zodiac. The killer is gone. The letters are over. And even The Zodiac is disappearing. But that doesn't mean nothing happens.

In September 1972, Toschi and Armstrong serve a warrant on the trailer of Arthur Leigh Allen. He's not living at home anymore.

Toschi's affidavit in support of the warrant demonstrates that nothing has changed since August 1971. It's the same information in Jack Mulanax's reports. But now Toschi has been in touch with Don Cheney. Again. And Cheney remembers something new. During that almost 5-year old conversation with Allen, the pedophile said that he knew how to disguise his letters. He'd go to the library and take out books about how the cops identify handwriting. And use these as instruction manuals.

This is enough to get a warrant.

The cops raid Allen's trailer. He's not home. The cops go inside. There are sex toys and animals in cages. Allen arrives after a while. The cops search and catalog his material. They read him his rights. They get handwriting samples. Nothing matches Allen. Nothing says Zodiac.

This happens again in 1991. After Graysmith's *Zodiac*. The book doesn't use Allen's name but identifies him while getting a thousand details wrong. Vallejo PD re-opens its investigation into the murder of Darlene Ferrin, talks to more people, Vallejo PD gets more information, Vallejo PD gets a warrant, Vallejo PD raids 32 Fresno Street.

Allen's parents are dead. Allen still lives in the house. Hereditary wealth favors the degenerate. He's down in the basement. The house is full of weird shit and bombs and weapons. Vallejo gets more forensics off Allen. Later, when Allen's dead and SFPD develops a dubious DNA profile, it doesn't match Allen. Nothing will ever match Allen.

Brother, he's a creep, he's a pervert, and he's a pedophile.

But he is not Zodiac.

chapter sixteen

the return of the king

JANUARY 1974. SAN FRANCISCO. An oil crisis, punishment on countries seen to support Israel during the Yom Kippur War, is in full effect. People can't get heat, gas for their cars. In this month, 18 people will be murdered in San Francisco. In the fullness of the year, the city will clock 131. But there's more than the official record. There are always the people who matter so little in life that no one notices when they're gone. Unless the bodies are found. And there's no promise that will happen.

The violence starts small, two suicide jumpers on 1 January. Someone shoots a pellet gun at a bus at 23rd & De Haro. Days go by. A heroin addict kills the manager/co-owner of a grocery store in the Sunset. Two members of the Symbionese Liberation Army, a Maoist group that will soon kidnap heiress Patricia Hearst, are arrested after a gun battle. Thirteen uniformed members, swastikas & brownshirts, of the National Socialist White People's Party attend a meeting of the San Francisco Board of Education. A riot breaks out. A criminal with the aliases Valentine Pure O'Day and Love the Magician is picked up after raping a 14-year old girl and confesses to an unsolved 1972 heroin murder in the Haight. A former circus clown, arrested and convicted in 1967 for an assassination plot against then-Mayor Jack Shelley, is killed by a hotel clerk. The circus clown pulls a knife. The hotel clerk pulls a bigger one. The head nurse of the delivery room at the University of California San Francisco is found in the trunk of her own car. Shot through the head.

Evidence ties her death to a murder-suicide in a Hayes Valley housing project. In Daly City, less than a block from San Francisco city limits, 33-year old Pansy Leong strangles her 7-month old son and then shoots her husband and herself. Richard Emilan Newell is found, nude and butchered, in a van near 12th & Folsom. Newell's grandfather was the first person in the United States to be inoculated against rabies. Newell's great-grandfather attempted to murder Newell's great-grandmother. Someone takes a shot at the Hall of Justice with a .38. On 26 January, police arrest William P. Hanson for a series of murders and attacks that occurred throughout 1972 and 1973. Before he's captured, the crimes are attributed to The Paper Bag Killer, after Hanson's habit of using firearms hidden in shopping bags. Hanson's attorney, son of the 1952 Progressive Presidential Party candidate Vincent Hallinan, says that, in 1972, Hanson's girlfriend had been raped and this caused the Paper Bag Killer to, quote, go on a mad quest like Don Quixote. Unquote. On 27 January, the body of Gerald Cavanaugh, a transplant from Montreal, is found on Ocean Beach at the end of Ulloa Street. He was 50-years old and worked as an upholsterer. Stabbed seventeen times in the chest and the back. It's the beginning of a series of serial murders of gay men. The assailant will be called The Doodler, after his habit of picking up victims while sketching their likenesses in bars.

A tide of blood runs through the streets.

Each crime is its own tragedy, its own horror.

But none competes with what happens on 28 January.

†

It starts in Autumn 1973. There are multiple acts of attempted and successful murder. There's no real pattern, nothing to suggest any connection between the killings. Other than the race of the victims and the race of the assailants. All victims are White. Witnesses have identified the suspects as Black. One survivors is Art Agnos, a living vision of the well-meaning liberal. In a few decades, he'll be Mayor. He's shot in Potrero Hill, a neighborhood famous as the origin point of O.J. Simpson.

On the night of 28 January 1974, Muhammad Ali is fighting Joe Frazier. It's a rematch, second of an eventual three fights. Ali is the most famous member of the Nation of Islam, an American new religion founded in 1930s Detroit by W.D. Fard.

Fard was of Middle Eastern extraction by way of New Zealand, and the message that he preached went something like this: the original man is the Black man. A scientist, named Yacub, on the island of Patmos, used tricknology to create a hybrid off-spring of the original man. This is the colored man, whom we now identify as the White man. The White man is a kind of devil. Not necessarily a literal Satan, but close enough. Fard labels his religion Islam, calls its adherents Muslims, but far from Sunni belief. It's not even identifiable with the more elaborate versions of Shi'a.

The group is almost always in the news, the Black Muslim as nightmare figure ever since the advent of Malcolm X.

This time it's with reason. On 25 January 1974, the Berkeley police pull over a van. The words NATION OF ISLAM are painted on the vehicle's side. IMPORTED FISH across the rear. Things go wrong. A man in the van, Larry Ray Crosby, is shot in the back. He's 24-years old. The story gets out, yet another incident involving police harassment and the NOI.

On 28 January, while Ali is fighting Frazier, things go wronger. Across two hours and twenty minutes, five people in San Francisco are stalked and shot. The responsible individuals are identified by witnesses, of multiple races, as Black. Four victims die, one survives. They're all ages, male and female. Like the earlier incidents, the only pattern is that the victims are White. It's America's nightmare come true, the race war that everyone's been thinking about since Nat Turner's rebellion or the Los Angeles Watts Riots of 1965. The Manson Family were sent down for trying to provoke the cataclysm. And now it's here, it's happening, jack, the *Helter Skelter* prophecy is true.

The murders will be known as the Zebra Killings, supposedly after the Z radio band that the SFPD uses to coordinate its response, but everyone grasps the instant symbolism. Black on White. Or is it White on Black? When the case resolves in May 1974, it's a miscarriage of justice that never gets sorted, never gets a Netflix docuseries. The prosecution is based on a theory circulated by SFPD and San Francisco Mayor Joseph Alioto.

They go back to the founding documents of the Nation of Islam, in particular the catechism *Lost-Found Muslim Lesson No. 1 (1-14),* which says:

> 10. Why did Muhammad and any Muslim murder the devil? What is the Duty of each Muslim in regards to four devils? What Reward does a Muslim receive by presenting the four devils at one time?
>
> Answer: Because he is One Hundred Percent wicked will not keep and obey the Laws of Islam. His ways and actions are like a snake of the grafted type. So Muhammad learned that he could not reform the devils, so they had to be murdered. All Muslims will murder the devil they know he is a snake and, also, if he be allowed to live, he would sting someone else. Each Muslim is required to bring four devils. And by bringing and presenting four at one time, his Reward is a button to wear on the lapel of his coat. Also, a free transportation in the Holy City Mecca to see Brother Muhammad.

Linking this text with murder is a tradition from the Detroit days. In 1932, one of Fard's followers, Robert Harris, sacrificed James Smith on a makeshift altar. Back then, the press coverage was about a "Voodoo Cult."

In May 1974, the SFPD are contacted by Anthony Cornelius Harris (no relation to Robert) who says he's got info on the Zebra killings. There's a back and forth. Harris ends up with immunity from prosecution, granted by the Mayor himself. Harris tells a story about a group inside the Nation of Islam known as the "Death Angels." Membership requires that each new applicant kill a certain number of White devils. When the quota is met, the member earns their wings. Harris says that the Zebra killings were planned and executed by people working in and around the Black Self-Help Moving and Storage Company at 1645 Market Street. Mayor Alioto goes public with the story, suggests that the Deaths Angels are responsible for at least 71 murders in California. The SFPD rounds up people at Black Self-Help. Four stand trial and are found guilty. Harris is the star witness.

The story is told, now, through Wikipedia and paperback True Crime. A cohesive narrative, fashioned by prosecutors and police, worn smooth after tumbling through criminal justice. Black Muslims want to kill Whites. Black Muslims have a secret sect within a sect. Black Muslims kill Whites. Black Muslims are so enraged by the shooting of Crosby that, on the night of 28 January, they unleash a wave of terror. Black Muslims are captured. Black Muslims are imprisoned. The terror stops.

SFPD fashioned the cult theory before Harris's phone call. The headline of an article in the 31 January 1974 *Examiner:* FRIGHTENING EVIDENCE OF A BLACK SECT MURDER RITUAL. It's almost every detail of Harris's story. Months before he told it. One might want to assume that this was the result of good police work and the authorities guessing the cause before the evidence presented itself, but, prior to being contacted by Harris, the SFPD's major investigative work was unconstitutional traffic stops on every Black man driving a car. Stop and frisk. Widespread violation of civil rights, indiscriminate of religious belief. Then there's an even bigger problem. With the exception of the first attack, no witness describes more than two assailants. Usually one, and the described person described bears an uncanny resemblance to Anthony Cornelius Harris. Which he himself acknowledges while testifying in court. Then there's an even bigger problem. All of the evidence presented at trial was circumstantial. At best. And driven by Harris. Who was the only person that hard evidence linked to the crimes. The lone fingerprint was his. Read the source material and it's seems like he committed at least one of the killings. Very possible all. And then worked with the SFPD and received reward money, immunity, and a new identity.

Did the crimes stop because the SFPD rounded up a super criminal conspiracy of murderous voodoo Black men? Or did the crimes stop because the culprit was given cash and moved out of town?

These questions can't be answered.

Not here, not now, not in this book.

The shootings occur early enough on 28 January to make the nightly television news. Blood broadcast at 11PM on multiple stations across the Bay. And the 29 January morning edition of the *San Francisco Chronicle*.

Someone was watching.

Or reading.

†

That morning, an unknown individual goes to an unknown destination somewhere in San Mateo or Santa Clarita County, down in the South Bay below San Francisco and Oakland and Berkeley, and deposits a letter in a post box.

The letter reads like this:

> **I saw & think "The Exorcist" was the best saterical comidy that I have ever seen.**
>
> **Signed, yours truley:**
> **He plunged himself into the billowy wave**
> **and an echo arose from the suicide's grave**
> **titwillo   titwillo**
> **titwillo**
>
> **PS. If I do not see this note in your paper, I will do something nasty, which you know I'm capable of doing.**

If Zodiac sends this letter, it's in response to 28 January. The Zebra shootings look like the crimes promised back in November 1969. "When I comitt my murders, they shall look like routine robberies, killings of anger, & a few fake accidents, etc."

But something's off. This looks and reads exactly like the Zodiac letter you'd write if you're a sophisticated copycat. It sounds like the original, but it's like a cover band performing someone else's greatest hits. The notes are right but the timbre is wrong. Other than the symbols, which have no apparent connection to previous Zodiac symbology, there's nothing here. And these symbols are lame, mean nothing. It's as if someone looked at the Flying V on the Halloween Card and saw random noise. And copied what they thought was nonsense. No innovation. And then the letter quotes from *The Mikado*:

> *He sobbed and he sighed, and a gurgle he gave,*
> *Then he threw himself into the billowy wave,*
> *And an echo arose from the suicide's grave—*
> *"Oh, willow, titwillow, titwillow!"*

And *The Exorcist?*

Satanic demonic possession occultism. Just like The Zodiac.

Everything is calculated. *I'm Zodiac, I love Gilbert & Sullivan!* Zodiac's never made that calculation. Zodiac is Zodiac. Once he sends in Paul Stine's shirt, he doesn't have to convince people. He does what he wants. He doesn't make an argument for himself. He glues a pumpkin on a greeting card.

There's a passage in Mike Rodelli's 2017 book *The Hunt for Zodiac* that throws this letter's authenticity into question. Rodelli recounts a conversation with Alan Keel, once the head of the SFPD's crime lab:

> Keel went on to say that one of the forgeries was Zodiac's controversial April 24, 1978 letter that had initially been declared an actual Zodiac letter based on handwriting but which had later been deemed a forgery by many handwriting experts. The other forgery, Keel said, was "one of the (four) 1974 letters" attributed

to the killer. However, Keel stated that he "could not recall" which 1974 letter was the second forgery. I am sure I sighed audibly when he said that. That is because I was literally salivating to know which one of the four 1974 letters was not authentic, since each of these letters had been used by various researchers at different times to point a finger of guilt at someone due to the content of a given letter. Which one was a phony!?

According to the chart of DNA testing results compiled by SFPD's lab in ca. 2000, the *only one* of the 1974 letters that had been tested by Keel up to that time for DNA was the January *Exorcist* letter.

On 31 January, the *Chronicle* publishes an article about this letter from an old friend. The Zodiac's back. But the timing is bad.

No one knows it, but The Zodiac's only got about four days.

The Bay Area's biggest crime story, ever, is about to break.

†

On 4 February, the Symbionese Liberation Army kidnaps Patty Hearst. Patty's a good girl, she's 19-years old, she's from a famous family, she's engaged to a man with the unfortunate name of Steve Weed, she's a student at UC Berkeley. Her grandfather was a Twentieth Century press baron, inspiration for Orson Welles's *Citizen Kane,* her great-grandfather was a United States Senator who made his fortune by ripping precious metals out of the Earth, and her daddy is the editor of the *San Francisco Examiner.* The SLA are White Maoists with mega motor spirit. They connect with an African-American prison escapee named Donald DeFreeze. The Maoists decide DeFreeze must be their leader. True revolution can only come when they submit to the right-on leadership of a Black man. They're from what might be called the Rhetorical Left, so it doesn't matter which Black man. Any Black man will do. All brothers are righteous when you can't tell them apart. DeFreeze renames himself, calls himself Cinque, and accepts the vocation. The SLA go on a Maoist reign of asynchronous terror. They emerge into public knowledge when they make a strike against The Establishment. They assassinate Oakland's first African-American school superintendent. The SLA use cyanide laced bullets to murder this fascist pig who's trying to help Black kids get an education. The SLA issue a series of tedious communiqués. Dispatches from their unquiet war. Zodiac style. And then, in February, they kidnap Patty. They break into her Berkeley apartment. They smash Steve Weed over the head. They steal Patty. She's such a good pretty girl. And now she's in the arms of those animals. To have this happen to her. In his book *The Voices of Guns,* Paul Avery notes a difference between Leninist-Marxists and Maoists. Leninist-Marxists believe in expulsion, in the death sentence, in the gulag. Maoists believe in re-education. The SLA are Maoists. The SLA re-educates Patty. She learns that she's an insect who preys upon the lifeblood of the people. Patty starts releasing audio communiqués. She denounces her family, her privilege, everything that made Patty into Patty. She's not Patty anymore. Now she's Tania, homage to the *nom de guerre* of an Argentinian-born East German revolutionary who fought with Che Guevara. Patty's on board with urban violence. The SLA release a photo of Patty dressed as a revolutionary, gun in her hand. The photo is way sexy. Patty's got the appeal of a rich girl who's never eaten canned food and whose parents can afford cosmetic enhancement. Her legs are spread and her delicate unlabored fingers wrap around the cold steel of a sawed off. She's in Che drag. Patty's on the cover of *Newsweek.* Patty's daddy's paper is reporting on Patty. Patty's a bad girl. Patty's sex appeal juices Berkeley revolutionaries. The Berkeley revolutionaries turn the photo into a poster. The poster says TANIA. And then Patty's in a bank, Patty's helping the SLA rob the bank. Patty's screaming *UP AGAINST THE WALL, MOTHERFUCKER!* On the way out, Patty's comrades are committing murder. And Patty's there, she's watching death, gun in her hand. The story continues until September 1975. Ends in the most predictable way. More innocents die. Most of the SLA are killed. But not Patty. Patty's arrested. Patty's family hires F. Lee Bailey. The attorney requested by The Zodiac for Jim Dunbar's morning show. Bailey blows it. He delivers an abysmal performance. Somewhere in San Francisco, Melvin Belli is weeping. Patty gets a sentence of thirty-five years. Patty goes to jail. President Jimmy Earl Carter commutes Patty's sentence. Patty gets released. Patty becomes a Hollywood star. Patty's on the cover of *People*. Patty doesn't have a gun in her hand. Now she's holding a baby. Another heir to the Hearst fortune. Patty's starring in movies. Patty visits Televisionland. On his last day in office, 20 January 2001, President William Jefferson Clinton pardons Patty. Her record's cleansed, the conviction never happened.

†

Another letter comes into the *Chronicle*. Postmarked 3 February 1974, a day before Patty Hearst is kidnapped. Postal delays keep it from arriving until 14 February 1974. It makes no contemporary news, doesn't hit the papers, but the SFPD sends it to the FBI.

The letter reads like this:

Dear Mr. Editor,

Did you know that the initials SLA[indecipherable character, possibly a Y, possibly a colon] (Symbionese Liberation Army) spell "sla," an old Norse word meaning "kill."

a friend

An FBI report of 28 February 1974 states that this letter is postmarked with a 913 zipcode. The northwest of Los Angeles County. In years to come, when the heat is on, the SLA retreat to Los Angeles. The date too must be considered. Had this letter been delivered properly, it would have arrived at the *Chronicle* on the day, or the day after, of Patty Heart's kidnapping.

This one can safely be dismissed. But it gives us information. The *Chronicle*'s mailroom bad boys are hunting The Zodiac.

On 10 July 1974, the *Chronicle* publishes an article by Duffy Jennings. Page 2. ZODIAC'S LETTERS TO THE EDITORS. Two correspondences have arrived. One was postmarked 8 May 1974 but did not arrive until 4 June. It's a pre-paid postcard, stamp printed on the stock. Just like a PEEK THROUGH THE PINES. The other letter is postmarked 8 July, sent from Marin County, arrives 9 July.

The 8 July letter looks like this:

Editor—
Put Marco back in the ,hell-hole from whence it came — he has a serious psychological disorder— always needs to feel superior. I suggest you refer him to a shrink. Meanwhile, cancel the Count Marco column. Since the Count can write anonymously, so can I————
the Red Phantom
(red with rage)

Count Marco is the tradename of advice columnist Marc H. Spinelli. He writes in the voice of a 1950s male chauvinist. Much of this persona is a put-on, the ethics of professional wrestling disguised as quasi-journalism. Marco is loathed, people buy the paper to hate-read his column. And as the women's liberation movement takes off, the schtick is tired.

On 8 July, the day that this letter is mailed, the *Chronicle* runs a Marco column about "the male menopause." Why do men's sex drives decline as they age? Marco's conclusion, directed at a female readership, is this: "If you're not getting any sex from him, it's not because he's too old or too tired, but because you've lost your touch—you've lost your sex appeal."

If Zodiac is the Red Phantom, he's changed his handwriting and become a feminist.

†

The 8 May 1974 postcard looks like this:

> Sirs— I would like to express ~~an~~ my ~~constrant~~ consternation concerning your poor taste & lack of sympathy for the public, as evidenced by your running of the ads for the movie "Badlands", featuring the blurb - "In 1959 most people were killing time. Kit & Holly were killing people." In light of recent events, this kind of murder-glorification can only be deplorable at best (not that glorification of violence was ever justifiable) why don't you show some concern for public sensibilities & cut the ad?
>
> A citizen

(rear)

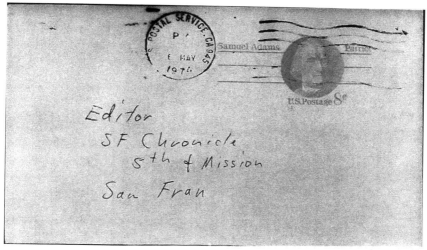

(front)

The text reads:

> Sirs—I would like to expression my consternt consternation concerning your poor taste & lack of sympathy for the public, as evidenced by your running of the ads for the movie "Badlands," featuring the blurb—"In 1959 most people were killing time. Kit & Holly were killing people." In light of recent events, this kind of murder-glorification can only be deplorable at best (not that glorification of violence was <u>ever</u> justifiable) why don't you show some concern for public sensibilities & cut the ad?
>
> A citizen

The card arrives. The press and the cops think ZODIAC. As the decades go by, researchers come to believe that the mailing is not attributable to the killer. It's wrong to call it a hoax—it never uses the magic word, never pretends to be part of the dialogue.

More than any other 1974 mailing, this one feels like Zodiac. The tone is right, the jerky insincerity, a knowingness that knows that everyone knows that this isn't what the writer believes, someone telegraphing that this is not their real self, that they've adopted the language of a Victorian schoolmarm on a Temperance crusade.

Then there's Terrence Malick's debut film *Badlands*. The film fictionalizes the story of Charles Starkweather and Caril Ann Fugate. In 1958, the two embark upon on a nine day rampage. They murder ten people. Including Fugate's father. Malick picks up the squalid barebones and fashions an existential meditation on youth and death and America. Starkweather and Fugate announce the arrival of the spree killer, of the murderer who kills multiple people in a short period of time. In 1958 and 1974, there is no categorical classification. But it's coming.

An advertisement for *Badlands* first appears in the *Chronicle* on 28 April and continues across the next two weeks. As the days go on, the advertisement grows progressively smaller. In the beginning, full-size, 28 April, this is what appears:

If the card is from Zodiac, then might it not fit the previous pattern? Might there not be mention of The Zodiac in the *Chronicle*?

It's there. Page 38 of the 7 May edition. The day before the card is mailed. A letter to the editor from Jay A. Miller, executive director of the American Civil Liberties Union in San Francisco. Like any good editorial correspondent, Miller is mad as hell. He's pissed about how the police and city handled the Zebra case, the stop-and-frisk of every Black man with the misfortune to turn down the wrong street. In the days leading up to 7 May, Mayor Joseph Alioto announces that Zebra is solved, that they've got the perpetrators. The solution, such as it is, does not derive from stop-and-frisk. An informant called the cops. The widespread violation of civil rights was for nothing. All it did was make life harder for Black people.

Alioto defends the tactic by suggesting it was not racially motivated, that similar methods were employed in previous cases. Including the Zodiac Killer. In Miller's final paragraph, he writes: "You dismiss the charge of racism. A check of your own files would demonstrate that widespread dragnets such as Operation Zebra were not conducted for either the Zodiac killer or the Nob Hill rapist, both cases in which the alleged suspect was white..."

For what it's worth, the FBI performs handwriting analysis on the 1974 correspondences. They think the 29 January letter is possibly genuine, 3 February is not, the Count Marco letter is unlikely, and that the 8 May card shares multiple consistencies with previous Zodiac correspondences.

This short note about murder-glorification is written on a pre-paid postcard. Just like PEEK THROUGH THE PINES. The mailing of 22 March 1971. It might mean that one, too, is genuine. But there's a difference. When the 1971 card is sent, it's ages old, invalid postage, can't get to the *Chronicle* without special intervention.

On 2 March 1974, the postal service raises its rates. Again.

8¢ for a postcard, 10¢ for a letter. This pre-paid card, with its 8¢ stamp of SAMUEL ADAMS PATRIOT, is a recent purchase. Zodiac never fucks up delivery. Even if this mailing falls victim to recent slowdowns brought on by a budget crunch and the introduction of automatic machine sorting. Even if it takes a month to arrive. It gets there in the end.

This card is sent after news tying The Zodiac to Zebra. The same story that appears to have motivated the 29 January correspondence. But there's that question of DNA. Which may never be answered.

One thing's certain. The 8 May card does not get tested for DNA. It can't. Potential sources are stamps and envelope seals. And this one has neither.

But it does have a postmark.

US POSTAL SERVICE, CA 945 PM 8 MAY 1974.

A 945XX zipcode. An exact location is not specified.

945XX covers Berkeley and Oakland.

But also the North Bay.

Vallejo.

†

A little postcard, taken as genuine in the moment and since dismissed. But it fits a pattern, it's got the right tone, it innovates the form, and the FBI thinks it's consistent.

It's the real deal.

This is the last Zodiac correspondence. For as long as there is the postal mail, there will be letters from The Zodiac. But the genuine issue original is retired. He isn't dead, no suicide, didn't go prison, not in jail, not in a mental hospital, hasn't moved. Zodiac is where he always been. In the Bay Area. He's taken off the hood. And put away the tradename. Dropped the crosshairs. He's stopped pretending that he can't spell. He does not write this card with a blue felt-tip pen. But he's out there. Doing what he's always done. Reading newspapers. Writing letters. There were so many predictions and diagnoses. Zodiac wants to be caught! Zodiac can't stop! Zodiac is a gibbering psychotic! Zodiac's sexual dysfunction will bring him to heel! Nonsense offered by hacks, people with the same desire as Zodiac, people hoping to see their names in print. The killer did the murders, Zodiac wrote the letters, Zodiac stopped writing. Zodiac got away. Zodiac won.

The killer might have a body count in the hundreds. Anything is possible. But there's a difference between the killer and Zodiac. The killings happen on California dirt. Zodiac happens in the mail and in the papers. Zodiac is gone. He's a penitent pilgrim, thrown his weapons to the sea. Zodiac is done. Zodiac is gone. Zodiac has no place in a world with Zebra and the SLA. Now he is a citizen. One last joke. Not that glorification of violence was <u>ever</u> justifiable. He's returned to the nameless and anonymous masses of American flesh. Back in the hell-hole from whence it came. A citizen. The first letters lacked the tradename. As does the last. The beginning is the end.

Citizen.

Ghost.

Gone.

chapter seventeen

a to z

IN 1975, THE ZODIAC re-emerges. Sonoma County Sheriff Don Striepeke holds a press conference where he announces a new idea. The thought emerges with the help of a computer. There's been a string of unsolved murders in Santa Rosa County. Where Arthur Leigh Allen had his trailer. The victims are female, young. Striepeke and his computer tie the killings to The Zodiac and other young women murdered in Seattle, in Utah, in Colorado. Striepeke believes these are witchcraft crimes, black magic, that The Zodiac kills to form an occult Z on the map of America. But when Striepeke draws his pattern on a map, it's not a Z. It's an N.

It looks like this:

Striepeke isn't an idiot. And he exists in a context. When Mayor Alioto announces that Zebra is solved, he advances a theory. The Zebra murders are a small part of a pattern. The Death Angels are more than a local group. They're nationwide. They're responsible for countless attacks. Alioto circulates a list of 73 crimes that he attributes to the group. It's madness, untrue, but here it is, Mayor of the big city, and he's saying, *this inexplicable rise in death? It's not that California has motor spirit. There's a better answer.*

Striepeke's so close. But gets distracted by the magic word. He's got fever. He looks at the map and sees ZODIAC. N can be Z. All it takes is a change in perspective. Turn your head 90°. You'll see it.

Striepeke doesn't know it, not yet, but he and his computer are right. He's found a murderer. But it's not The Zodiac. Man and machine have stumbled across the wake of Theodore "Ted" Bundy. Who will most define the idea of the serial killer.

Ted's one of those guys, man, he's a dysfunctional loser with a bad child-hood. And he kills a certain type. Young White women with hair parted in the middle. When he's caught, he's so average, so boring, that no one can reconcile the non-entity with its crimes. Society invents a new story. Ted's a genius, Ted's really handsome, Ted's charming. *He's not what you'd expect!* But Ted's none of these things. He's not hideous. But Ted's nothing special. He's not a genius. He's a reasonably well-educated White male adult who speaks with a dialect shorn of any obvious lower economic markers. And he's definitively not charming. Extant footage shows a man with no idea how to talk to people, who's always telling jokes that never land. If you're a sociopathic genius, and you want to manipulate others, humor is the first thing that you figure out. Being funny isn't a perfect substitute for the so-cial lubricant of natural beauty. But it's the next best thing. Ted's got none of it. Neither the brains nor the beauty nor the humor. Ted Bundy is the dog's breakfast of heterosexuality, representative of the equation's inherent imbalance. For every thousand remarkable women, the individuals who are smart or funny or beautiful or capable of amazing things or all combined, there's about one reasonably decent guy. Before he's revealed as a serial killer, that's how people see Ted. He's that decent guy. Ted's the default choice. He's the compromise. He might be mediocre but he represents an unspoken promise. He might not be on your level but he'll be okay enough and won't brutalize your existence with his upper body strength and pathologized resentments. In the day's parlance, he seems like a good provider. But Ted doesn't provide. And Ted isn't decent. He's remarkable in the least remarkable way. Ted's not the dog's breakfast. Ted's two eggs and bacon spiked with a lethal dose of arsenic. He's a shitty little guy who likes to kill, who cuts off women's heads and has sex with the result. The cognitive dissonance of the good provider being a mass murder is so profound, and threatens to expose so many uncomfortable truths about heterosexuality, that the press transforms Ted into a beautiful stunning genius.

Striepeke announces the theory in Spring 1975. Utah cops arrest Ted in August. He's driving with tools of the trade. Crow bar, ski mask, ice pick, rope, handcuffs, flashlight.

In November, there's a meeting in Aspen, Colorado. Over thirty cops attend. Each comes from a jurisdiction in the Western United States. Each cop has a back catalog of unsolved murders. Victims who meet the pattern.

Striepeke's there.

It's plausible that Ted did some Santa Rosa murders. Not all. Some. The official Bundy body county starts in Seattle 1974. While awaiting execution in 1989, Ted indicates that he killed earlier than anyone imagined. He confesses to a homicide in California. Ted doesn't say where it happened. Ted probably doesn't know the victim's name. Those were the bad days before Mr. Bundy got organized. Before 1974.

In 1992, the FBI releases a document.

Ted Bundy Multiagency Investigative Team Report. It contains a timeline of Bundy's movements, works off credit card receipts. There are glaring holes, long stretches during which Ted is missing.

In the Summer of 1967, Ted's in the Bay Area. He's attending classes at Stanford University. In January 1968, Ted's in San Francisco. In May 1969, Ted's back in San Francisco, crashing with friends. On 8 August 1970, Ted's hitchhiking on the 101 in Marin County. The cops give Ted a ticket. Ted gives the cops a Seattle address.

In early 1972, the first three Santa Rosa victims are abducted and killed. Where's Ted? No one knows. November 1972. The fourth girl goes missing. Where's Ted? No one knows.

It was there. Right before Striepeke, maybe in his own backyard. He thought it was Z on a map. It wasn't. But Striepeke's not an idiot. Striepeke did something that no one else did. He saw the pattern. But couldn't rid himself of the word. Or cure the fever. He saw the pattern and thought ZODIAC. When he should have been thinking TED.

Details of the November 1975 meeting are lost, only echo in newswire articles and Ann Rule's *The Stranger Beside Me.* But it's this place when Bundy is identified as the thing for which there is no name. A fear is born.

Given Striepeke's attendance, we have to imagine that someone asks the one question that accounts.

Can it be that Ted is The Zodiac Killer?

†

On 24 April 1978, an unknown man goes to an unknown destination and deposits a letter. It's addressed to the *San Francisco Chronicle.*

It reads like this:

Dear Editor

This is the Zodiac speaking I am back with you. Tell herb caen I am here, I have always been here. That city pig toschi is good but I am ~~bu~~ smarter and better he will get tired then leave me alone. I am waiting for a good movie about me. who will play me. I am now in control of all things.

yours truly:

⊕ - guess

SFPD - O

It's a forgery. In the shock of the moment, in the excitement, everyone treats the letter with credulity. An old friend has come to visit. The cops, the press, Dave Toschi. Everyone is on board.

The handwriting doesn't look the same, but maybe Zodiac's aged, maybe he's changed his style. There's another telltale difference. Not a single word is misspelled. And the letter is about Herb Caen and Dave Toschi and movies. The genuine issue original had one subject and one subject only. Citizen card excluded. His subject was himself. Every authenticated letter, even when it mentions other people, is about Zodiac. The people of the Bay Area had better wear my buttons. Help me Melvin I am sick.

A successful forger never recreates the real thing, never duplicates a Jackson Pollock. They're not painting a copy, they're painting the moment's perception of the artist. People can't see a thing for what it is, people see with the eyes of their era. It's why, twenty years after acceptance as genuine, successful forgeries always look fake. The moment ends, perceptions shift. A new idea of Pollock takes hold. Looking back, everyone can see that the forgery does not match the new perception.

It's been years since the genuine issue original. Graysmith's book hasn't been released. There's no Internet. People only have the memory of the thing and their moment's perception.

And that perception is shaped by events on the other side of America.

Something happens in 1976 and 1977. Out in New York City. There's a Zodiac cover artist named Son of Sam. A paperback reaction to the Bay Area crimes. Son of Sam kills couples with a gun. Son of Sam writes letters to the police and the press. He makes obvious spelling errors and taunts the press and pigs. When he's caught, police find an unsent letter, signed with Son of Sam's own symbol, dim echo of Zodiac's crosshairs. The story is huge. International news. A crazed manic in New York City. Center of the American imagination. Blood, death, letters.

When the 1978 forgery arrives, it more than an echo of 1969/1970. It's an echo of Son of Sam. Who infects memories of The Zodiac.

Whoever forges the letter has access to the originals. Either newspaper reproductions or the genuine articles from 1969-1970 and 1974. The letter starts with the classic opening: "This is the Zodiac speaking." But "yours truly," that's a dim echo of Jack the Ripper and London 1888 and only appears in one other Zodiac letter. The 29 January 1974 mailing. If Mike Rodelli's DNA story is accurate, these words support the thesis that the 1974 letter is another forgery, that these two letters have the same author.

Whomever he or she may be, whoever wrote this 1978 letter, they're not Zodiac. That much is certain.

†

The Zodiac is back. Dave Toschi is on top. Tips flood in. More cops are assigned to The Zodiac.

And then it goes sideways.

In 1974, the writer Armistead Maupin begins serializing a soap opera in Marin County's *Pacific Sun,* an alternative weekly. *Tales of the City.* His stories are about a San Francisco apartment building's residents. A significant number of the characters are homosexuals. In May 1976, *Tales* moves to the *Chronicle.* Maupin's from the Deep South, got the Confederacy in his blood. Now he's in San Francisco. The mint julep charm scores the bodies of other men, serves as fodder for the writing. *Tales* will explode, become books, decades of television adaptations.

In 1976, before any of this happens, in his first year at the *Chronicle,* Maupin introduces a storyline excised from the collected editions. There's a new killer in town. He's called the Tinkerbell Killer because he spreads glitter on the corpses. Tinkerbell is chased by a cop named Henry Tandy.

Maupin doesn't know word one about crime or law enforcement. To give Tinkerbell verisimilitude, he needs to talk to a real cop. Maupin asks colleagues at the *Chronicle.* A message comes back. Speak with Toschi. Maupin gets in touch. Toschi is happy to help. Other than his professional hunt for The Zodiac, this is Toschi's most defining aspect. He loves the press. Other cops speak with reporters when necessary, when it'll break a case. But say as little as possible. Toschi's a maximalist. He can't stop talking. He's got that big brash San Francisco personality. He says whatever gives the best copy. He charms Maupin.

Maupin includes Toschi in *Tales.* A fictive Toschi gives Tandy advice. Tells him how to conduct an investigation into this new kind of killer. Bitches about The Zodiac. If it seems like a terrible idea to have a real life cop appear in fan fiction published by a newspaper that reports on that cop's real life activities, well, at the time, some people thought the same thing. But the SFPD let it happen anyway.

A week after Toschi's first *Tales* appearance, Maupin receives fan mail. They're not about Maupin or *Tales*. They're about Toschi. One of these letters is sent by four students at San Francisco State University. Sally, Mary, Pam, Sue. They sign the letter: "the gals from 'State.'" The gals think the world of Toschi. He's *soooooooooo* dreamy. The other letters say the same thing. *Isn't Toschi the best? Don't you think he should be in more installments?*

Maupin doesn't pay much mind. Not at first. But the letters keep coming and he realizes that they're all on same paper stock and composed on the same typewriter. Maupin gets it. Toschi is writing his own fan mail. It's gross and embarrassing. Not for the ego that it displays. Maupin knows ego better than anyone. But it's so crude. And so amateur.

Maupin files the letters in his archives, writes Toschi out of the column. In the denouement of the Tandy/Tinkerbell saga, Toschi discovers that Tandy is Tinkerbell. To really make it in this city, says Tandy, you've got to generate your own press. Maupin intends this as a message to Toschi.

In April 1978, Maupin is readying the first collected volume of *Tales*. His editor asks him to remove Tinkerbell. It's too ridiculous. Which speaks volumes. People have said many things about Maupin. No one's ever described him an author of the plausible.

The new Zodiac letter arrives. That city pig toschi is good but I am better. The *Chronicle* prints the story. Maupin's having coffee with a friend named Daniel. The friend reads Maupin the letter. It's one of those moments when clocks seem to stop ticking.

Maupin *knows*. As sure as Toschi *knows* that Arthur Leigh Allen is Zodiac. This sounds like Toschi's fan mail. Maupin remembers that in one of their conversations, Toschi said the same thing as the Zodiac letter. I am waiting for a good movie about me. I'm the inspiration for *Bullit*. I'm *Dirty Harry*.

Maupin and his publicist contact someone in the upper echelons of the SFPD. Maupin will only ever refer to this individual as "Blue."

Maupin tells Blue his story. He gives Blue copies of the fan mails. Blue says that he's not surprised. Blue says that Toschi can get anything into the newspapers. But isn't good for much else. It implies a great deal of intradepartmental resentment. Of Toschi and his publicity.

There's a month of silence. Maupin reaches out again, talks with Blue. The SFPD knows that Toschi wrote the fan letters, can't confirm that Toschi wrote the Zodiac letter. There's a second meeting. This time with Toschi's direct supervisor. He confirms that there's an official investigation, that there are "definitive discrepancies" in the Exorcist letter of 1974, that the police only authenticated the 1978 letter because they knew the *Chronicle* would print it, that no one was suspicious of Toschi prior to Maupin, that handwriting analysts in Sacramento are attempting to discern if Toschi wrote earlier Zodiac letters. Maupin has contracted to write an article for *New West* magazine. About the fan mail. About Dave Toschi. The SFPD brass knows the story is coming.

A few days later, the SFPD goes public. They're trying to scoop Maupin. Toschi is removed from the Zodiac investigation, Toschi is transferred from Homicide to Robbery, to the pawn shop detail. Toschi admits writing the fan mail. But Toschi did not write the Zodiac letter. Which the SFPD says is a forgery. But also says that Toschi didn't write it.

Maupin holds his own press conference. He faces a hostile press. He's just removed their best source in the SFPD. There are accusations that this is publicity for the forthcoming book. That Maupin is as big a press hound as Zodiac or Toschi or Melvin Belli.

The story is national news. The SFPD remains firm on one thing. Toschi did not write the Zodiac letter of 1978. Or the Exorcist letter of 1974. Despite rumors, despite the background chatter, despite a later FBI report that states Toschi's definitive authorship of both.

Toschi continues working for the SFPD, but it's the end of the Toschi who emerged after Paul Stine. Blue is punished. Toschi's supervisor is punished. They kept the Chief of Police in the dark. And the Chief is pissed.

Toschi has several high profile defenders. Including Dianne Feinstein. She's not yet Mayor, not yet a United States Senator. She sits on the city's Board of Supervisors. She's the President. These twelve people are the most powerful officials in the city, have more juice than the mayor. It's a quirk of local governance. Feinstein is the most powerful of the twelve.

She thinks Toschi has been, quote, crucified, unquote.

Feinstein knows Toschi through The Zodiac. There's a Tenderloin drunk called Old Tom. The drunk writes Zodiac letters. He's been at it since forever. Old Tom has another nickname. Old Tom is called The Valiant Crusader. In August 1976, The Valiant Crusader sends Feinstein a letter from The Zodiac. "Do you miss me? Was busy doing some nefarious dastardly work, for which I am well suited."

Everyone hits the wall. Is The Zodiac coming for Feinstein? Toschi soothes the nerves. *Don't worry, this isn't the real deal, he's just an old Tenderloin drunk.* He's harmless. By sight alone, Toschi can differentiate Old Tom's letters from those of the genuine issue original. Toschi earns a future defender.

The supervisors control the city. But no one controls the cops. There's no redemption narrative. Jesus doesn't come back from death. Toschi suffers in Hell. He'll have to wait for the publication of Graysmith's *Zodiac.* The book is the result of a not-so-secret collaboration between its author and the cop. Graysmith writes of Toschi in glowing terms. Describes him as the inspiration for *Bullit,* as Supercop. It's said that the two men talk every day. Toschi gives Graysmith the lowdown on Arthur Leigh Allen. Graysmith hears and sees. He *knows.* Arthur Leigh Allen is Zodiac. The book is shaped towards this conclusion. Allen is still alive, appears under a false name. *Zodiac* is as much about Allen as The Zodiac. They're one in the same. Toschi said it.

Publication is eight-and-a-half years in the future. Now Toschi is just another grunt chasing bad checks and hotel robberies.

He had it, he held it in his hands, thought that it was his forever, and then it disappeared in a flash. Toschi believed that people liked Toschi for being Toschi, that they dug the big brash San Francisco personality and the underarm holster that inspired Steve McQueen. But he was wrong. No one cared about Toschi. They cared about what Toschi gave them. Information that became newspaper copy. They cared about The Zodiac. And Toschi was Mr. Zodiac. But that's gone. And there's nothing left.

†

Toschi dies in 2018. Gone, gone, gone. There's no reason to besmirch the dead. He was like anyone else on this planet. He did his best in a situation over which he had no control. Question the actions, not the judgment. Toschi wasn't an inhuman machine that produced justice, he wasn't Robocop. He was a man who, repeatedly, came up against things that no person should see. One time is enough to distort the human psyche. But a hundred motor spirit murders? Toschi held Ann Jiminez's hair in his own hands.

Toschi was better than average. There's no available record of him being accused of brutality or corruption. He landed a case in October 1969. Another dead cabbie. Bog standard. It turned into something else. With a letter and a piece of cloth. It gave him the one thing that he never expected.

Fame.

It's like any other drug. Some people snort it up and never want another dose. Some people can handle the casual on/off. And then some people get the tiniest taste and never recover. They're never the same. They need it. They crave it. They will do anything to keep the high. There's never enough. There's always one more fix. There's no end goal. Its pursuit structures life, gives meaning to the pointlessness of daily existence. Like any other job.

In 1978, the story plays out like this: Maupin puts Toschi in *Tales*, letters arrive from Toschi about Toschi, written under fake names. Maupin worries about the 1978 Zodiac correspondence. Maupin ends Toschi. Toschi denies writing the Zodiac letter, says that all he did was write letters about himself. An immature stupid thing. But he did not compromise an investigation. The two are different, separate. He'd never jeopardize police work. The SFPD says Toschi wrote the fan letters. Says the Zodiac 1978 letter is fake. But not faked by Toschi. This is the official narrative, the one that's easiest for a police department that screwed up the Zodiac investigation at its beginning. And may have screwed it up again.

What Toschi says is this: I was so impressed by seeing myself in *Tales* that I wrote fan mail about myself. It was a stupid thing to do. Toschi never mentions writing letters to anyone else, makes it sound like this was a one time thing, as if he were overwhelmed by the power of fiction.

Maupin contradicts this before the news breaks. Herb Caen, the world famous gossip, is mentioned in the forgery. Maupin calls Caen's assistant Carol Vernier and asks, have you guys ever gotten mail about Dave Toschi? Carol says, yes, whenever Herb writes about Toschi. We get funny letters.

In the reporting of the moment, no one asks Herb Caen about letters from Toschi. But it's something that journalists know. In the 14 July 1978 *Chronicle*, this appears: "A number of local reporters have received notes from [Toschi], praising their work, most usually when they mention Dave Toschi. Sometimes he made up names. Sometimes he signed them 'Anon.' Others were signed 'Deputy Dave.'"

Something happens in 1975. Bill Armstrong wants out of homicide. He's been Toschi's co-pilot since 1968. The split causes rumors.

The 17 September 1975 *Examiner* prints a gossip item. It says that the rumors aren't true, that Armstrong and Toschi remain friends, that Armstrong switched partners because he lives near another detective. Armstrong and the other detective decided to carpool. Beyond the Hall of Justice, no one cares. No one's asking for this question to be answered. If the gossip item is intended to kill the rumors, it has the opposite effect. Suspicion wafts where there was none.

Without Armstrong, Toschi appears in the press with much greater frequency. On 3 October 1975, the *Examiner* publishes a story about Toschi helping the child of an overdosed woman. On 24 October, the paper prints mail from a reader named Mrs. G. Richel. She, supposedly, lives in San Francisco. She read the 3 October article. She writes: "I was pleased too by the questioning conducted by Inspector David Toschi. The gentleness he displayed shows we still have some decent policemen in San Francisco."

Each year, R.L. Polk & Company publishes a weapon-sized directory that lists almost every citizen in the city of San Francisco. It includes names and addresses. For 1975, 1976, and 1977, Polk's offers no evidence of Mrs. G. Richel. Searching through online genealogical databases, there is no evidence that she lived.

On 24 December 1975, the *Examiner* runs JUST A NOTE TO LET COP KNOW. It's about how Dave Toschi and his new partner Frank McCoy [2] received a letter. Its author is a 17-year old girl named Angel Marks. Toschi and McCoy had to find Angel and her mother in a downtown hotel. This happened, quote, last October, unquote. Angel's older sister, Danni Price,

---

2   Articles of the period sometimes identify Toschi's partner as Frank McCoy, other times as Frank Falzon. This happens, on and off, across years and with no discernible pattern. Order can not be brought to this.

was arrested in Kentucky along with Jim Stewart of Portland, Oregon. They were accused of killing an Iranian general's son. Angel's letter is a follow-up. Danni has been exonerated, Jim Stewart has confessed to everything. Angel thanks the two cops. She wants to give them a sense of pride and accomplishment and say how much respect she has for people like Toschi and McCoy.

There is no media record of an Iranian general's son being killed. In either 1974 or 1975. Not just in Kentucky. Anywhere in America. There is no evidence of an Angel Marks with a sister named Danni. Portland has so many Jim Stewarts that it's impossible to isolate a single individual.

Last October. Quote, unquote.

Is this October 1975 or October 1974?

If it's 1974, then the story can't be true. McCoy was not yet Toschi's partner. Angel should be writing to Dave Toschi and Bill Armstrong.

On 7 January 1976, the *Examiner* publishes a letter. Mrs. John Walsh says that she's impressed by the story of Toschi and McCoy and Angel. She concludes with the following line: "Obviously, both detectives displayed tact, courtesy and professionalism in their work." There are so many men with the name John Walsh that the Mrs. can not be traced.

On 1 February 1976, the *Examiner* runs an article by its columnist, Guy Wright. It's about a Vietnamese immigrant assisting the police. The immigrant helps Dave Toschi and Frank McCoy. The two cops nominate the young man for a Citizen's Award. Even though he's not a citizen.

On 23 February 1976, Wright runs reader responses to the column. One is from a Mr. William Chalker. He commends both Toschi and McCoy for doing a fine bit of community relations service for their department. Another letter is from Mrs. J Whipple, who writes that she is particularly impressed by Dave Toschi's recognition of the young Vietnamese immigrant.

In the 1975 and 1976 Polk's directories, there is no evidence that Mrs. Whipple ever existed. She isn't present in any genealogical databases. In the 1975 and 1976 Polk's, there is an entry for "W. Chalker." No first name is specified. Genealogical databases do not tie any William Chalker to the address of W. Chalker.

On 27 February 1976, Wright publishes a column about a man named Lon Nansell. He was released from a psychiatric hospital in Nebraska. Declared sane by psychiatrists. Nansell comes to San Francisco and kills

Steven McCurn, stabbing and beating the 23-year old man with a garden stake. Nansell tries to drive the stake through McCurn's heart. He says: "I am Jesus Christ. He is Satan." He might as well have said: *I have motor spirit.* Toschi calls Nansell's father, who's a minister in Nebraska. The father says that he can't understand why his sick son was made out-patient.

The murder did happen.

On 15 March 1976, Wright runs responses to his 27 February column. THE COP AND THE JESUS CHRIST KILLER. The correspondents are Tom Dougherty, Mrs. Murial Sanchez, and Fred Woebber. Dougherty thinks that Toschi is the only person who knows how to do his job. Mrs. Sanchez can't believe that Toschi hasn't said to hell with it. After all, he faces the stupidity of the liberal establishment. Fred Woebber has the same thought, has no how idea how Toschi can deal with murderers, let alone lawyers and psychiatrists.

Polk's directories for 1975 and 1976 reveal no trace of either Dougherty or Woebber. On the basis of her last name and marital status, Mrs. Sanchez can not be traced in the directory. Genealogical searches reveal no one of this name living in San Francisco or its surrounding counties.

On 13 August 1977, the *Examiner* runs THE CITY'S SUPER COP.

Puff piece, the Toschi myth made manifest.

On 21 August 1977, the *Examiner* publishes a response. William Chalker has written again. He compliments the article, thinks Starr really captured the thoughts and feelings of the well-known detective. He hopes Toschi stays with the SFPD for many years to come. In 1977, there is even less evidence for Chalker's existence than in 1976.

On 6 November 1977, *Examiner* columnist Dwight Chapin asks his readers to write in and tell him whom they love in public life. Chapin offers his own eleven suggestions. One is O.J. Simpson. On 20 November, Chapin publishes the results of his reader poll. When he's done with the top ten, he adds the following note: "The second week of my poll was like the first—filled with interesting surprises. For example—Dave Toschi, San Francisco Homicide Inspector, got several impassioned votes."

†

On 25 June 1976, the *Examiner* runs an article about how Dave Toschi has a secret pal. She's a high school student at Presentation High School. It's all girls, Catholic. As a class exercise, this girl, named Janice, wrote a letter to someone whom she admires. None other than Dave Toschi. Janice imagines that Toschi sees all kinds of horrible things but wants him to know that he's a very special policeman.

Janice exists. She's in Presentation's yearbooks.

The article neglects to mention that Janice lives across the street from Dave Toschi.

†

The case against Toschi's authorship of the 1978 letter rests on the idea that he wouldn't screw up an investigation. Not this investigation. Above all else. Especially not this one. He might write to Maupin, yes, but why would he jeopardize the hunt for Zodiac? A core part of the defense—that Toschi only wrote to Maupin—is known to be untrue even before it's offered. Journalists know that Toschi writes under assumed names. There is a demonstrable pattern of duplicity, of manipulation around letters, of faked news stories. One has to ask the bigger question. Who benefits from a hoax Zodiac letter?

The answer's there in the months between April and July 1978. After the *Chronicle* prints the letter, the Zodiac case gets new resources, new officers, and Toschi gets publicity. A *Chronicle* sub-header on 26 April 1978 says it all: MASS SLAYER TAUNTS OFFICER WHO TRAILS HIM.

Nobody cares about Toschi like Toschi cares about Dave Toschi. Not his fellow cops, not journalists, not any criminal that he's arrested. They might have strong feelings. But not as strong as those of Dave Toschi. No one else has spent years faking letters about Toschi.

But maybe Maupin faked the letter to gain the publicity. It's possible, maybe, except Maupin doesn't need the publicity. Maupin's San Francisco famous. The first book is going to be a success. There's an enormous untapped market of homosexuals who are ignored by the straight establishment. And then, again, there's a bigger question. If Maupin faked a Zodiac letter, why does he mention another writer and a cop and not himself? Maupin's written about Zodiac, Maupin's burlesqued Zodiac as Tinkerbell, and Maupin's San Francisco famous. He's a perfectly viable candidate. That'd be the real publicity. And that's not what happens.

The letter doesn't look like a Zodiac letter. It looks like people's memories of a Zodiac letter. The original letters never use a cop's name. Just like they never use a victim's name.

The Old Toms of this world never demonstrate much capacity for detail. These are not the people who remember a cop's name. They barely remember Zodiac, even when they've got a pile of clipped articles.

The letter states that city pig Toschi is good. Just like every other fake letter Toschi has written. That's the connective tissue.

The demonstrable frauds praise Toschi's looks, his professionalism, his dignity, his bearing. They're as naked as the hoax letter. And if one thinks about this statement—that city pig Toschi is good—and assumes that it wasn't written by Toschi, then then letter makes no sense.

Toschi is a good cop. Generally. But he's awful at closing serial murder. He's had nine years to catch Zodiac. In 1975, Toschi is put on the homocide beat. Things have changed since SATAN SAVES ZODIAC. There's someone called the Black Doodler, later shortened to the Doodler. He starts killing in 1974 and continues into 1975. He appears to be a young African-American man. His victims are predominantly middle aged White males from other countries. Based on accounts of surviving victims, there's a theory that the Doodler meets his victims in gay bars and catches their attention by drawing their likenesses on napkins and tablecloths. Hence the tradename. The theory is tenuous. Many of the men considered definitive Doodler victims are murdered nowhere near bars. They're found at known cruising spots, public spaces used for homosexual assignations. And then there are two other sets of contemporary gay serial murders. There's someone who slashes and mutilates drag queens in the Tenderloin. And a group of murders that the police believe revolve around the BDSM and leather scenes. The lines of demarcation are porous.

In February 1974, a man named Stig Lennart Berlin is murdered. He's found in apartment #9 at 725 Hyde Street. He'd been stabbed with a knife in the chest and other areas. A bloody towel in the bathroom. Gore in the sink. He was a 37-year old immigrant from Sweden, a naturalized American. He'd served in the US Army. He was 5 feet 6 1/2 inches tall. He was a homosexual. His killing meets every criteria of the Doodler.

1973 issues of the *Bay Area Reporter* establish that Berlin is a habitué of gay bars. The first public acknowledgment of the Doodler's existence is in the 14 November 1974 *Examiner*. In this article, Berlin is posited as a Doodler victim. In the same article, Joseph "Jae" Stevens is not listed as a Doodler victim. In a few years, Jae will be enshrined as a canonical victim.

Which is complicated because Jae is a self-described female impersonator. And there's a killer of drag queens in San Francisco. Whom the SFPD does not believe is the Doodler. When the cops catch a break on the Doodler case, it's because a European Diplomat picks up the Doodler and brings the Doodler to the Diplomat's apartment. There's a back and forth about cocaine and the Doodler goes into the bathroom for about an hour. The Doodler emerges from the bathroom and stabs the Diplomat. Somehow the Diplomat survives and tells the tale but refuses to do so in a formal context, which hinders law enforcement. The Diplomat's apartment is in the Fox Plaza, a 29-storey apartment complex off Market Street. It's about a block from where Bobby Salem dies. SATAN SAVES ZODIAC. A week later, the Doodler attacks another gay man in the Fox Plaza. The Doodler breaks into the apartment, ties up its occupant. He's ready to kill. The occupant is saved by his own screaming. He makes enough of a ruckus that the neighbors bang on the walls. The Doodler flees.

These attacks complicate the narrative. At some point, the SFPD discount Berlin as a victim because he's found at home. The five canonical victims are found outside. But the Doodler theory is based on surviving victim statements. All of whom are attacked indoors. Both the Diplomat and the other Fox Plaza survivor are assaulted in July 1975. Two months later, on 27 September 1975, a 32-year old lawyer named George Gilbert is murdered in the Fox Plaza. He's stabbed to death. The police attribute Gilbert's murder to the BDSM killer. The basis for this attribution appears to be witness statements placing Gilbert in a leatherbar on the night of his death. But, in its first reporting on Gilbert, the *Chronicle* states that he's killed after having a small party at home. And he's killed in an apartment building where there have been two attacks by the Doodler.

Good luck making sense of this.

Toschi and his partner Frank McCoy handle the leather murders. There's traces of this in the contemporary newspapers and also one of the worst articles ever written. Published in the June 1976 issue of *Hustler*, it's by the gonzo journalist Bill Cardoso. "The S.F. Fag Murders." It opens with Cardoso listening to his neighbors screaming in agonizing pleasure and then remembering a time in his youth when he was sucked off by someone named Antoine and felt so ashamed after orgasm that he beat the shit out of Antoine. Cardoso believes that Antoine liked the beating as much as the sucking. Then the article gets worse.

Nothing is more distasteful than sitting in judgment on the sexual politics of an earlier era. They're always bad. Give it thirty years and our own will look awful. And intent matters. If Cardoso was attempting to use, however poorly, street vernacular to make a point, that'd be one thing. But he's not. The article is an example of the most socially toxic homophobia: the presumed straight who amps up the hatred hoping that it will disguise his own homophilic desire.

Toschi is the article's sole point of sanity. Even judged by latter day standards, he doesn't sound homophobic. Just square. And he's concerned with keeping people from dying. He's a good cop. But when it comes to the press, he's got awful judgment. Why did he ever agree to be in this article?

Toschi fails with the S&M slayings. They go unsolved.

Just like Zodiac.

If someone follows Toschi in the newspapers, and does it with enough regularity to discern his quality as a cop, then they must also see the failures. This is why Blue says what he says to Maupin. Toschi can get anything in the newspapers. But he's not good for much else. On his highest profile cases, Toschi has failed. Only one person in the Bay Area thinks that nine years and no Zodiac constitute a good job. And that's Dave Toschi.

There's the possibility that someone who hates Toschi writes this letter knowing that Toschi sends out fake letters. Knowing that if the ruse falls apart, Toschi will be in hot water. If journalists know that Toschi sends bogus letters that praise Dave Toschi, so do the other cops. That's normal gossip, the cross pollination of two interlocking industries. And what's happened for years? Everyone's turned a blind eye. Toschi has sent in letters that are demonstrably fake, Toschi's planted stories that aren't true. And he's never suffered any rebuke. For this to be an act of vengeance, someone would need a crystal ball. They'd have to guess that Armistead Maupin is the one person with the bad taste to break a longstanding gentleman's agreement.

People have suggested that Robert Graysmith wrote this letter. In 1978, he's shopping a book proposal. But, seven months later after the forgery, Graysmith believes that the April 1978 letter is genuine. He uses it to crack the second cipher, the one that isn't solved until December 2020. This isn't a retroactive narrative shoved into his book. There's an FBI file dated 15 February 1979. It details Graysmith's contact with the Bureau, offering them his solution, using the names Herb Caen and Dave Toschi to solve the code. People have accused Graysmith of many things. He's got his problems. But his issues don't emerge from dishonesty. Graysmith's got Zodiac fever. Someone who believes they can see the truth and disregards anything contradicting that truth. Graysmith thinks the letter is real.

The simplest and saddest explanation is that Toschi forges the letter. If DNA rumors are true, then he also forged the 29 January 1974 letter.

But why?

†

The answer that affords Toschi the most humanity, and which also makes the most sense, is that it comes back to Arthur Leigh Allen.

In August 1971, Toschi takes one look at Allen and he *knows*. This dude is all wrong. This dude stinks worse than stink itself. This dude is The Zodiac. Toschi carries this belief to his grave. He states it to Graysmith. With great frequency. He states it to Mark Ruffalo, the actor who plays Toschi in Fincher's *Zodiac*. The belief shapes Graysmith's book. Toschi puts Graysmith onto Allen. The cop and the cartoonist are in near daily communication. Toschi feeds Graysmith. The info points to one person. Arthur Leigh Allen. Zodiac. Yes. The 1972 raid did not pan out. But. Zodiac is a diabolical genius who plans in advance. And. Allen is Zodiac. Thus. Allen is also a diabolic genius. Do you really think he'd leave anything around, waiting to be found? His fingerprints didn't match the ones taken from Paul Stine's cab. Remember that letter? Zodiac used airplane cement to disguise his fingerprints. Of course the prints don't match! He told us they wouldn't! Do you think a guy who knows how to disguise fingerprints will hold on to an executioner's hood?

Zodiac is a genius.

Arthur Leigh Allen is Zodiac.

Thus, Arthur Leigh Allen is a genius.

In September 1974, Allen is arrested in Santa Rosa on a molestation charge. The victim is 9-years old, brought into Allen's trailer for nefarious dastardly work, is given money for his silence. On one occasion, Allen says the following to his victim: "I know you don't like it, but I'm just a nasty man." In 1975, Allen gets a functional insanity defense, is sent to the Atascadero State Hospital for the Criminally Insane. He stays in the hospital for two years, gets released in August 1977. By which time the Zodiac investigation is fallow. There are no new leads. And no new crimes.

In public, Toschi never speculates on Zodiac's responsibility for new murders beyond the known five. And Cheri Jo Bates. But there are those young girls in Santa Rosa. Who might be victims of Ted Bundy. Z on the American map. Santa Rosa. Where Arthur Leigh Allen lived. The death cycle starts after the August 1971 interview with Allen and ends around the time of his arrest. Toschi doesn't say it. Not in the press. But Toschi *knows*. The murders never stopped. They just changed. As promised in a letter.

Now, in 1978, Allen is free. Has been since August 1977. Thanks to the liberals and the lawyers and the psychiatrists. They say that Allen is no longer insane, that Allen is a cured man. But Toschi knows. Allen isn't a garden variety child molester. Allen is The Zodiac. And The Zodiac is a genius. The Zodiac has to be a genius. How else could he evade Dave Toschi? Only genius beats Supercop. The Zodiac's clever enough to fake his way out of a hospital. Much stupider people do it every day. Remember that dumb kid who thought he was Jesus Christ and tried to stake Satan through the heart?

Allen's back in Vallejo. Back at 32 Fresno Street. But Vallejo isn't interested. The case is closed. Bill Armstrong is gone. Maybe he and Toschi had a fight, maybe not. Ken Narlow of Napa Sheriff's Department is still interested. But Napa's small. Napa doesn't have any juice. Toschi is the only one left. And each and every week, he gets what he always got. People call him up, maybe three people every seven days, and tell Toschi that their ex-husband is The Zodiac. Toschi is a good cop. He duly investigates. But it eats time. And these leads do not matter. None of these people are The Zodiac. Toschi *knows*. Arthur Leigh Allen is The Zodiac. The leads are useless. The Zodiac is at 32 Fresno Street, down in a basement. Planning to re-offend, contemplating how to kill the poor innocents whom Supercop has sworn to protect. Toschi believes this as much as he believes that Allen killed Cheri Jo Bates. As much as he believes that Allen wrote the poem on the desk at Riverside City College. It's clear as day.

Toschi spends six months with this knowledge. Every week he's called out to the scene of another horrible murder. Motor spirit visions go into the brain. Toschi *knows* about Allen. And Toschi *knows* something else. He knows how low humanity can go. He's seen it in the motionless dead, in their rigor mortis, in pools of blood, in shattered bone, in the slime and gore that slips from the flesh of the raped dead like satin lingerie.

He's waiting for another letter. But none comes. He knows why the letters stopped in 1971. Allen met with Toschi and Armstrong and Jack Mulanax. Allen realized Supercop was on his tail. That's when the killings started in Santa Rosa. And then, in 1974, Allen wrote again. Maybe the 1974 letter isn't forged by Toschi. But if it is, it did the trick. It shook Allen loose. Zodiac sent the Citizen card. Zodiac was red with rage at Count Marco. And then Allen got arrested. And the letters stopped. Zodiac kills and Zodiac writes. And now Zodiac is free. Even if Toschi did forge the Exorcist letter, Zodiac wrote the Citizen card. Zodiac was the Red Phantom. And remember. If Toschi forged the Exorcist letter, then he knows that the Citizen card is genuine in a way that no one else can know. So he's waiting. Allen is free. He knows it's coming.

But it never arrives.

Half a year goes by. Half a year of waiting. Of Allen out there. Maybe he's killing again. Maybe he's molesting some poor kids.

Toschi can't go after Allen. Not without new, substantial evidence. The 1972 raid was a disaster. It turned up nothing. They got Allen's handwriting and it didn't match. If anything, the raid produced evidence that exonerated.

But Toschi can explain that. Allen is ambidextrous. And they made a mistake. They only raided the trailer in Santa Rosa. Not the parents' house in Vallejo. 32 Fresno went untouched. Who knows what Allen had there? And who knows what he destroyed? The past failure makes the evidentiary threshold too high without anything new. And there's no resources. Just poor David Ramon Toschi. Working alone. Carrying a tattered photocopy of the Exorcist letter in his wallet, taking it out for every journalist.

There are nine cabinets filled with dead ends.

And one file labeled ALLEN, ARTHUR LEIGH.

Toschi's had good luck in the past. Look what's happened with the *Examiner.* They've published so many of his letters. Toschi got what he wanted. No one found out. One well timed piece of writing can change everything. The cause is good. It's righteous and just. And it's overdue. It's long past time that they catch this bastard Allen who is Zodiac.

So he does it.

He writes the letter.

The genuine issue original demonstrated something in 1970. With no new material, it's not easy to write a Zodiac letter. You fall back on your personality. The inner self emerges. Your hobbies and obsessions. Buttons and comic books and dragons. Toschi writes a letter and has no new material. Toschi is like any of us. The one thing that he can't escape is himself.

Toschi writes about Herb Caen. Caen's a famous man, got that column. Toschi reads it with the religious fervor of a preacher thumbing the Bible. Caen is San Francisco currency. That's how to get coverage.

Toschi lived through 1976-1977, read about Son of Sam. Like everyone else, his perception of Zodiac is infected by the last famous letters sent by an occult killer. What did Son of Sam do? He left notes for the cops, yes, but he also wrote to Jimmy Breslin, a columnist for the *New York Daily News.* It's copycat of the Halloween Card to Paul Avery. Breslin took Son of Sam's letter and ran with it. Breslin made Son of Sam a celebrity. Jimmy Breslin isn't in San Francisco. But San Francisco isn't New York. San Francisco is Herb Caen. That's how to get coverage.

And then, yes, Zodiac should write about cops. Zodiac wrote about cops before. As did Son of Sam. When Zodiac mentions cops, the police take notice. But it must be plausible. 1978 isn't 1970. There are no unsolved cop homicides. Patrolman Robert Hooper got shot in February. The suspect was picked up the same night. Son of Sam was different than Zodiac. Son of Sam wrote to the top cop working his case. Son of Sam used the man's name. Who's the top cop most associated with Zodiac, who's one of San Francisco's most famous men? Dave Toschi. And if, in the process, Toschi earns a little more press, well, what's the harm? Any press for Toschi is press for Zodiac. And any press for Zodiac moves Allen towards prison.

Doesn't Zodiac like movies? The 1974 letter says *Exorcist.* The Citizen card says *Badlands.* Toschi asks the question that's always in his mind. Who will play me. In a movie. Toschi knows that Zodiac wrote the Citizen card, that it's an evolution. What does Zodiac do in that anonymous note? He doesn't misspell anything. This new letter must partake of the evolution. Toschi doesn't misspell a word.

Toschi does it.

He writes the letter.

†

When the letter arrives, Toschi is called to the *Chronicle.* The letter needs authentication. Toschi doesn't send it to the places that have authenticated past Zodiac correspondences. It doesn't go to Sacramento. He doesn't even bring the original. He takes a photocopy to John Shimoda, head of the postal service crime lab in San Bruno. Shimoda has never authenticated a Zodiac correspondence. It takes two hours before he declares the letter genuine.

Toschi knows that photocopies are useless for authentication. The knowledge is there in the beginning, in an FBI file of 17 October 1969: "The other specimens have been photocopies, some of which were made after the evidence had been treated for latent fingerprints. Such photocopies do not show sufficient detail to permit an adequate handwriting examination." It there's again on 20 October 1969: "It could not be determined whether the questioned hand printing... was prepared by one or more persons, because the photocopies of these specimens do not show sufficient detail for a satisfactory explanation..."

When the scandal breaks, Shimoda backtracks, changes his opinion. He tells the *Chronicle*: "All of the [past Zodiac letters] were on the same 7½-by-ten (inch) stationary with the same envelope and watermark... This last one was on standard 8½-by-11 bond and in a legal sized envelope."

This is demonstrably untrue.

Through the November 1969 mailings all Zodiac letters, including the second cipher, are on Woolworth's FIFTH AVENUE stationary. Starting with the Melvin Belli letter of 20 December 1969, Zodiac switches to different paper.

This is not to impugn Shimoda. He worked with what he was given.

Toschi took the letter to someone who didn't know the material.

†

For a while, it works. It really works. Toschi gets coverage, Zodiac gets coverage, the investigation gets more resources. SFPD remembers. The city remembers. Toschi isn't alone. And it's not like 1969. This time, there's no mystery. They know who did it. Arthur Leigh Allen. He lived in Riverside. He said it himself. He practically confessed to killing Cheri Jo Bates. And wrote those letters. Then came to the Bay Area and did it again. More killing, more letters. 1972. Santa Rosa. Hitchhikers. No one's working blind. Now they know where to direct focus. It's not like before. Toschi's got it, he's holding it in his hand, and it's his.

But.

Then.

One day.

David Ramon Toschi.

Gets the call.

†

After news breaks and Toschi is reassigned to the pawn shop detail, an article appears. *San Francisco Chronicle*. 14 July 1978.

INSPECTOR TOSCHI TALKS.

Written by Mike Weiss.

It's the same piece that mentions the anonymous notes, the ones signed by other people and Deputy Dave.

Weiss begins with the latest. SFPD are investigating Toschi's possible authorship of the January 1974 Zodiac letter. Then the reporter moves to the meat. Excerpts of an interview with the disgraced detective.

Weiss describes his subject like this:

> In 2½ hours of highly emotional, often rambling and sometimes nearly incoherent conversation in his living room Wednesday night [12 July 1970], Toschi told his story of the years of his life that were devoted to the hunt of the Zodiac....

> As Toschi talked rapidly and nervously, skipping from subject to subject like a man who has too much feeling inside him to control or regulate, he never mentioned any of the 100 other homicide investigations in which he participated. Only Zodiac...

> He titled back in a brown naugahyde recliner and nervously pulled at his nail bitten fingers...

> ...As [Toschi's wife] spoke Dave Toschi's head slumped towards his chest. He was perspiring heavily. Once again tears welled in his eyes.

On the surface, this is a portrait of the man beset by misfortune. An unexpected blow has rearranged his mental landscape. Toschi's lost the most merciful thing in the world, the inability of the human mind to correlate all of its contents. Now he can see. And the vision has left him shattered.

But this is an era of journalism where the omissions are as important as the details. It's Bobby Salem, SATAN SAVES ZODIAC. The *Chronicle* meticulously catalogues every aspect of the victim's life: his furniture, his clothes, his cats, his friends. While avoiding the defining aspect of his existence: his homosexuality. If the reader is an adult, or has the right frame of reference, the true message comes through.

Bobby's queer.

Bobby's a homo.

Bobby's strange lusts went and plumb got ol' Bobby killed.

Read Weiss's 14 July piece now, in the future, and it's obvious that Toschi isn't telling the full truth. Regarding the letters that sent to Maupin, the detective says this: "I just signed them with the first names that came to mind... A couple of female names."

Two weeks later, Maupin's article is published in the 31 July 1978 issue of *New West* magazine. It includes full reproductions of the letters. One is from the gals at San Francisco State. Who think Toschi is *soooooooooooooooooooo* dreamy. The letter is written in the royal we, provides context, says the gals live in a dorm. It's a fully thought out document. From start to finish.

Later in his piece, Weiss provides the operative quote, the thing that ties it all together. Toschi describes receiving news of his reassignment. He says: "I was doing pretty well... Not drinking. Not taking any pills. I had been hit in the face. I'm 25 years in the department."

Weiss is more than a beat journalist. In about six years, he'll publish *Double Play*, a masterful work about the assassination of Harvey Milk and Mayor George Moscone. The killings will happen in five months' time. They elevate Dianne Feinstein to the Mayorality. From which office, on 23 August 1985, she holds a news conference and temporarily botches the investigation of Richard Ramirez A/K/A The Night Stalker.

Another murderous bore impossible without The Zodiac.

But none of that has happened. Not yet.

What does happen, back in 1974, is publication of Weiss's first book. *Living Together: A Year in the Life of a City Commune*. It's a diary of Weiss's life with seven other people in a Philadelphia commune. Against a backdrop of serious historical turbulence. The book's selling point is the implied turn-ons. For the square audience. Drug. Sex. Wild Youth. The diary has more sex than drugs, but the substances are present. There in the first ten pages. And there's the mescaline/LSD/orange juice cocktail taken by Chris, Dan and Joan. Or the marijuana plants in a vegetable garden that are taller than Weiss. The drugs are a wave that resonates without being measured.

Weiss has an expert eye.

He knows it when he sees it.

Motor spirit.

And how to describe it.

Without writing a word.

Like Weiss's piece, Toschi's quote says more in what it doesn't say.

"I was doing pretty well. Not drinking. Not taking any pills."

When one does well, one is not drinking, one is not taking pills. This implies its opposite. When one is not doing well, then one is drinking, one is taking pills. Toschi must have seen both sides.

Doing well. Not doing well.

Which asks the question: against whom is the comparison made? Himself, in the past? Other cops? Both? Civilians? Where? When?

The dreamy haze of pills and booze. That's enough to give you the idea. You do it. Once. And it works. You do it. Again. And it works. And again. And again. You do it until it stops working.

And now, here on 12 July 1978, Dave Toschi is no longer doing well. He's a man with too much feeling inside himself to control. Or to regulate.

Nine-and-a-half years in the past, David Ramon Toschi waded into the aftermath of Ann Jiminez's turn-out. A month after *Bullit*. Before Zodiac. Before Paul Stine. Before fame. Before *Dirty Harry*. Before Supercop. Before the letters. Before Maupin. Before *Tales*. Before the leather murders. Before the forgotten and bloody corpse of Stig Berlin. Before the Doodler. Before the articles. Before the fan mail.

Toschi saw it.

Held the hair of a lonely fat misfit in his own hands.

He went from Ann to Zodiac.

One man history of California in its decade of woe.

A to Z.

Toschi witnessed the birth of motor spirit.

And now he's caught a case of his own.

epilogue

15,594 Days

WHEN SHARON TATE DIES, a seed is planted. There's a black cat around every corner, witches in wooded groves. *Hail Satan!*

Then Manson and his acolytes are found, and yes, they're shocking, but they aren't what people imagined. Manson's weird, he's crazy, he's the hippie nightmare. But dig it, jack, Charlie ain't a Dark Lord of The Pit.

The seed grows. People kill other people, write on doors, on walls. The Death Angels are proclaimed. Ted Bundy draws an N on the American map. Son of Sam waters the grounds. Motor spirit tends the garden. It takes ten years to blossom.

In late 1980, St. Martin's Press publishes *Michelle Remembers.* The book has a simple premise. A Canadian psychiatrist helps a patient remember that she's the victim of a Satanic cult and its ritualistic abuse. In one instance, the titular Michelle says the ritual lasts for more than eighty days and involves several hundred people. It's Halloween drag porn, presented with enough Christian myth to disguise the turn-ons, the sexual kinks that its audience can't admit, the perversions that are engaged only when presented as evil. Despite both patient and psychiatrist being Canadian, this is perhaps the most American thing about the book.

None of what they write is true.

Which presents a problem.

People need for memory to be absolute, impermeable.

If people's understandings of their own lives are corrupt, then who are they? Michelle is so average and ordinary that there's no way this wellspring of Black Masses can come from anything but lived experience. She had to have been there. Ted Bundy in reverse. The average person anointed.

Every individual has two intelligences. There's the surface intelligence, the one that society attempts to measure through standardized tests. People's performance is variable, everyone's unique. But there's a symbolic intelligence beneath the surface. On this level, everyone's a genius, experiences the same semiotic chaos. It can be tapped at will. But most people don't have an excuse. Michelle undergoes regressive memory therapy, a discredited pseudoscience that exists beyond a replication crisis, and bores down into her second intelligence. And it turns out that Michelle likes to write hardcore Christian porn. The innocence of her exterior, which rests on demeaning assumptions about gender and class, requires that the results be presented as truth. As something that happened. That was real. *Michelle Remembers* isn't exactly True Crime, but the book vibrates on the genre's most unspoken frequency: the socially acceptable presentation of sexual perversion. If it isn't real, if it didn't happen, if it's not true, then everyone must face and live with the shame of their own arousal. The collapse of XXX into Trigger Warnings, identical function under a new name: *watch out, you're gonna be turned on.* The book launches a decade of American credulity. Of people who recover memories and destroy themselves, their families, and their societies. An untold number of lives are ruined. All the while, there are people in the media who want more, more, *more!* Who can't get enough Satan, who mint coins from the pain. Later, some will be disgraced. Some will become sainted figures. None will suffer rebuke for their participation in the fraud, in the credulity, in the wide-scale manufacture.

The Satanic Panic begins.

†

In 1986, St. Martin's Press issues Robert Graysmith's *Zodiac*. To his credit, Graysmith isn't interested in demonology or the occult. He doesn't believe that Zodiac is the result of a wide conspiracy.

The killer and his victims are gone from popular memory. They linger in certain recesses—there's that early warning network of California's speed freak crazies, and there's people who remember the crimes when they happened, and there's the obsessives who think they've got the answer—but, by and large, no one remembers Zodiac. He was just a thing that happened back when hippies had serious motor spirit and the Rhetorical Left thought that a dimebag of speed was indistinguishable from radical politics.

Graysmith's book is like any other. Ninety-five percent of the people who buy the object will not read the text. But books are funny things. They don't need to be read. Hold them in your hand and you absorb the concept. The Zodiac symbol is on the dustjacket. People touch the book, see and feel the symbol. In the climate of the moment, they think SATAN. If Dave Smith's 15 October 1969 article in the *Los Angeles Times* gave birth to The Zodiac, then this is the resurrection, the second coming, slaves rising in the afterlife.

Our boy's back. And better than ever.

Graysmith writes with manic pulp fever. The factual flaws don't hurt. If anything, they help. As the present book demonstrates, the tedium of accuracy can only slow the breakneck pace. And although *Zodiac* makes feints towards multiple suspects, there's only one destination.

Arthur Leigh Allen. A fat balding pedophile in Vallejo. A degenerate, a criminal, a destroyer of lives. But not exactly someone at whom you can point and shout *Hail Satan!*

This is Graysmith's major insight. If Zodiac is ever found, he'll be like every other crappy killer. Tiny and broken. The insight doesn't match the text's jagged paranoia. Time rewritten, events running backwards. Everything planned out and executed to perfection.

It's Dave Toschi's last testament. Credulity becomes the game. It's there in the 1972 affidavit, written to get a search warrant. To dig through the hell of Allen's trailer. This is the template.

To create The Zodiac, all you need is about three thousand words. These can be anything. Recovered memories, circumstantial nonsense, years old testimony from an enemy, not much more than a hunch. If it's contradicted by physical evidence, like, say, Allen looking nothing like any description of the Zodiac, or, say, Allen being too tall, then the disconnect is ignored. Or written around.

Zodiac opens the floodgates.

The next book is published in 1987. *Times 17: The Amazing Story of the Zodiac Murders In California and Massachusetts 1966-1981.* Written by an individual named Gareth Penn. He claims that Zodiac is a UC Berkeley professor named Michael O'Hare. The professor is lucky. He's the one Zodiac suspect whom no one takes seriously. Penn's theories are too obtuse, too weird, too complex.

That same year, Doubleday publishes Maury Terry's *The Ultimate Evil: An Investigation into a Dangerous Satanic Cult.* Theoretically, the book is about the Son of Sam. Zodiac cover artist from New York City. Who shot couples and wrote letters. Terry starts small, begins with the letters. These texts reference the killer's neighbors. Terry investigates, finds that the neighbors were part of the same cult as the killer. Then discovers a nationwide organization that spans from sea to shining sea. Not a single drop of American blood is spilled without the involvement of this cult. Terry can see. It's not a Z on the American map. It's an inverted cross, it's a pentagram.

The charitable interpretation is that Terry discovered something genuine, the potential involvement of the neighbors, and having been right once, believed that he could never be wrong again. Yet Terry's very first articles about Son of Sam, published in 1979, tell a different story. They demonstrate that Son of Sam worked alone. And contradict Terry's later narrative, one in which he's nagged by doubt about the NYPD's presentation of the case. The doubt becomes a worry that becomes a certitude. He pulls stray threads until he unravels the tapestry and sees that it'd been draped over a secret door. When he walks through the door, Terry discovers a Satanic temple. In 1979, there's none of this. His articles reduce Son of Sam to a sad neighborhood eccentric with a handgun. His early work is the most persuasive argument against his later publications.

In 1990, another cover artist gets on the charts. Again in New York City. He calls himself Zodiac. He sends letters to the cops and the media. There are eight victims, all of whom are shot, three of whom die. One of whom is stabbed. Zodiac II's letters are everything that people think they remember in those of the genuine issue original. Victims are chosen based on astrological signs, there's codes, there's references to the hood. It's dead certain that Zodiac II read Graysmith's *Zodiac.* And did what other readers did. Believed.

The climax comes in 1991. There's a tabloid hack named Geraldo Rivera. He used to be married to Kurt Vonnegut's daughter. He's the lowest of the low, a bottom feeder. Absolute scum. Geraldo's got his own syndicated television show. *Now It Can Be Told.* Schlock pornography disguised as journalism. Barely.

One episode of *Now It Can Be Told* is about whether astronauts survived the 1986 Challenger disaster. Another episode ropes former President Gerold Rudolph Ford into an appearance. He denies being paid money to pardon former President Richard Milhous Nixon. Another episode is about how guns, drugs, and prostitutes are purchased with food stamps.

The Zodiac episode airs in 1991.

A segment titled MANIAC IN THE MASK.

Geraldo sends a quasi-journalist out to Vallejo. Interviews are taped with former newspaper reporters, cops who worked the murders, and Darlene Ferrin's sister Pam. Maury Terry is interviewed. He claims that Zodiac is an occult Satanic killer.

A former staff journalist at the *Vallejo Times-Herald* claims that Zodiac's Lake Berryessa hood was an exact duplicate of one worn by Aleister Crowley. Which it was not. Terry says that the name Zodiac is an occult reference, that the letters are littered with occult references. Pam introduces the idea that the whole thing was about Darlene. She gets basic details wrong. Maury Terry invokes Stanley Dean Baker. SATAN SAVES ZODIAC.

Now It Can Be Told speculates that the Vallejo police were involved. Apparently, Darlene used to fuck a lot of cops. The segment doesn't end so much as dissolve into bathos.

Now it's out there, now it's mass media. Charlie was a bust. But Charlie started it all. Charlie planted the seed. Charlie was the farmer. The Zodiac is the crop. He's this guy about whom no one knows anything, someone whose anonymity means that he can't disappoint. He was an occult killer. And there's always been this hole, this emptiness, this place created when Charlie turned out to be a cheap pimp with an acid connect.

The Zodiac lives.

Now It Can Be Told airs a follow-up.

THE MAN WHO KNEW TOO MUCH.

The man in question? Michael Mageau.

Maury Terry's back. He claims everyone knows that Darlene was being followed. It's claimed that Darlene was into the occult. It's claimed that Mageau said that the killer called Darlene by her nickname before he shot her. None of this true. There's short clips of an interview with Arthur Leigh Allen. In shadow. Silhouette in a basement. Denying that he's Zodiac.

The segment has something else.

The most shameful thing in all of Zodiac.

Now It Can Be Told wires Darlene's sister with a hidden microphone and brings her to Michael Mageau's house. She confronts him on the front lawn. A television crew is down the street, films it all with telephoto lens. Ambush journalism of a crime victim.

Michael Mageau and Pam look destroyed. They're the walking wounded. They're the baseline of the killings. The decades of pain and trauma and unresolved questions.

And now they're residents of Televisionland.

†

The panic ends. As all panics do. Waiting to be revived. As all panics do.

By the mid-1990s, Satan's not on the radar. But there's this new thing, it's been coming, there were hints in the previous decade with the personal computer revolution. But mostly people aren't on it, it's not really available, but it arrives, eventually, through a variety of mechanisms. And it's called the Internet.

The first website comes online in the late 1990s. Zodiackiller.com. The most elemental name. It's the beginning of something, a process, and one of the few places that delivers on the promise of the early digital revolution. The operator of Zodiackiller.com, Tom Voigt, has a genius idea. He starts collating data. To give a sense of his achievement: in 1995, most Zodiac letters had never been seen in their original presentations, could not be seen by anyone but the cops. By 2002, every letter is available. Perhaps not in perfect reproduction. But in copies that are good enough. It's like this with every aspect of the case. The information is democratized, dissected, pored over. Message boards sprout up, individuals notice things that the cops could never see. They share the information, see it adopted, merge into this new body of knowledge, this reservoir of thoughts and concepts. Sometimes, it's blind alleys and dead ends. Sometimes, it's something more.

The only problem is that The Zodiac infects the enterprise. Birthed by Dave Smith, resurrected by Graysmith. This isn't the fault of any of the Internet people. They work with what they have, with what's available.

†

David Fincher makes the feature film *Zodiac*. It's released in Winter 2007. The second best film about San Francisco. Only *Dirty Harry* is better. On the surface, both films are about the same thing. *Dirty Harry* is directed by Don Siegel, the ultimate journeyman director. Fincher is, arguably, the last person who operates in the mold. And *Zodiac* is the last wide release American film that's about something. A year after it appears in cinemas, Marvel releases *Iron Man*. A process is complete. American filmmaking is reduced to cartoons, back to the spectacle where it began. There was a period, maybe half a century long, in which the film industry entertained the notion that its products could engage with the contours of the human experience. This notion ends as soon as Robert Downey Jr. puts on the plastic armor. Now there's only wise cracks, CGI explosions, re-staged 9/11, genocide simulators.

In *Zodiac*, Downey Jr. plays Paul Avery. He's a supporting actor in the last film of the old. And leading man in the first film of the new.

Fincher's film isn't about Zodiac. It's not even about The Zodiac. It's about the pleasure and terror of research. Of what happens when you wander so deep into the woods that you lose the path home. *Zodiac*'s narrative goes through the motions, disguises itself as Graysmith's *Zodiac*, takes factual liberties. But none of that matters. What matters is the center. When you are deluged with information, when you dive too far into the data, when you've got the itch that always needs to be scratched.

The film isn't a box office success. 2007 is too early. Give it another six years. Time reveals the fictional Graysmith, played by Jake Gyllenhaal. He becomes Everyman in a never ending morality play. He's what happens when you believe that data accumulation and Wikipedia entries are the same as knowledge, when coincidence does not exist because everything is connected by hyperlinks.

Everyman is every man who spends too much time on the Internet.

Within ten years of the film's release, it's widely acknowledged as the best American film of the Twenty-First Century. Not only by critics. But also the audiences who skipped its run in the cinema.

†

The last major development comes in 2008. A new name is floated. Richard Gaikowski.

He's unique amongst Zodiac suspects.

Prior to his 2004 death of lung cancer, he'd left a paper trail that wasn't confined to official documents and the machinery of mass surveillance. He'd appeared in those too, as does everyone who lives in the Western world's quasi-police state. Kommissar Karl Lohmann always gets his man. Digging through the files. But Gaikowski's self-generated trail was long and manifold. He'd worked as a mainstream journalist in the 1960s before disappearing into a countercultural haze after the assassination of Bobby Kennedy, re-appearing in 1969, living in the San Francisco Good Times commune and helping to produce its eponymous underground newspaper. When the paper closed down, he got involved in cinema, helped to open the Roxie Cinema on 16th Street in the Mission, and then transitioned into an interface with the 1970s punk scene. He'd merged the two interests, producing his own boy of cinematic work that focused, in part, on punk people. He'd started a film distributor that existed until the end of his life. At the dawn of the personal computer revolution, Gaikowski was the very first person to marry Left activism with the new technology. He established the NEWSBASE Bulletin Board, a proto-online messaging system used as a clearing house for information. If you wanted to know what the Sandanistas were doing, or learn about the war crimes of Alexander Haig, all you had to do was use your PC and its modem to connect to Gaikowski's system. He never abandoned San Francisco, lived for decades in the same storefront apartment on Guerrero Street. He was part of overlapping circles of artists and freaks and political nuisances. He was always there, always Richard, always Dick, a man who knew something about everything.

Gaikowski created message boards.

And now, in death, is a ghost on message boards.

He is The Zodiac.

Be careful what you wish for.

The ephemeral traces of Gaikowski's life, the articles that he'd written for the mainstream and alternative press, the hints of darkness in his films, all of it, becomes evidence of his imagined crimes. Clues in every scrap of writing, in every millimeter of celluloid. If a person browses Internet forums dedicated to The Zodiac, they can watch a body of knowledge being formed and fashioned from the detritus. It happens in real time and offers a vision of Gaikowski and the counterculture and San Francisco that is internally coherent and self-consistent. It just happens to be wrong.

Gaikowski is the entry point. As good a tool as any. There are mysteries upon mysteries. And these mysteries are not like the grand *whodunit?* They are the mysteries of San Francisco, of the counterculture, of the Californian psychic collapse. They are the mysteries of our present world and its birth. Our living future of motor spirit. Gaikowski is like Zodiac. There when the baby's delivered. Witness to history. He understands something before almost anyone else. The computer and information revolutions are real.

What he could not imagine is that the free flow of information, this sacred shibboleth of the press, will do something predicted by no digital utopist. Gaikowski could not see what it meant when each individual became their own press. No one could. This power, when extended to every living being, would murder knowledge. If every opinion is its own news, then there is no longer news. If every opinion is its own truth, then there is no longer truth.

The Zodiac can be anybody.

The Zodiac can be everybody.

Dick Gaikowski is The Zodiac.

†

Time is a Grade-A clusterfuck where no idea goes away.

1969 is 2007 is 2020.

The only new thing is each generation's belief that the ideas are new, a failure to establish institutional knowledge that might prevent the thing from happening again.

Richard Gaikowski hits Internet radar when Blaine, who worked with Gaikowski on *Good Times*, decides Gaikowski is Zodiac.

This happens, apparently, after the publication of *Zodiac*. Blaine reads Graysmith, realizes Dick was the killer, tries to involve law enforcement, records some conversations, goes on a sojourn to South Dakota and, under false pretenses, interviews Dick's mom.

Years later, Blaine gets on the Internet.

He writes to Zodiac researchers.

On 25 October 1969, Blaine publishes an article in the *Berkeley Tribe*. He advises Zodiac to throw his weapons to the sea, renounce war, become a penitent pilgrim. Blaine weighs Zodiac's crimes against Vietnam and police brutality and, in the purest expression of the Rhetorical Left, decides, *eh, what's five more dead people when we've got statistics?*

The 30 January 1970 *Tribe* runs another article by Blaine.

"Manson in the Hate."

Blaine, a former federal felon, recounts how he first heard of Manson. Blaine was in a special unit for homosexuals. Someone else transfers in after being Manson's "sweet boy." When Manson denied the sweet boy's affection, the sweet boy tried suicide.

That sweet boy's name?

Richard.

Blaine writes about a Haight Street death cult founded by Manson. Blaine identifies the cult as The Process Church, claims that Manson founded it and established the name.

This is, definitively, untrue. The Process is founded in England. In 1963. It's a Manichean thing, God and Satan, worship 'em both. Gnosticism's groovy when you have motor spirit. Gullible rich kids and useful poor kids come together and find out what it all really means before discovering that their leader can't talk to demons or control the wind.

Rinse, cycle, wash, repeat.

Branches all over the world.

Including Los Angeles and the Haight.

Blaine recounts a "medieval trial" in the death cult's Haight-Ashbury ashram. As far as the text can be followed, a member of the group named Pussycat insults someone named Father P... the 66th. The cult members tie and gag Pussycat and beat and insult him and debate staking him through the heart. The text is unclear on whether Pussycat is killed.

In the days after Manson's apprehension, December 1969, mainstream news outlets link Charlie and the Process. This story is planted by the Church of Scientology, which has a grudge: a lot of Process theology is stolen Scientology tech. And, in November 1969, two Scientologists turn up dead in Los Angeles, eyes cut out, mutilated in an alley. The girl is naked, raped.

Which leads to speculation: Sharon Tate + Scientology = ???

So the Process/Manson story is perfect distraction.

It enters the official narrative, features in the best-selling of best-selling True Crime. *Helter Skelter*.

Written by Los Angeles County's Vincent Bugliosi.

District Attorney. Who prosecutes the case. Puts away Charlie and his acid-eyed followers whilst preventing showbiz embarrassment. A good and loyal servant to the entertainment-industrial complex. Which must be kept functioning. To obscure the real Los Angeles money.

Aerospace. Cold War. Death machines.

The story makes stupid sense: Manson is the devil and the Process, putatively anyway, worship Satan.

The Process/Manson/Satan connection resonates all throughout the Satanic Panic. It's the main idea in Maury Terry's *The Ultimate Evil*.

Son of Sam wasn't a loner, Son of Sam worked for Process. And Process are killing everyone in America. Hide your children!

The Zodiac worked for Process, says Terry.

Blaine's story makes the unofficial narrative, Ed Sanders's *The Family: The Story of Charles Manson's Dune Buggy Attack Battalion*. Published in 1971. Blaine's inclusion is one of the things that provokes Process to sue Sanders and his publishers. First, in America, where the publisher capitulates. Then in the United Kingdom, where Process lose a multi-day trial.

In 1970, Blaine isn't breaking a new story.

There's been a month of Manson/Process.

In the news.

Blaine writes that Pussycat's trial happens in the "Devil House."

He gives the Devil House a vague address: Waller Street.

The Process do not have a property on Waller. The UK trial transcripts make this clear. The group is at 407 Cole and also Geary Boulevard, somewhere between the 2400 and 2600 blocks, and then on Oak Street. The transcripts fail to provide an exact address. Much later, some books give an address of 1820 Oak Street. Which is impossible. The even-side of Oak is the Panhandle. A park that runs along Oak and Fell.

There is no 1820 Oak.

None of the three Process addresses are anywhere near Waller.

But.

Waller is the subject of an recent article.

San Francisco Examiner.

5 December 1969.

Page 1.

VIOLENCE STALKS TERROR TERRACE.

Second and third paragraphs:

> The 1400 block of Waller Street – in the heart of the Haight Ashbury – has earned the name of "Terror Terrace" among many of its older habitues.
>
> One resident yesterday referred to the apartment house at 1480 Waller St. where Ann Jiminez was raped to death last Christmas, and to which the alleged attacker of a teenaged girl fled for sanctuary earlier this week as "the bloody bucket."

How does the story end?

To find out, read
How to Find Zodiac.

Printed in Great Britain
by Amazon

86702835R00181